"Life does not deliver a series of discrete events, but a tangle of overlapping experiences. The author was working on a mathematics degree, playing on a hockey team, and slowly coming out as trans and nonbinary when their mom was diagnosed with cancer. This book weaves memories from the author's childhood with scenes from the last few months of their mother's life into a tender story of acceptance, care, and love. The heavy moments are lightened by the portrayal of the family as penguins, with friends and strangers as a flock of other birds, but the story is deeply human."

—**MAIA KOBABE**, author of *Gender Queer: A Memoir*

"Will has created a beautiful, heartwarming family portrait, told thoughtfully with perfect spaciousness and pacing. Grief and growing up felt so tactile and close as I read this book, cover to cover, ending in tears, thrilled to be brought there by penguins."

—**NICOLE J. GEORGES**, author of *Calling Dr. Laura: A Graphic Memoir*

"Will Betke-Brunswick's *A Pros and Cons List for Strong Feelings* is a remarkable, but also chaotically specific, meditation on family and love. Will's personable and charming penguins navigate through the months after their mother's cancer diagnosis with an indomitable spirit and so so so much tender hilarity, even considering the subject matter. The rhythm of the lists Will uses in the book—final gifts from their mother, contents of a fridge, art in their house—are heartbreaking in how precisely they portray their family. I definitely have Strong Feelings about this book, and those feelings are largely that it is a stunning work that everyone ought to read."

—**SHING YIN KHOR**, National Book Award finalist and author of
*The American Dream?: A Journey on Route 66 Discovering
Dinosaur Statues, Muffler Men, and the Perfect Breakfast Burrito*

A PROS AND CONS LIST FOR STRONG FEELINGS

This is a work of nonfiction, except for a handful of names and identifying details changed to respect individuals' privacy.

Published by Tin House, Portland, Oregon

Distributed by W. W. Norton & Company

Library of Congress Cataloging-in-Publication Data

Names: Betke-Brunswick, Will, 1988- author.
Title: A pros and cons list for strong feelings / Will Betke-Brunswick.
Description: Portland, Oregon : Tin House, 2022.
Identifiers: LCCN 2022025071 | ISBN 9781953534453 (paperback) | ISBN 9781953534538 (ebook)
Subjects: LCSH: Betke-Brunswick, Will, 1988---Family--Comic books, strips, etc. | Cancer--Patients--Comic books, strips, etc. | LCGFT: Coming-of-age comics. | Genderqueer comics. | Autobiographical comics. | Graphic novels.
Classification: LCC PN6727.B48 P76 2022 | DDC 741.5/973 [B]--dc23
LC record available at https://lccn.loc.gov/2022025071

First US Edition 2022
Printed in the USA
Illustrations by Will Betke-Brunswick
Interior design by Diane Chonette

www.tinhouse.com

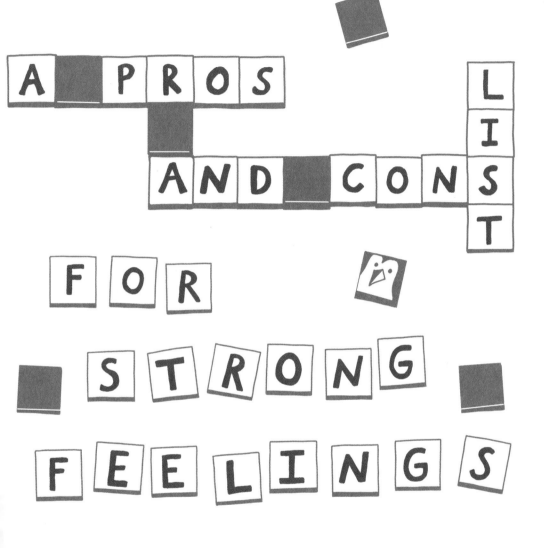

A PROS AND CONS LIST FOR STRONG FEELINGS

A GRAPHIC MEMOIR

WILL BETKE-BRUNSWICK

TIN HOUSE / Portland, Oregon

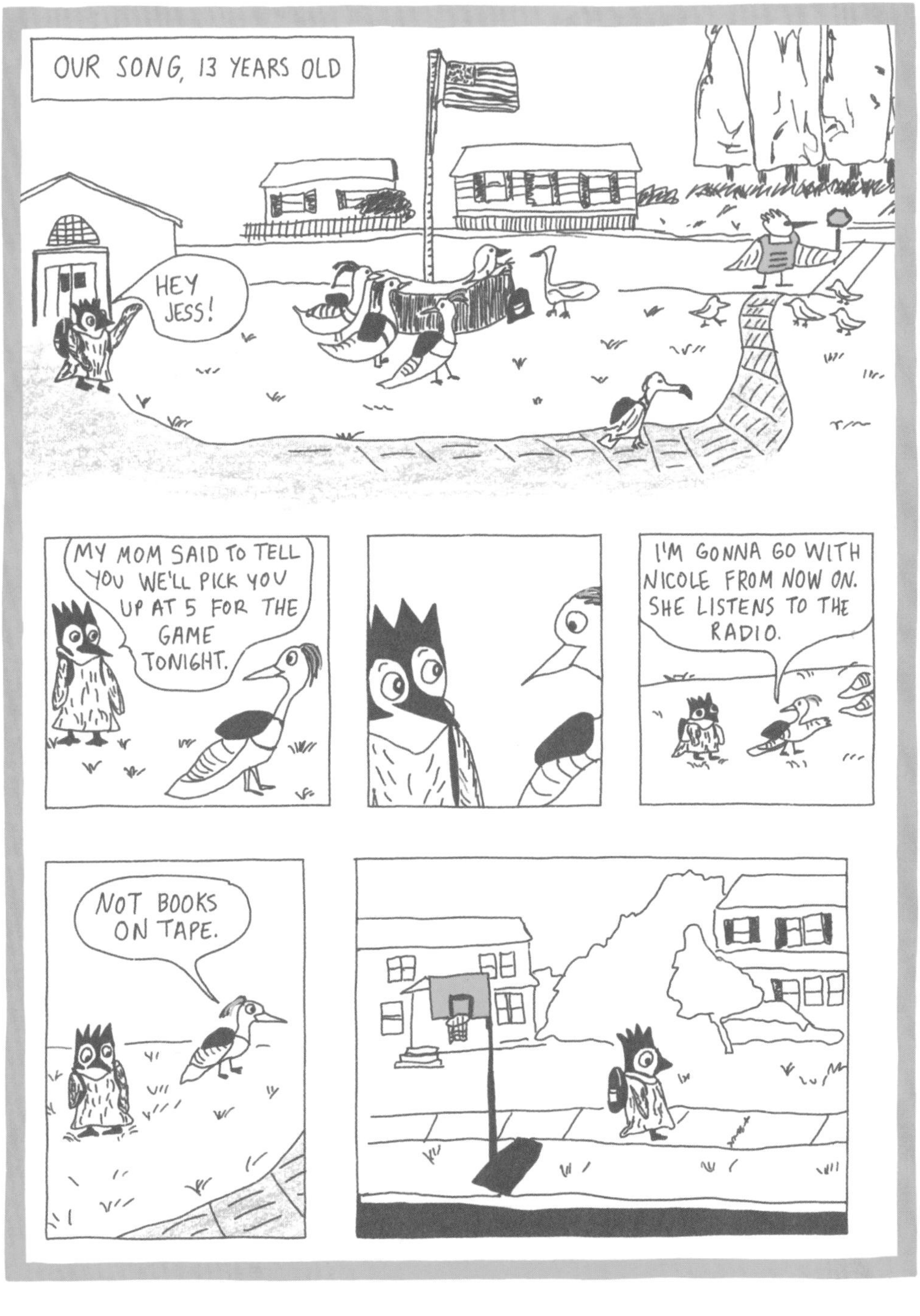
OUR SONG, 13 YEARS OLD
HEY JESS!
MY MOM SAID TO TELL YOU WE'LL PICK YOU UP AT 5 FOR THE GAME TONIGHT.
I'M GONNA GO WITH NICOLE FROM NOW ON. SHE LISTENS TO THE RADIO.
NOT BOOKS ON TAPE.

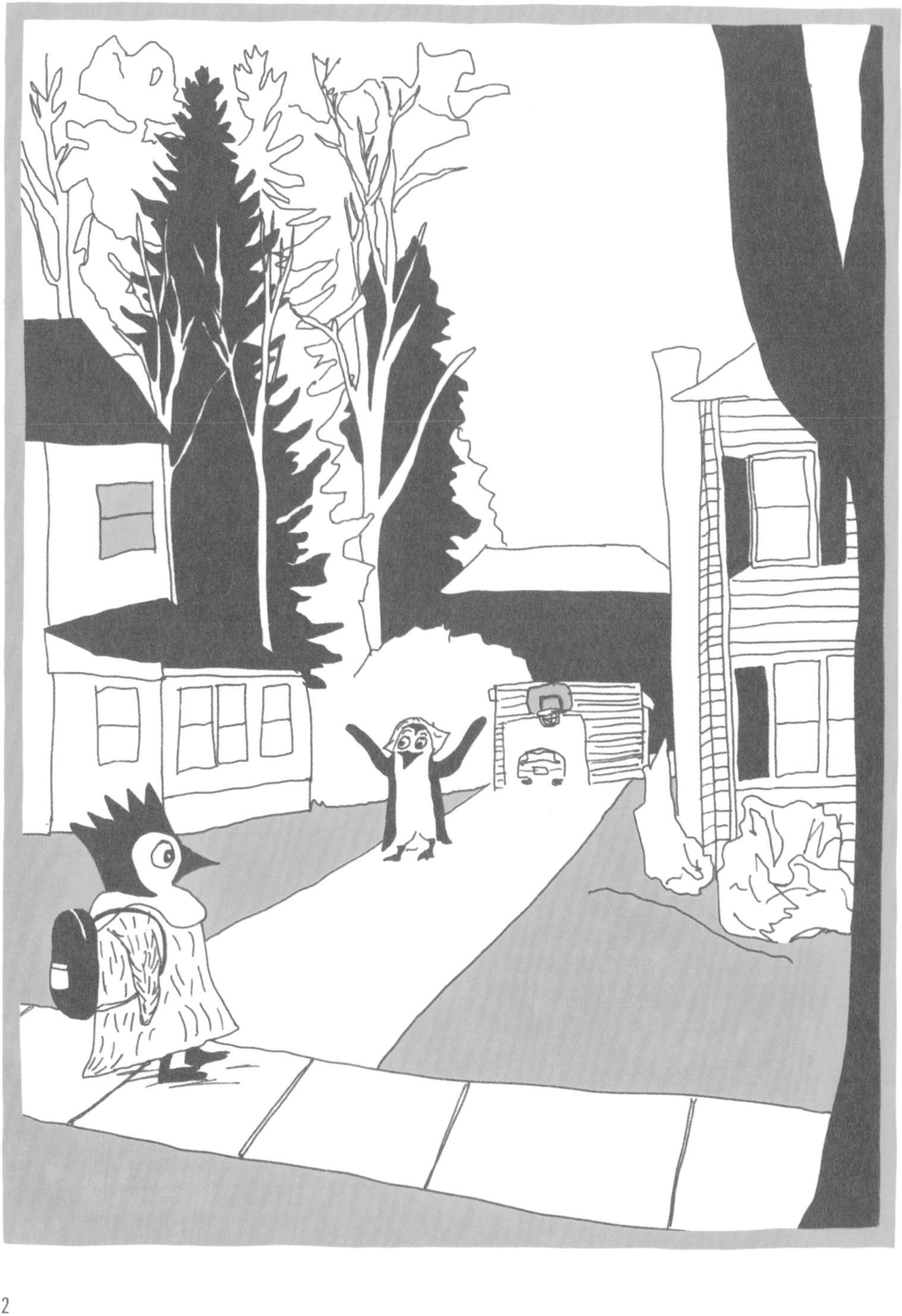

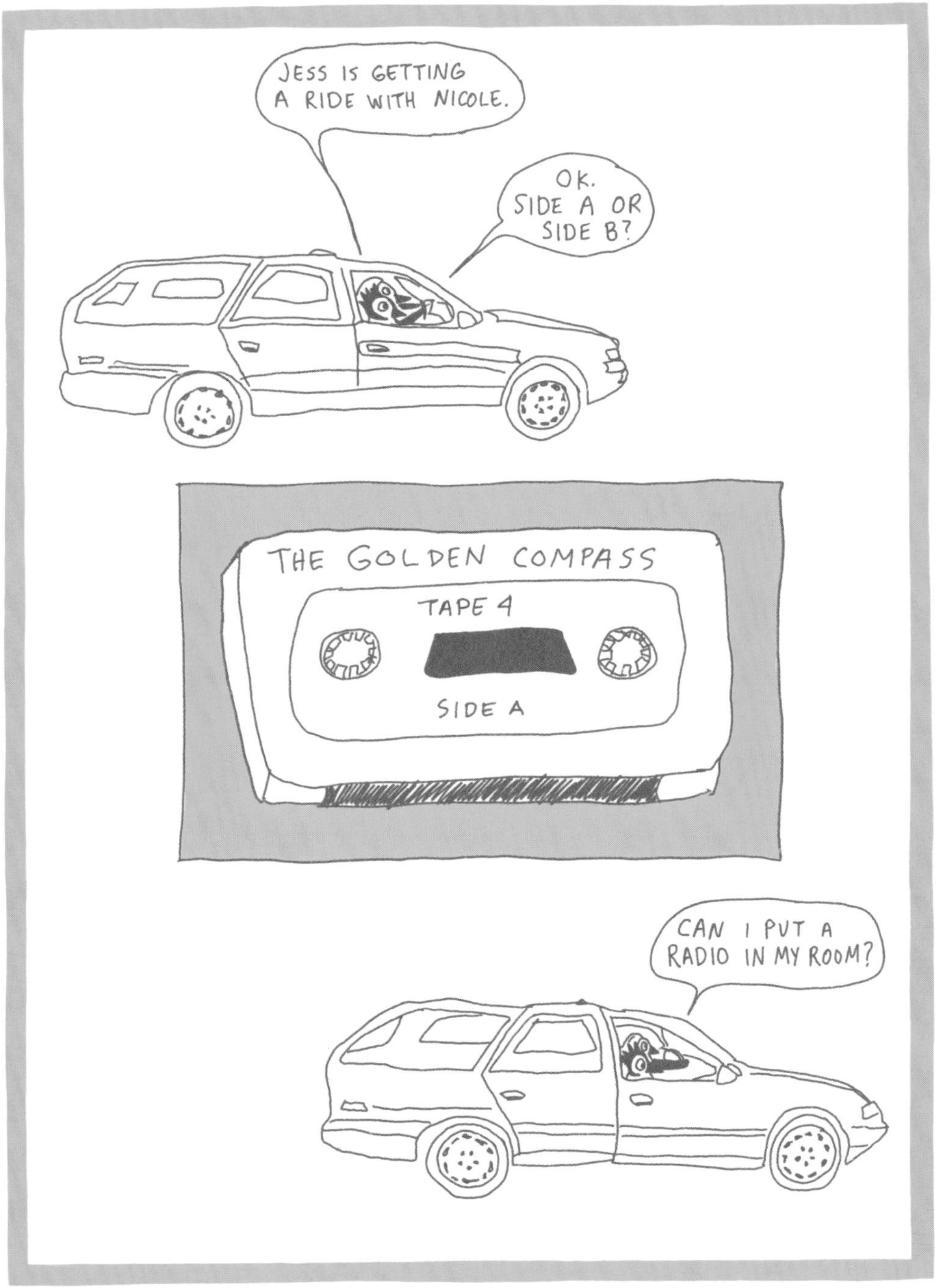
JESS IS GETTING A RIDE WITH NICOLE.
OK. SIDE A OR SIDE B?
THE GOLDEN COMPASS
TAPE 4
SIDE A
CAN I PUT A RADIO IN MY ROOM?

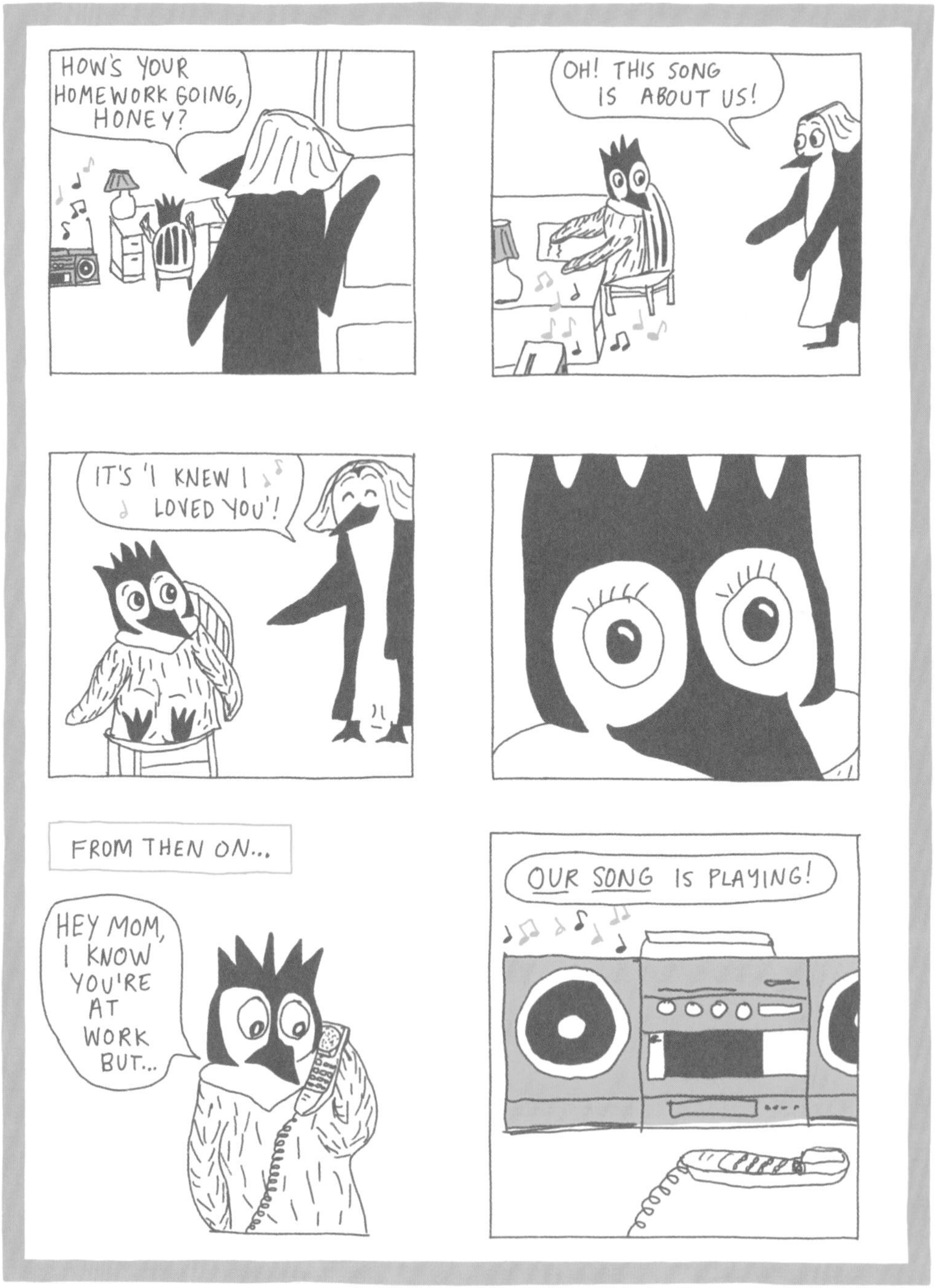
HOW'S YOUR HOMEWORK GOING, HONEY?
OH! THIS SONG IS ABOUT US!
IT'S 'I KNEW I LOVED YOU'!
FROM THEN ON...
HEY MOM, I KNOW YOU'RE AT WORK BUT...
OUR SONG IS PLAYING!

MARCH

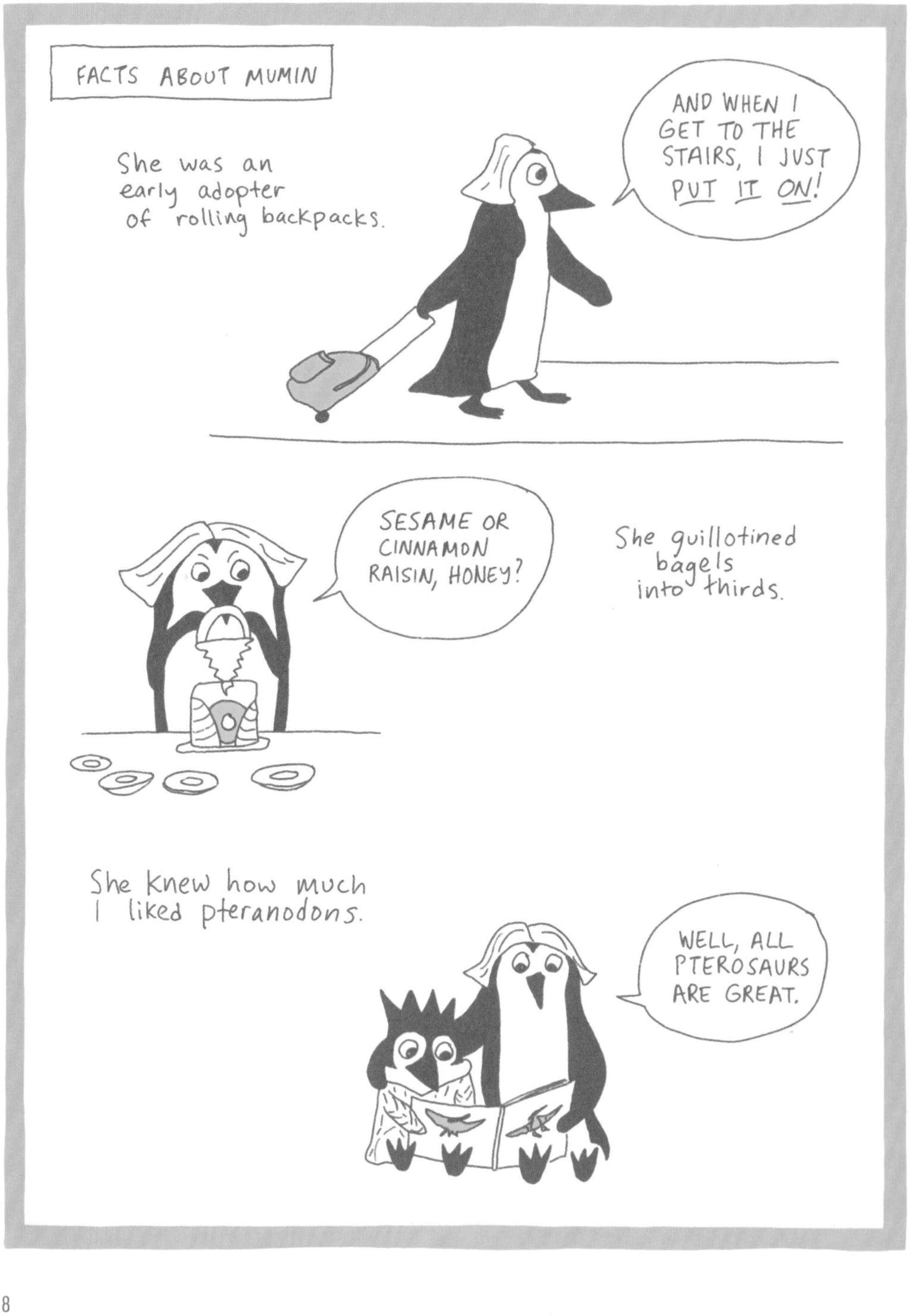
FACTS ABOUT MUMIN
She was an early adopter of rolling backpacks.
AND WHEN I GET TO THE STAIRS, I JUST PUT IT ON!
SESAME OR CINNAMON RAISIN, HONEY?
She guillotined bagels into thirds.
She knew how much I liked pteranodons.
WELL, ALL PTEROSAURS ARE GREAT.

DIAGNOSIS

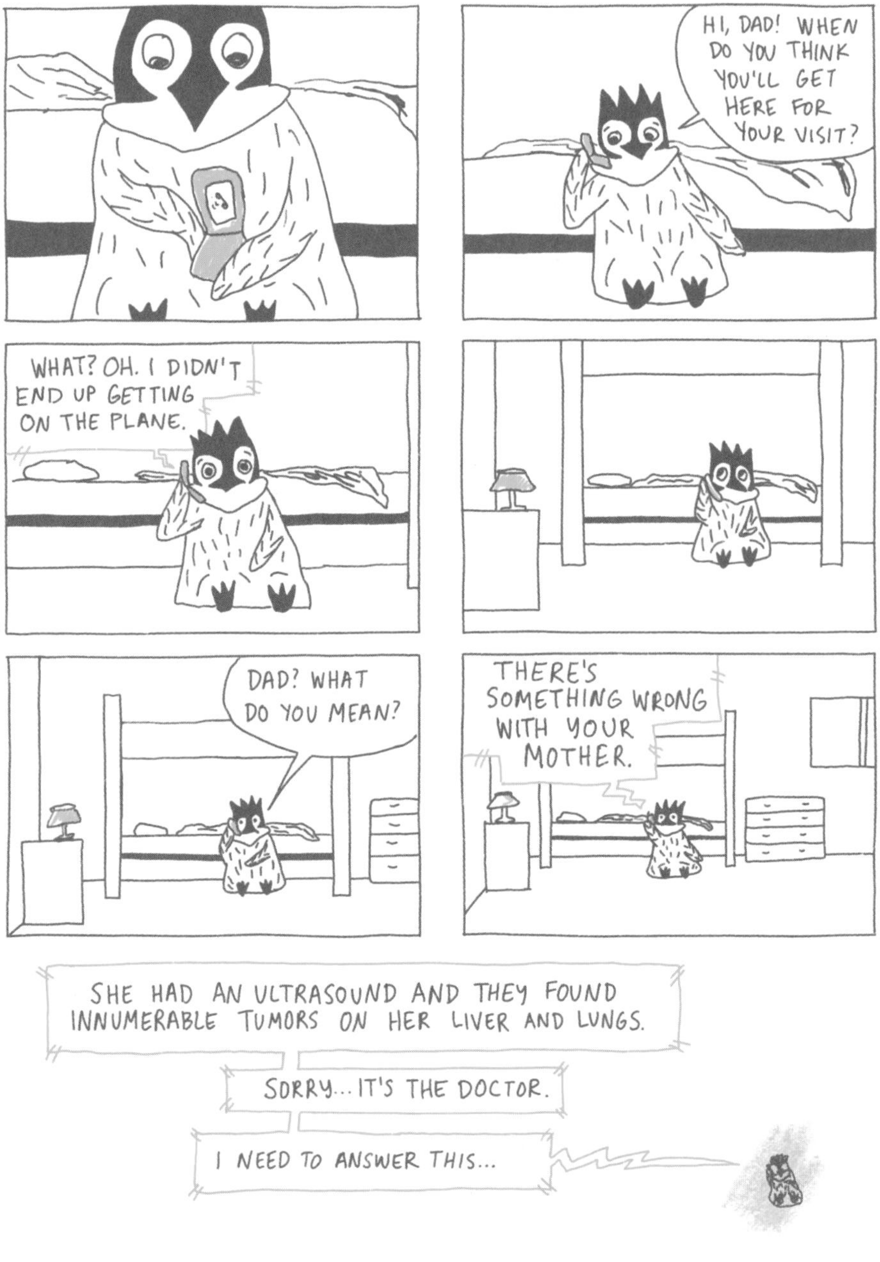

HI, DAD! WHEN DO YOU THINK YOU'LL GET HERE FOR YOUR VISIT?
WHAT? OH. I DIDN'T END UP GETTING ON THE PLANE.
DAD? WHAT DO YOU MEAN?
THERE'S SOMETHING WRONG WITH YOUR MOTHER.
SHE HAD AN ULTRASOUND AND THEY FOUND INNUMERABLE TUMORS ON HER LIVER AND LUNGS.
SORRY... IT'S THE DOCTOR.
I NEED TO ANSWER THIS...

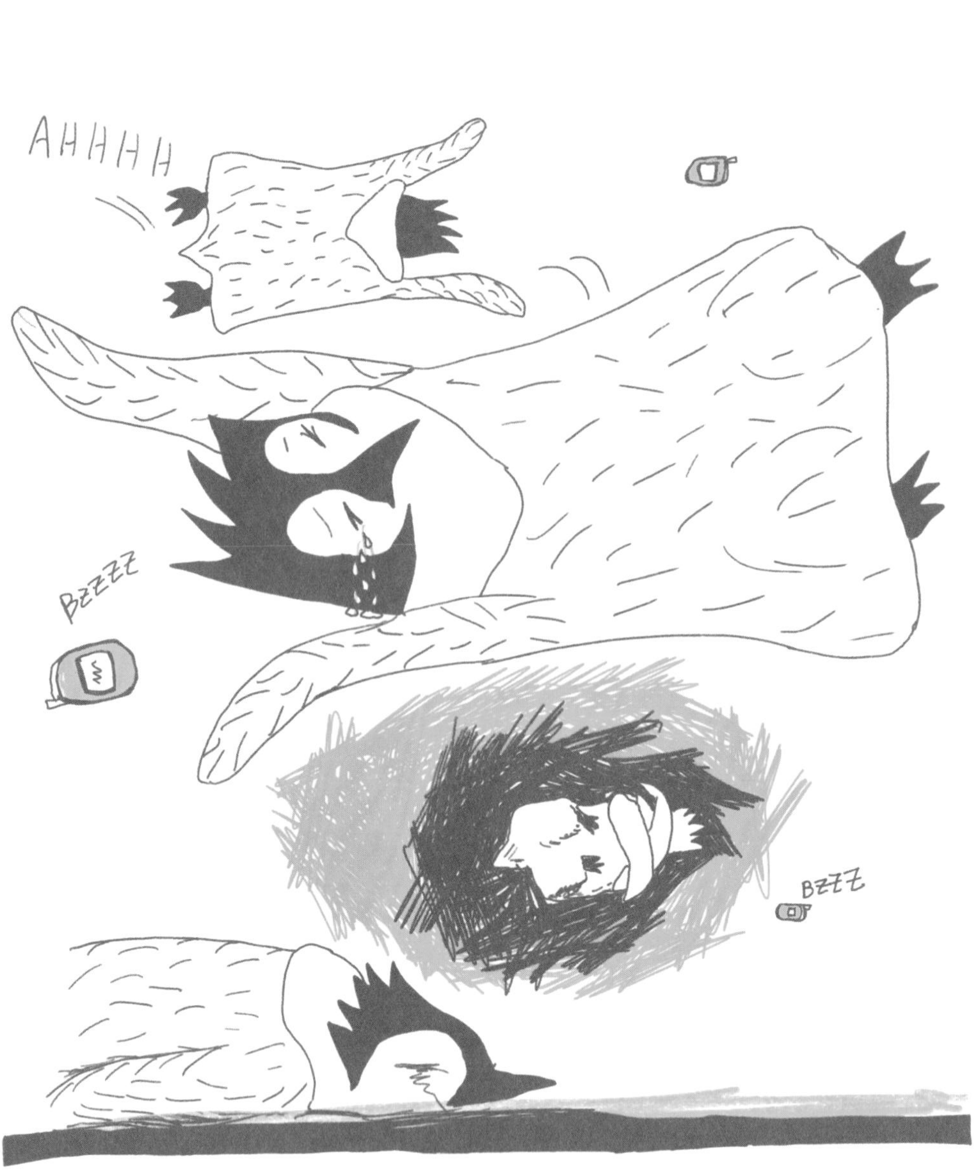
AHHHHH
BZZZZ
BZZZ

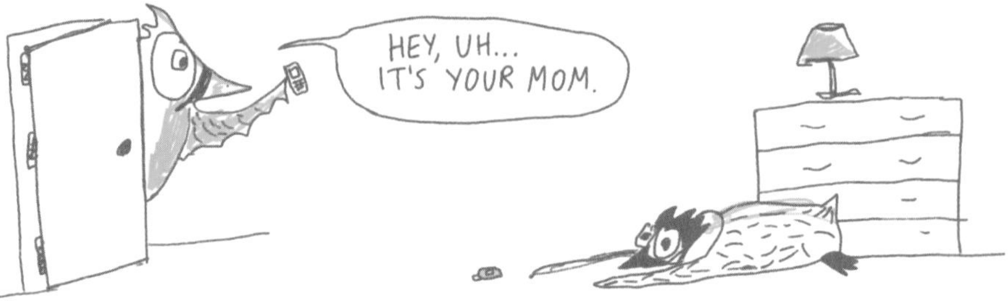
HEY, UH...
IT'S YOUR MOM.

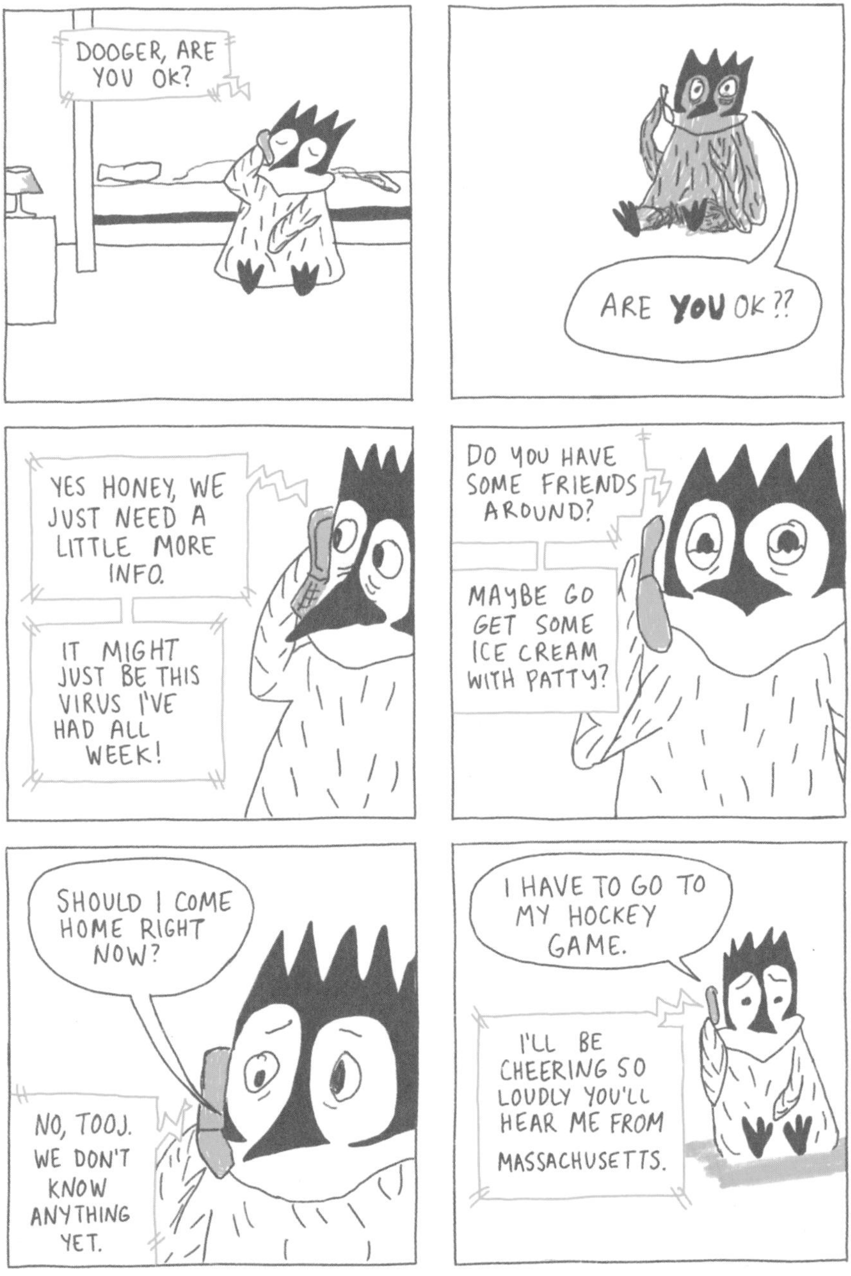

DOOGER, ARE YOU OK?
ARE YOU OK??
YES HONEY, WE JUST NEED A LITTLE MORE INFO.
IT MIGHT JUST BE THIS VIRUS I'VE HAD ALL WEEK!
DO YOU HAVE SOME FRIENDS AROUND?
MAYBE GO GET SOME ICE CREAM WITH PATTY?
SHOULD I COME HOME RIGHT NOW?
NO, TOOJ. WE DON'T KNOW ANYTHING YET.
I HAVE TO GO TO MY HOCKEY GAME.
I'LL BE CHEERING SO LOUDLY YOU'LL HEAR ME FROM MASSACHUSETTS.

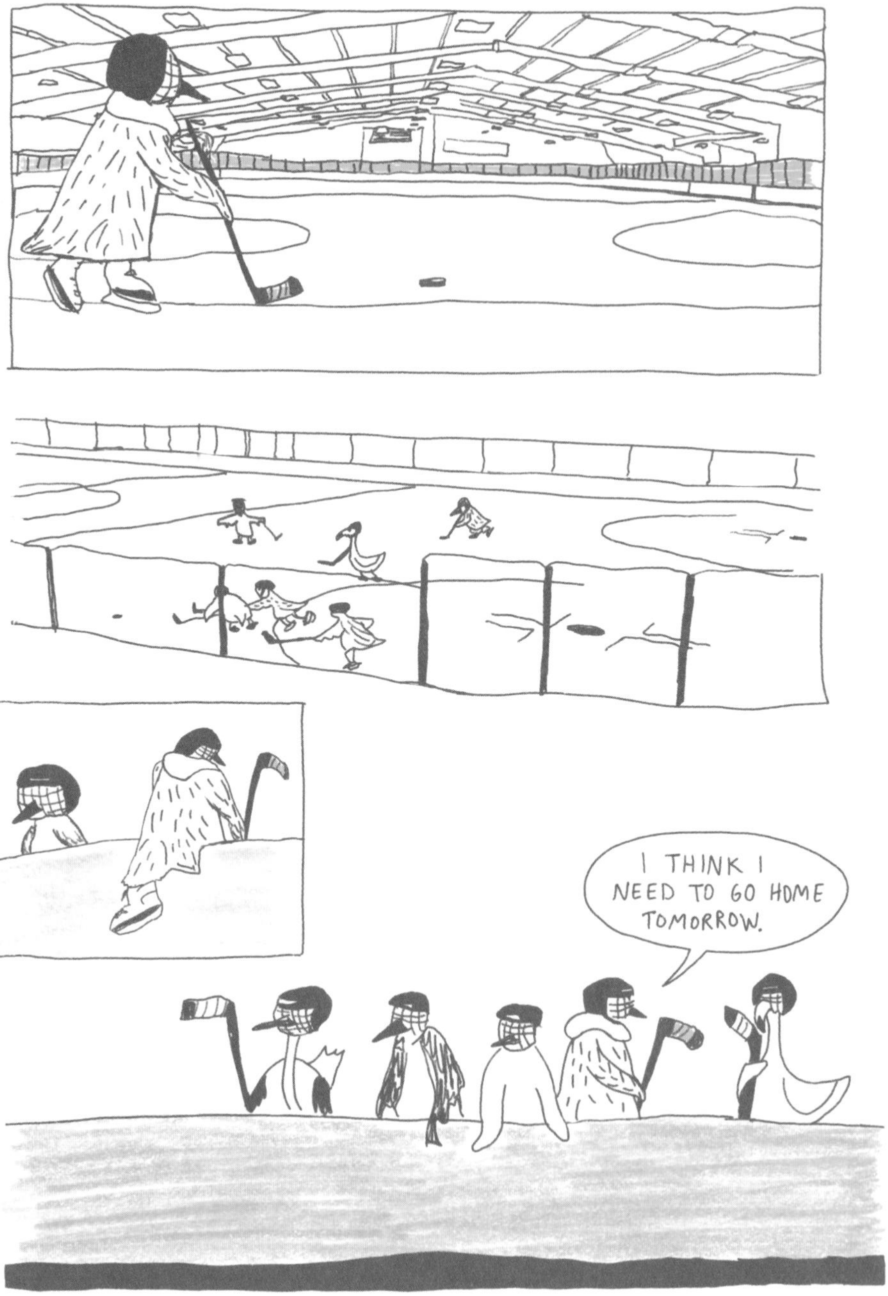
I THINK I NEED TO GO HOME TOMORROW.

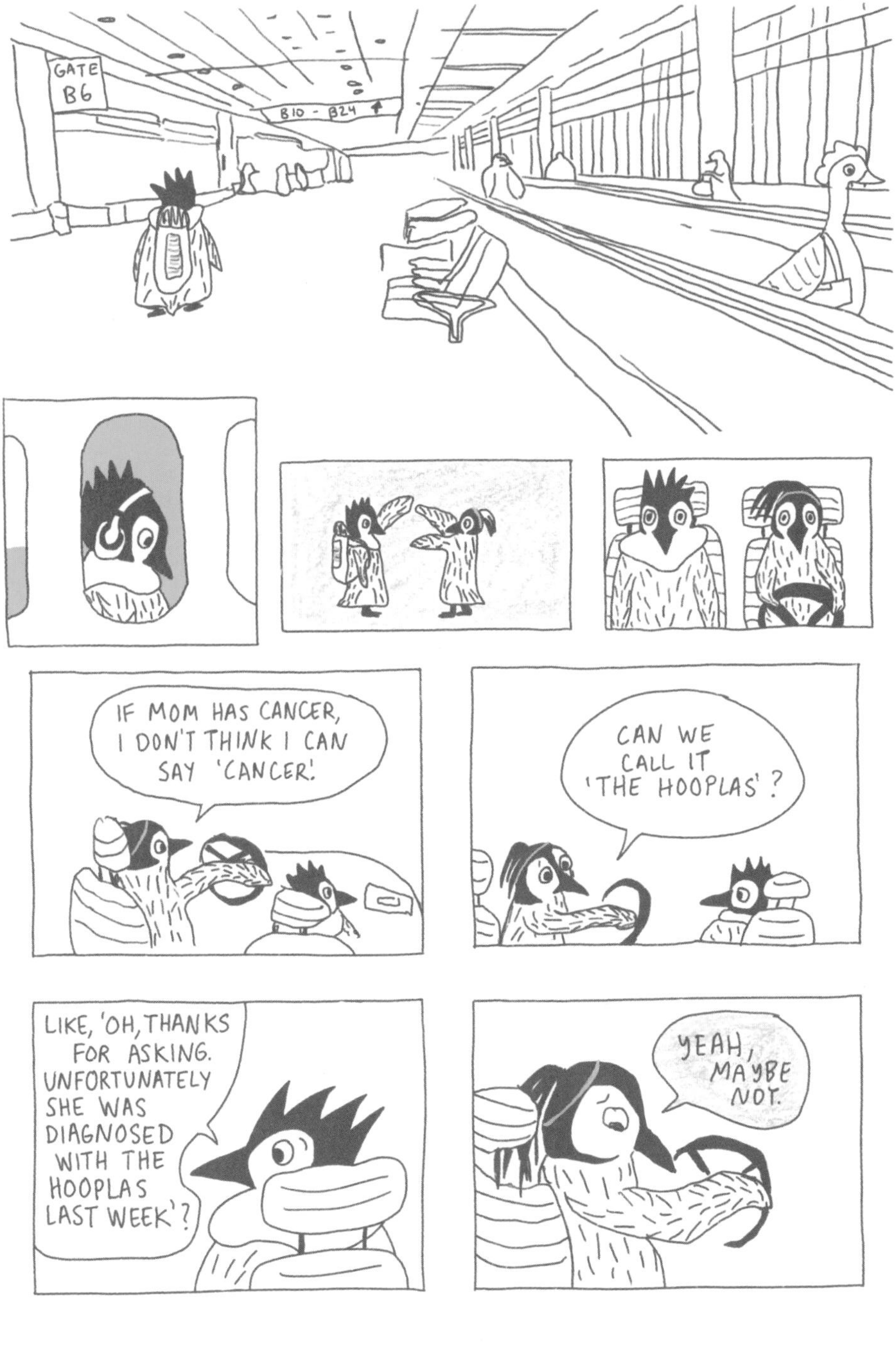
GATE B6
B10 - B24
IF MOM HAS CANCER, I DON'T THINK I CAN SAY 'CANCER.'
CAN WE CALL IT 'THE HOOPLAS'?
LIKE, 'OH, THANKS FOR ASKING. UNFORTUNATELY SHE WAS DIAGNOSED WITH THE HOOPLAS LAST WEEK'?
YEAH, MAYBE NOT.

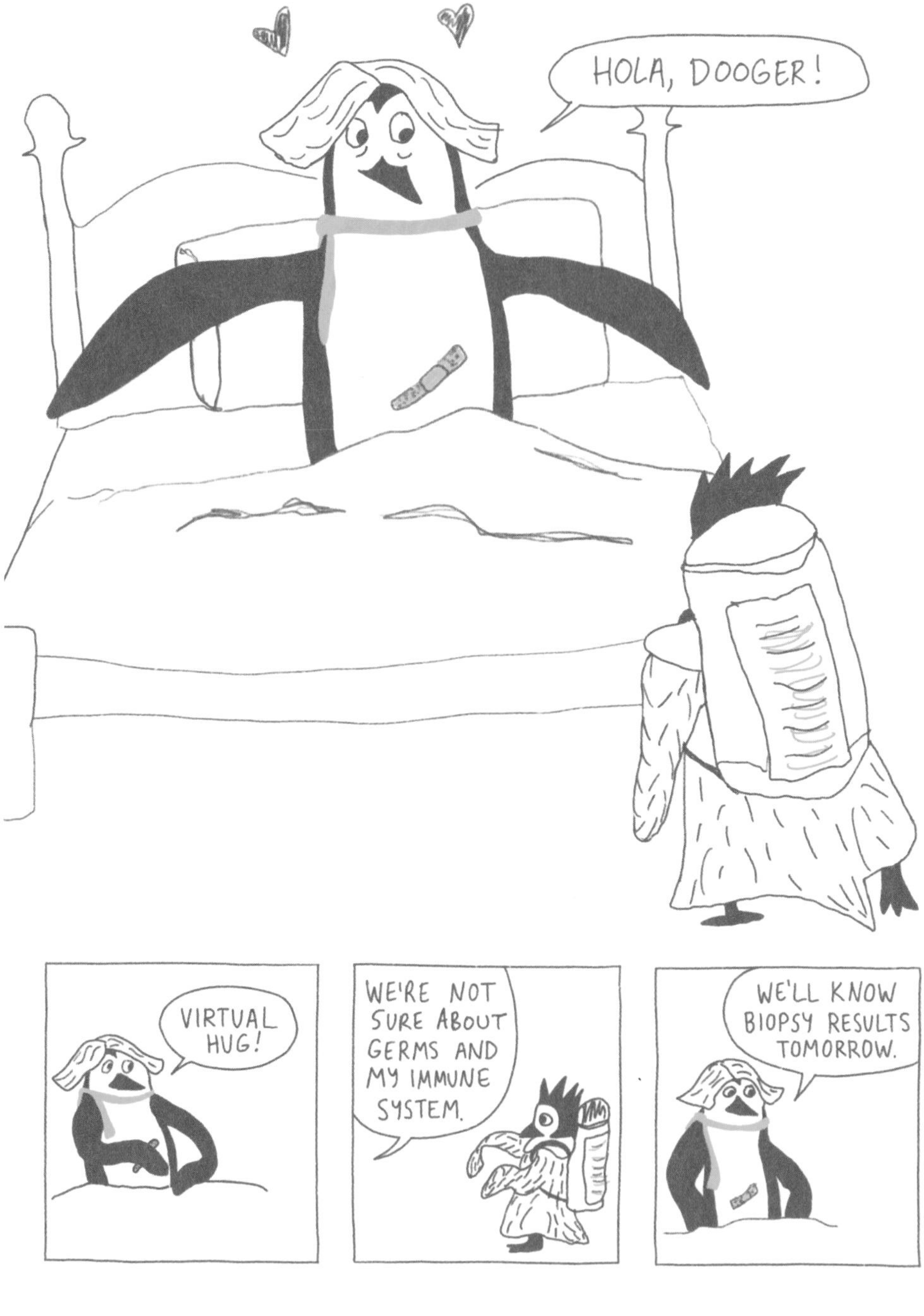
HOLA, DOOGER!
VIRTUAL HUG!
WE'RE NOT SURE ABOUT GERMS AND MY IMMUNE SYSTEM.
WE'LL KNOW BIOPSY RESULTS TOMORROW.

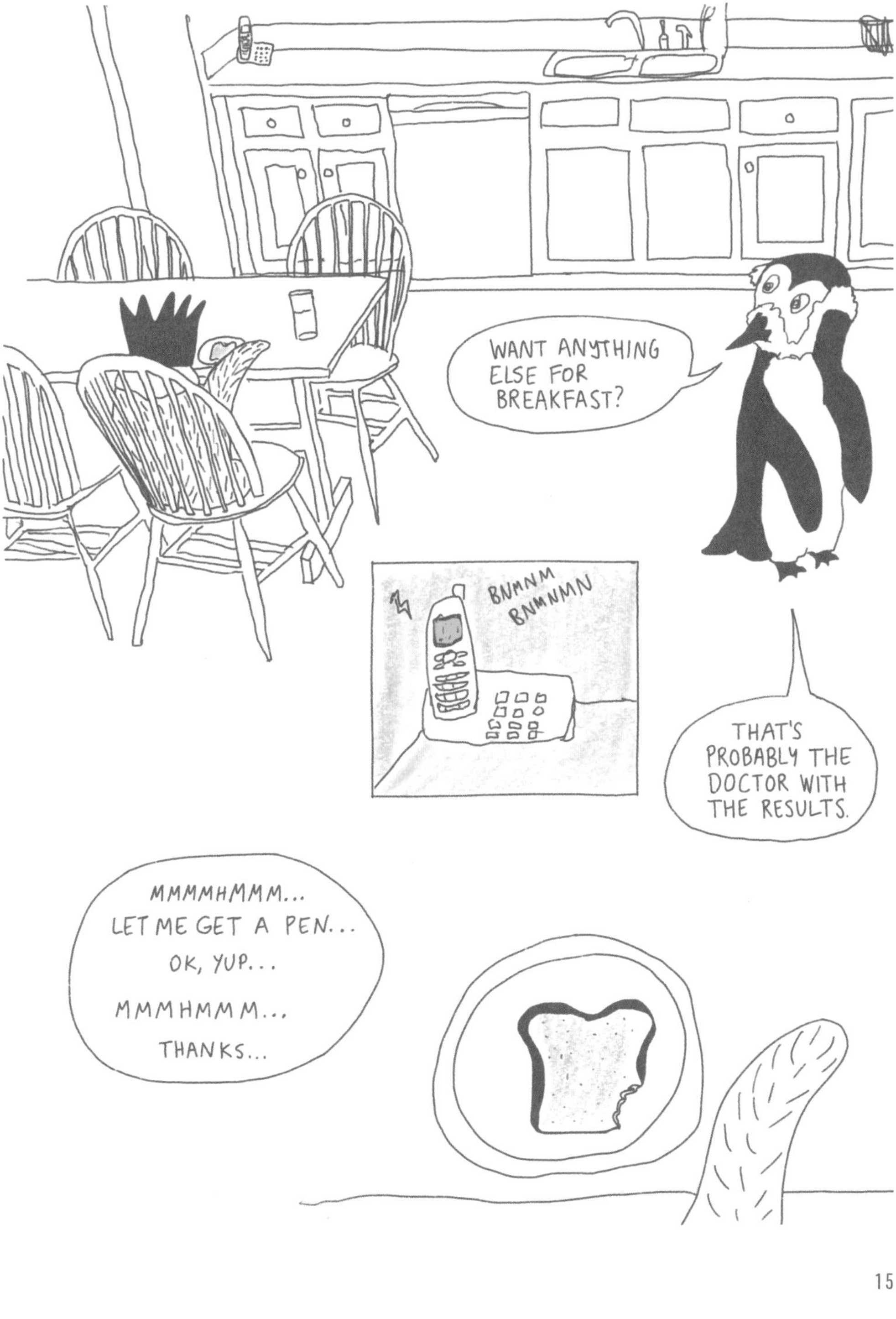
WANT ANYTHING ELSE FOR BREAKFAST?
BNMNM BNMNMN
THAT'S PROBABLY THE DOCTOR WITH THE RESULTS.
MMMMHMMM... LET ME GET A PEN... OK, YUP... MMMHMMM..., THANKS...

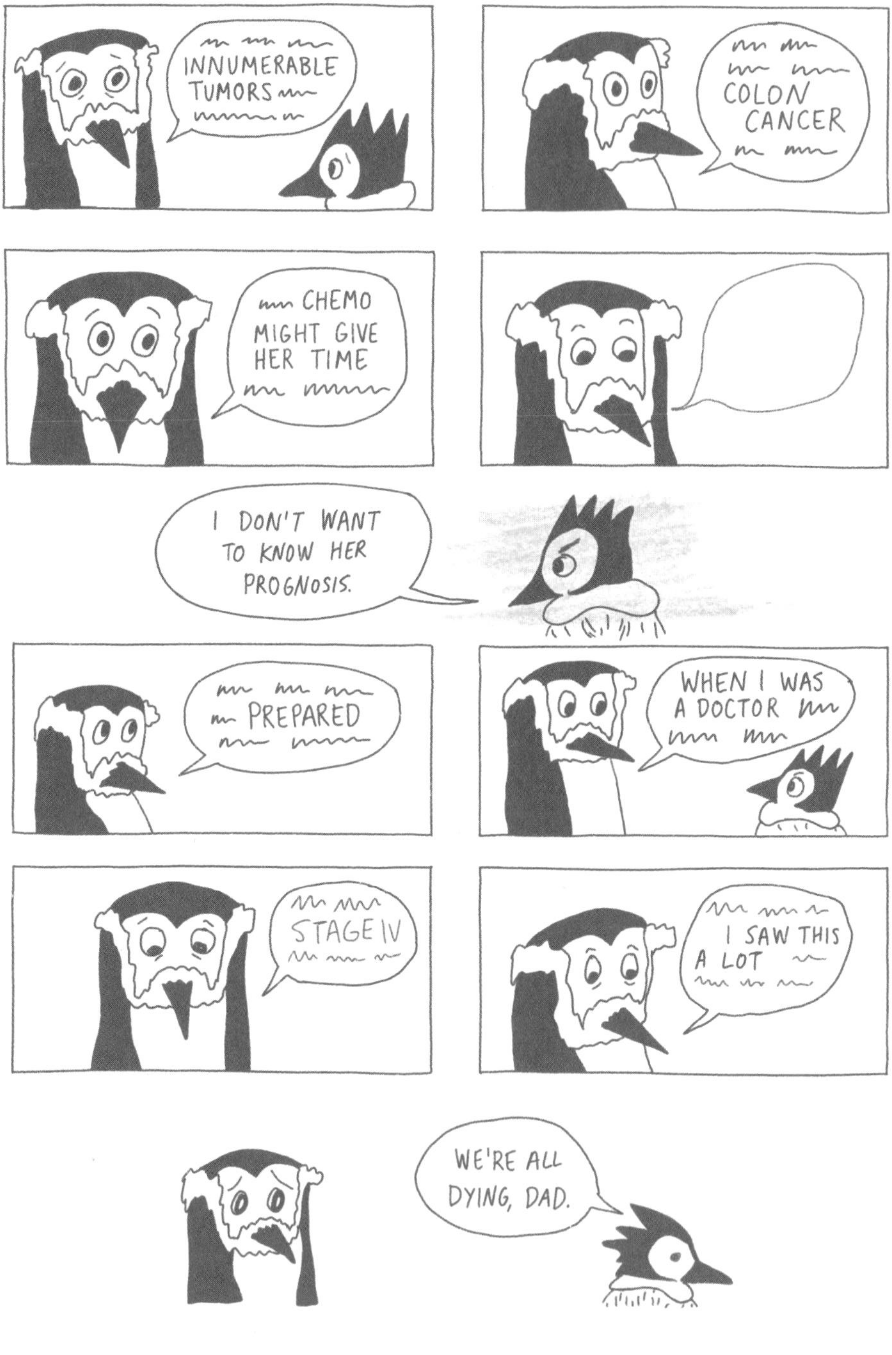
INNUMERABLE TUMORS
COLON CANCER
CHEMO MIGHT GIVE HER TIME
I DON'T WANT TO KNOW HER PROGNOSIS.
PREPARED
WHEN I WAS A DOCTOR
STAGE IV
I SAW THIS A LOT
WE'RE ALL DYING, DAD.

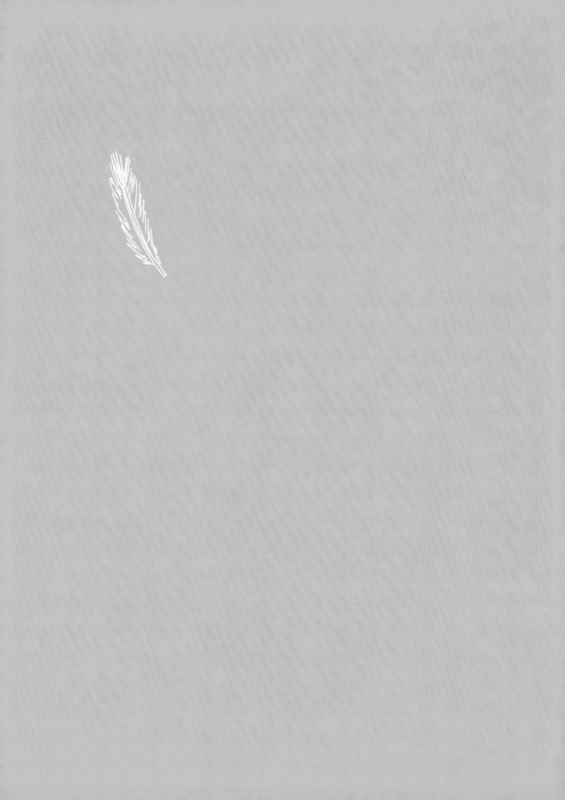

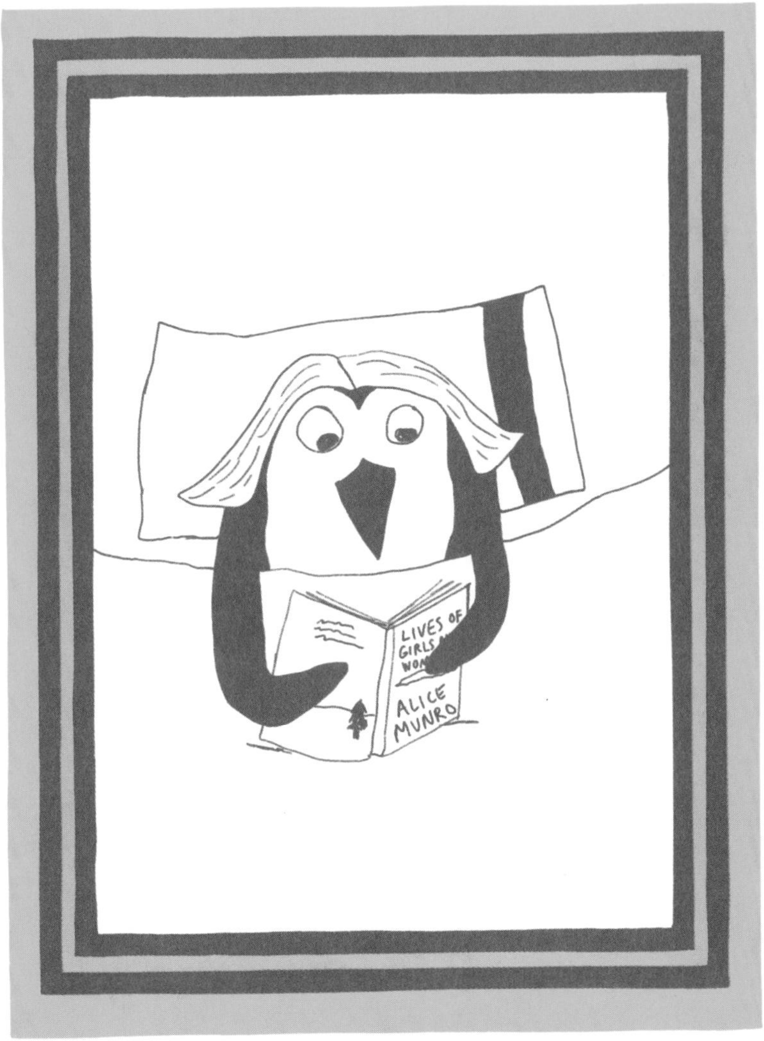
LIVES OF
GIRLS
ALICE
MUNRO

APRIL

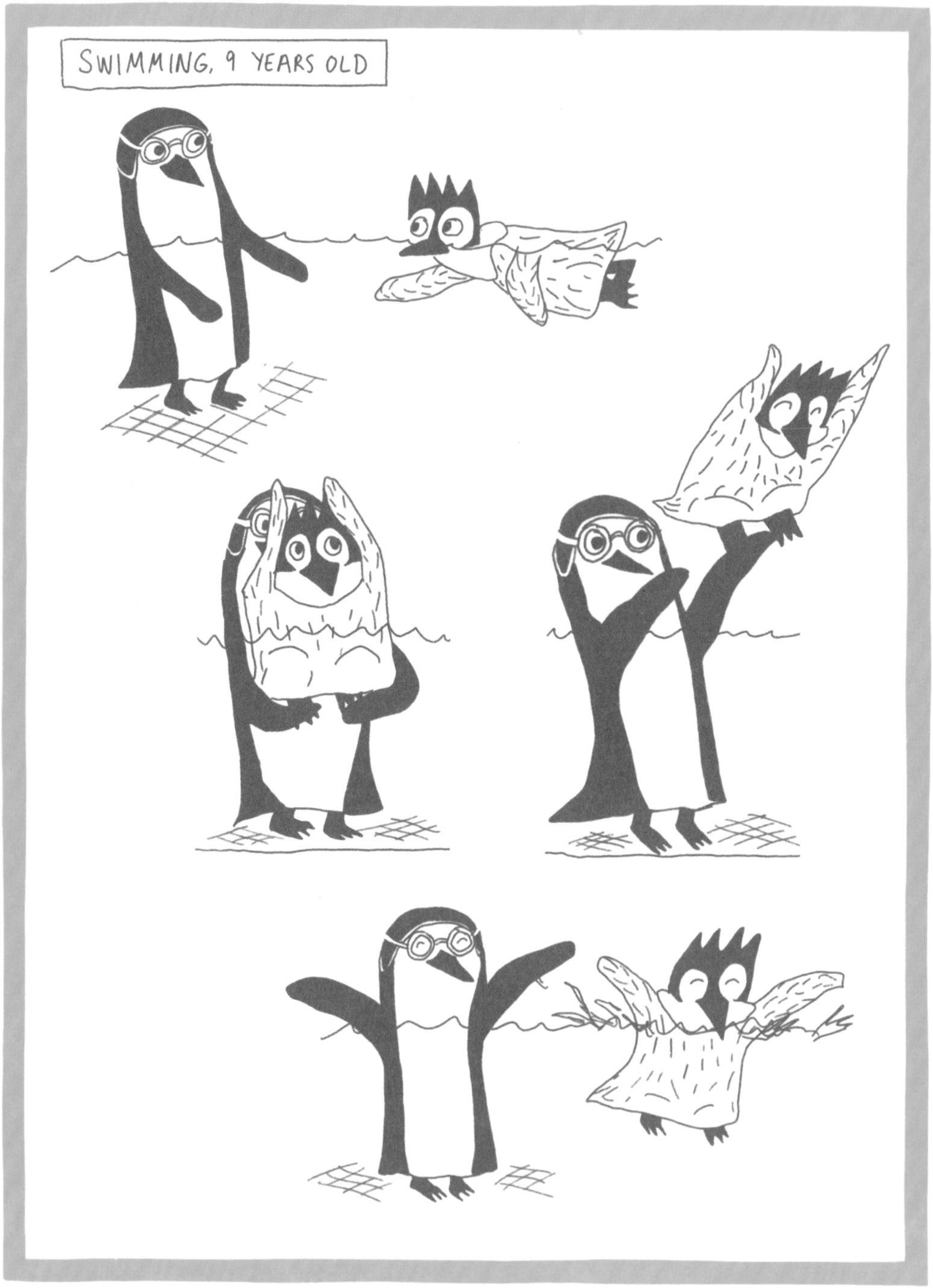
SWIMMING, 9 YEARS OLD

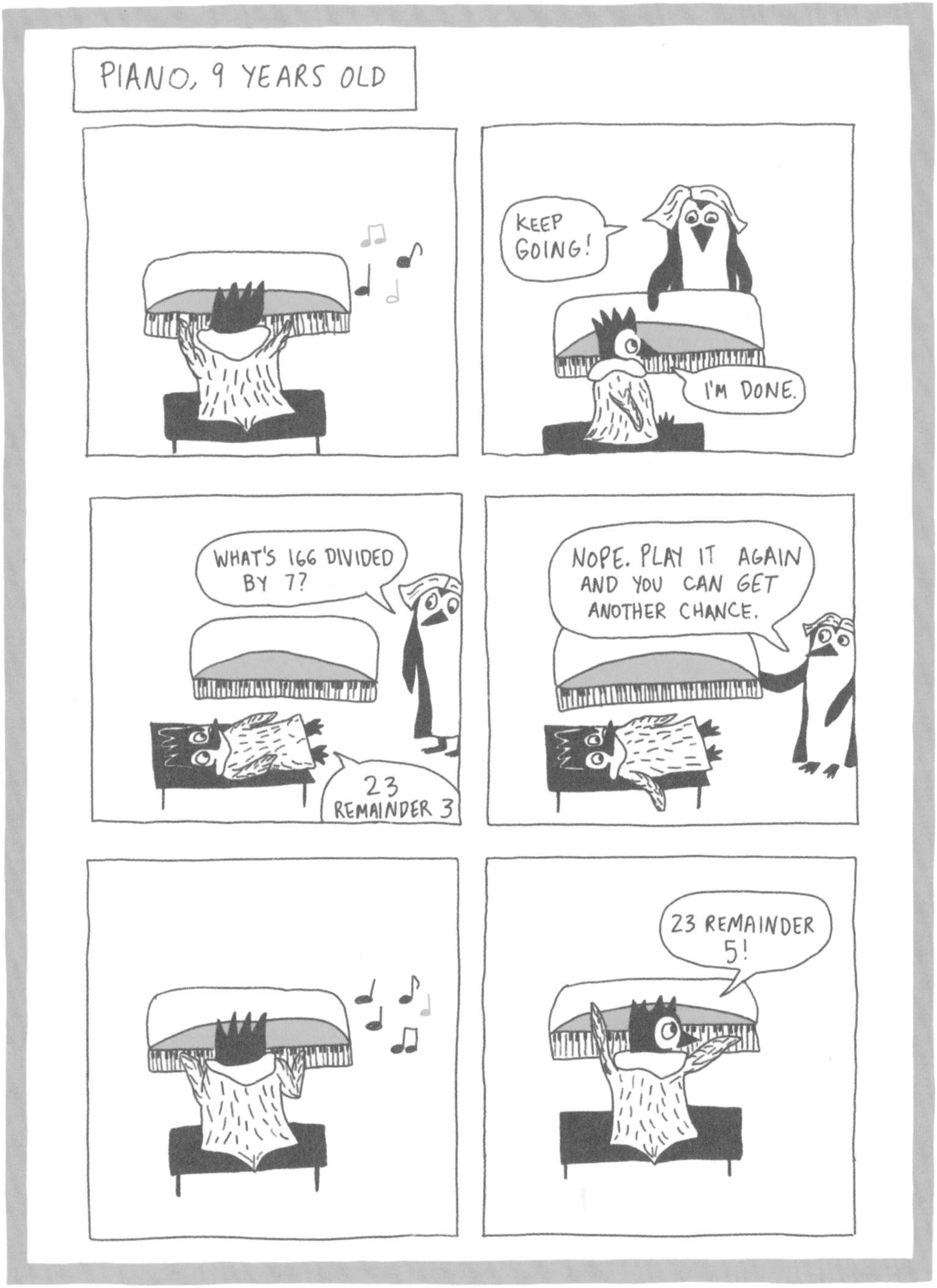
PIANO, 9 YEARS OLD
KEEP GOING!
I'M DONE.
WHAT'S 166 DIVIDED BY 7?
23 REMAINDER 3
NOPE. PLAY IT AGAIN AND YOU CAN GET ANOTHER CHANCE.
23 REMAINDER 5!

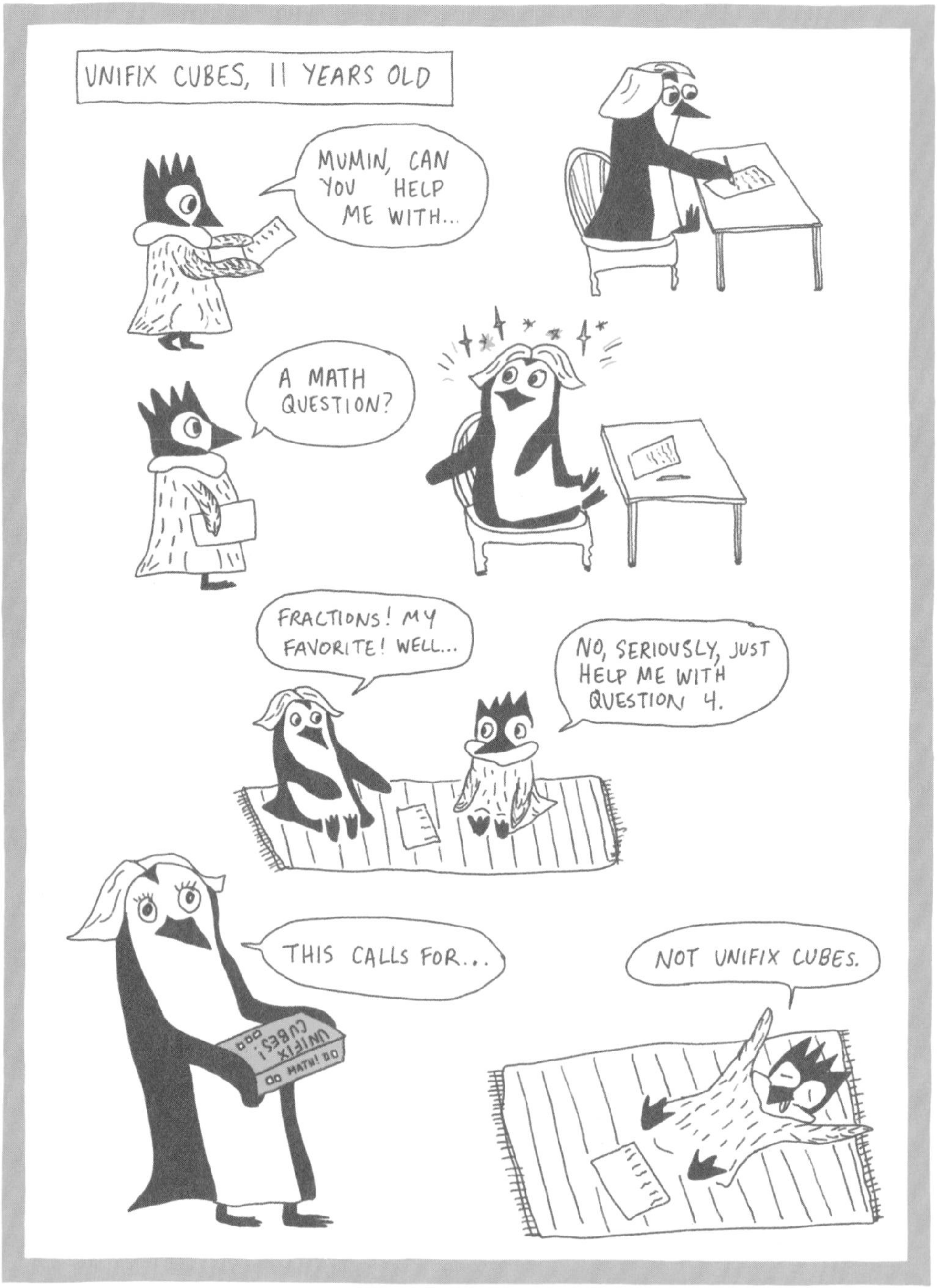
UNIFIX CUBES, 11 YEARS OLD
MUMIN, CAN YOU HELP ME WITH...
A MATH QUESTION?
FRACTIONS! MY FAVORITE! WELL...
NO, SERIOUSLY, JUST HELP ME WITH QUESTION 4.
THIS CALLS FOR...
UNIFIX CUBES!
MATH!
NOT UNIFIX CUBES.

NICKNAMES

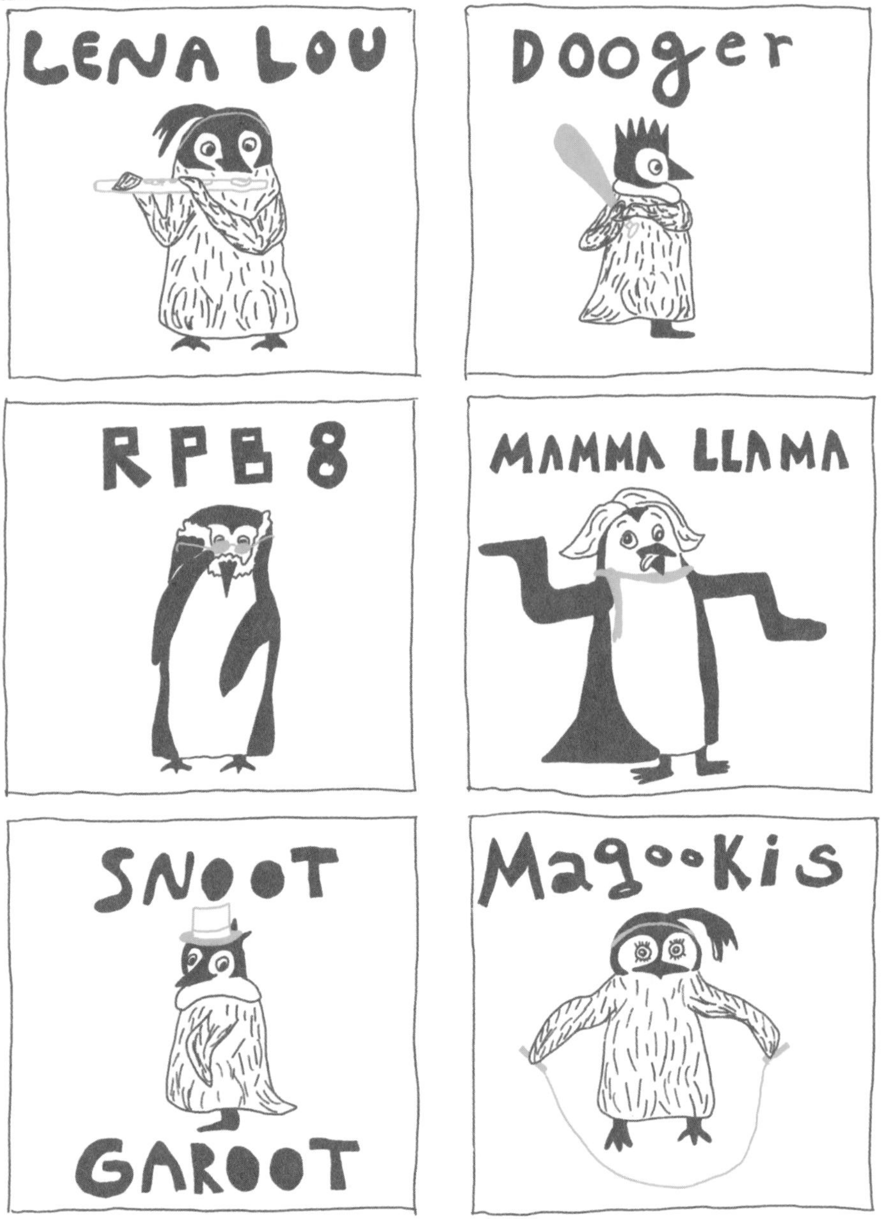
LENA LOU
Dooger
RPB8
MAMMA LLAMA
SNOOT GAROOT
Magookis

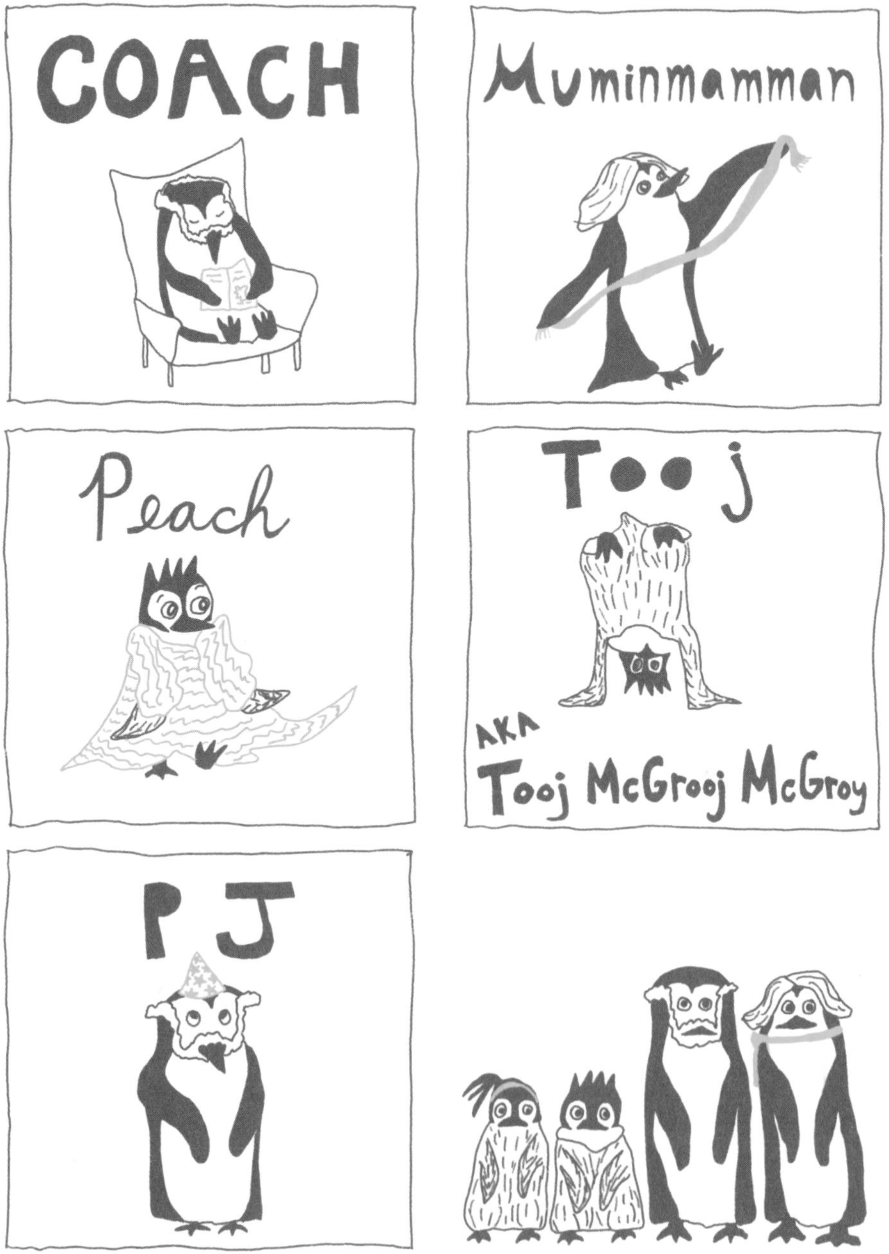
COACH
Muminmamman
Peach
Tooj
AKA
Tooj McGrooj McGroy
PJ

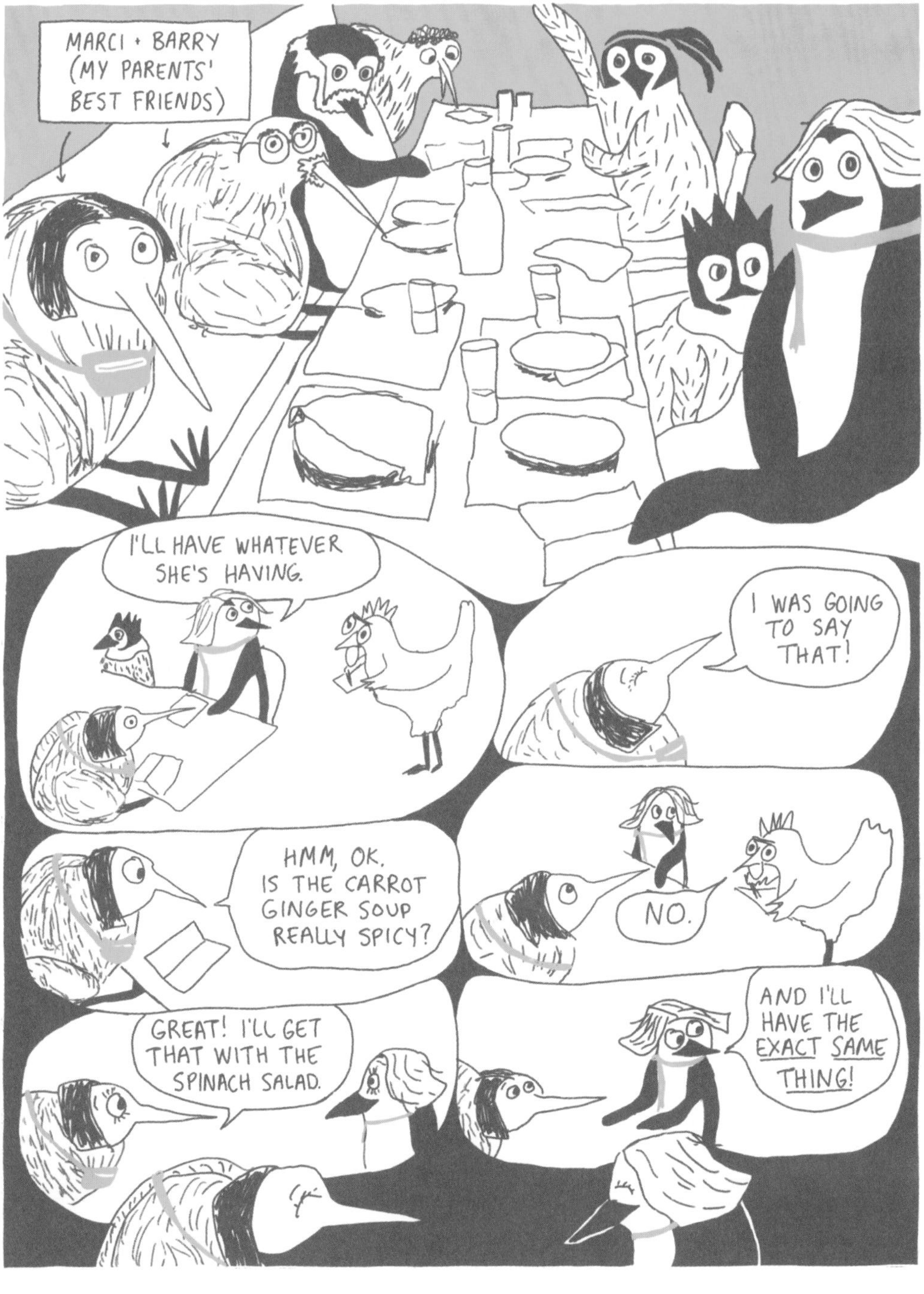
MARCI + BARRY (MY PARENTS' BEST FRIENDS)
I'LL HAVE WHATEVER SHE'S HAVING.
I WAS GOING TO SAY THAT!
HMM, OK. IS THE CARROT GINGER SOUP REALLY SPICY?
NO.
GREAT! I'LL GET THAT WITH THE SPINACH SALAD.
AND I'LL HAVE THE EXACT SAME THING!

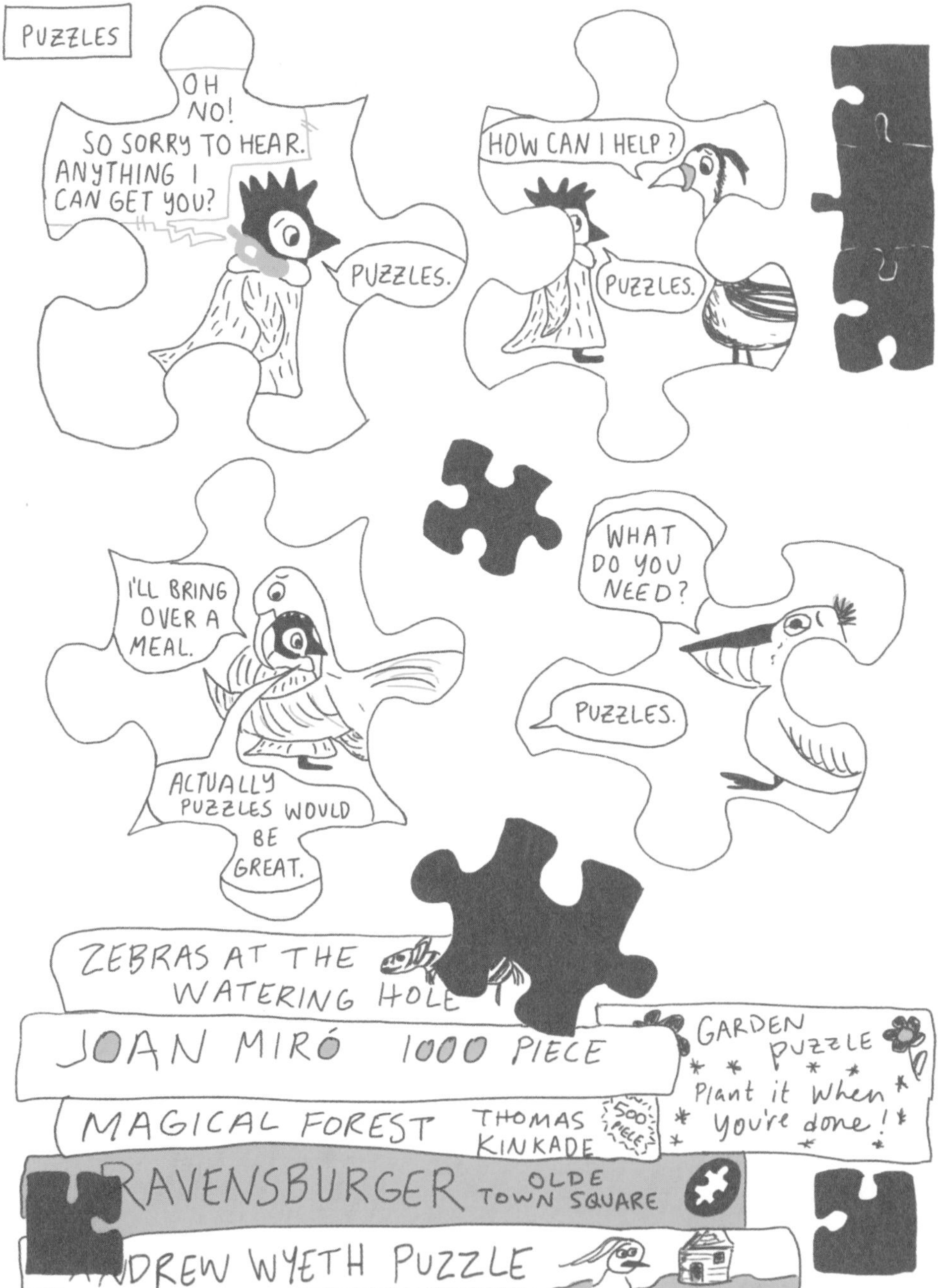
PUZZLES
OH NO! SO SORRY TO HEAR. ANYTHING I CAN GET YOU?
PUZZLES.
HOW CAN I HELP?
PUZZLES.
I'LL BRING OVER A MEAL.
ACTUALLY PUZZLES WOULD BE GREAT.
WHAT DO YOU NEED?
PUZZLES.
ZEBRAS AT THE WATERING HOLE
JOAN MIRÓ 1000 PIECE
GARDEN PUZZLE
Plant it when you're done!
MAGICAL FOREST THOMAS KINKADE
500 PIECE
RAVENSBURGER OLDE TOWN SQUARE
DREW WYETH PUZZLE

WAITING FOR THEM TO GET BACK FROM GETTING A SECOND OPINION

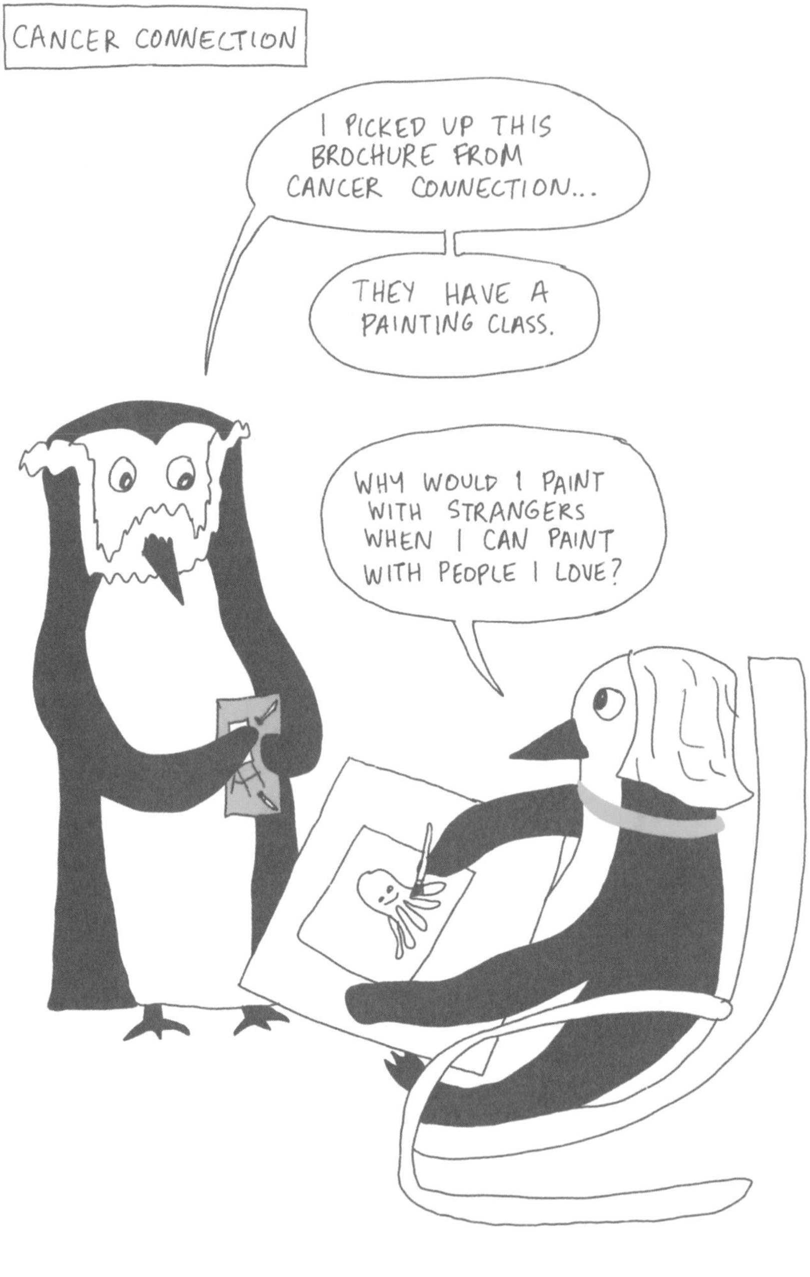
CANCER CONNECTION
I PICKED UP THIS BROCHURE FROM CANCER CONNECTION...
THEY HAVE A PAINTING CLASS.
WHY WOULD I PAINT WITH STRANGERS WHEN I CAN PAINT WITH PEOPLE I LOVE?

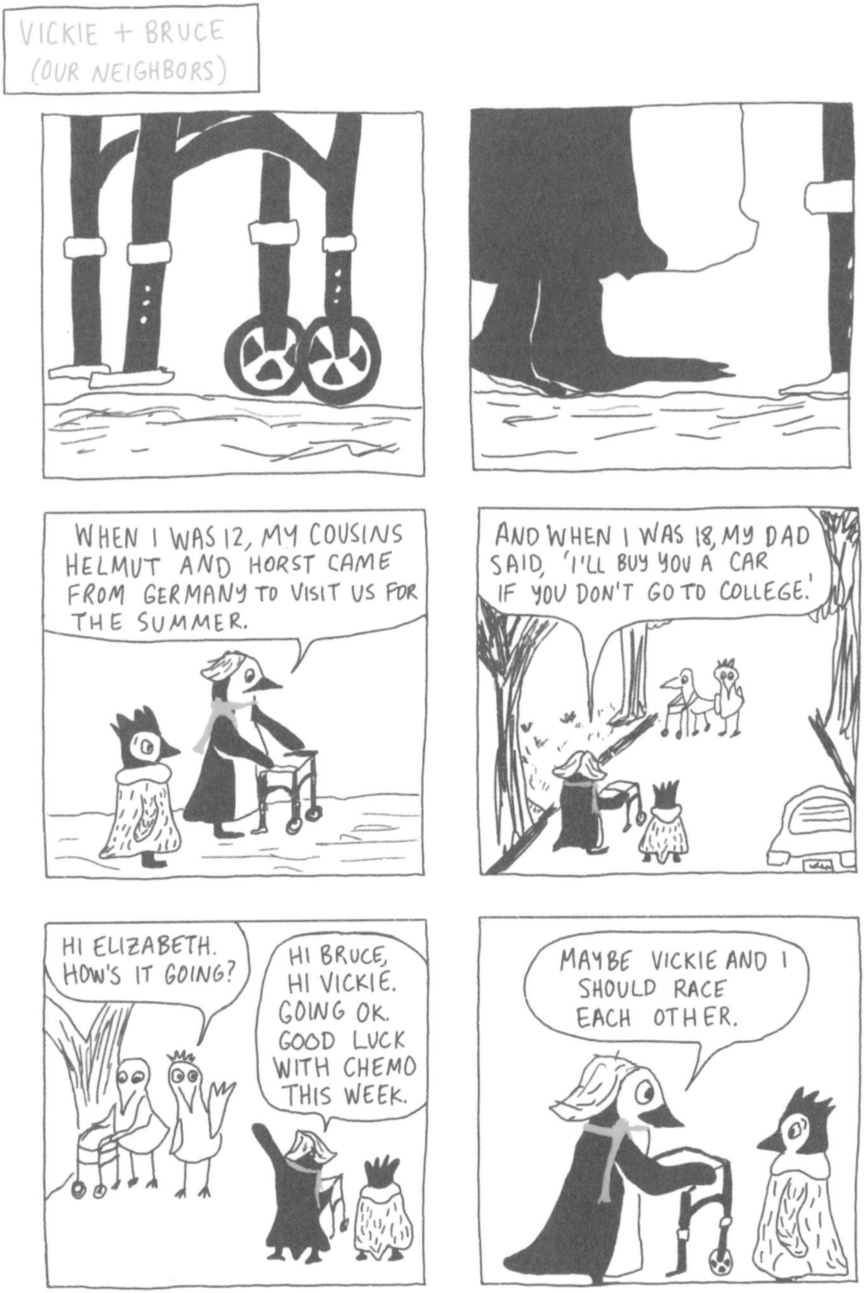
VICKIE + BRUCE
(OUR NEIGHBORS)
WHEN I WAS 12, MY COUSINS HELMUT AND HORST CAME FROM GERMANY TO VISIT US FOR THE SUMMER.
AND WHEN I WAS 18, MY DAD SAID, 'I'LL BUY YOU A CAR IF YOU DON'T GO TO COLLEGE.'
HI ELIZABETH. HOW'S IT GOING?
HI BRUCE, HI VICKIE. GOING OK. GOOD LUCK WITH CHEMO THIS WEEK.
MAYBE VICKIE AND I SHOULD RACE EACH OTHER.

ART IN THE HOUSE

'94 WORLD CUP

PAINTED PLATE FOR FATHER'S DAY

DARK (CREEPY?) KÄTHE KOLLWITZ PRINT ↓

THIS CORN BY ELENA IS 5 FT TALL

MY 8TH GRADE STLL LIFE

POSING WITH COOKIE MONSTER AT OUR COUSIN'S BAR MITZVAH

Van Gogh
at the MOMA
NOV 25- MAR 22

CHEMO

I'M SARITA! HOW'S YOUR TRANSFUSION GOING?

...AND THEN IN FEBRUARY I STARTED DOING SO MUCH BETTER.

TO CELEBRATE, WE EVEN NAMED OUR DOG 'CHEMO'!

SPELLED K-E-M-O.

MAY

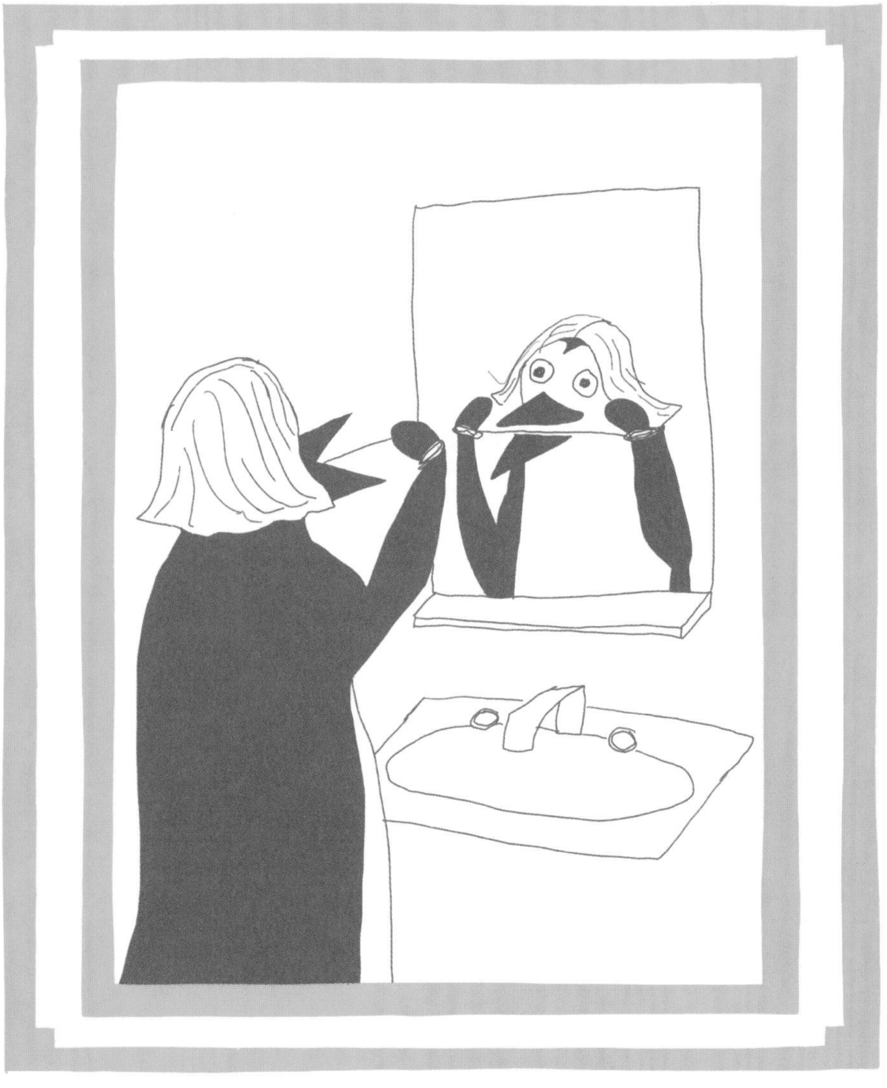

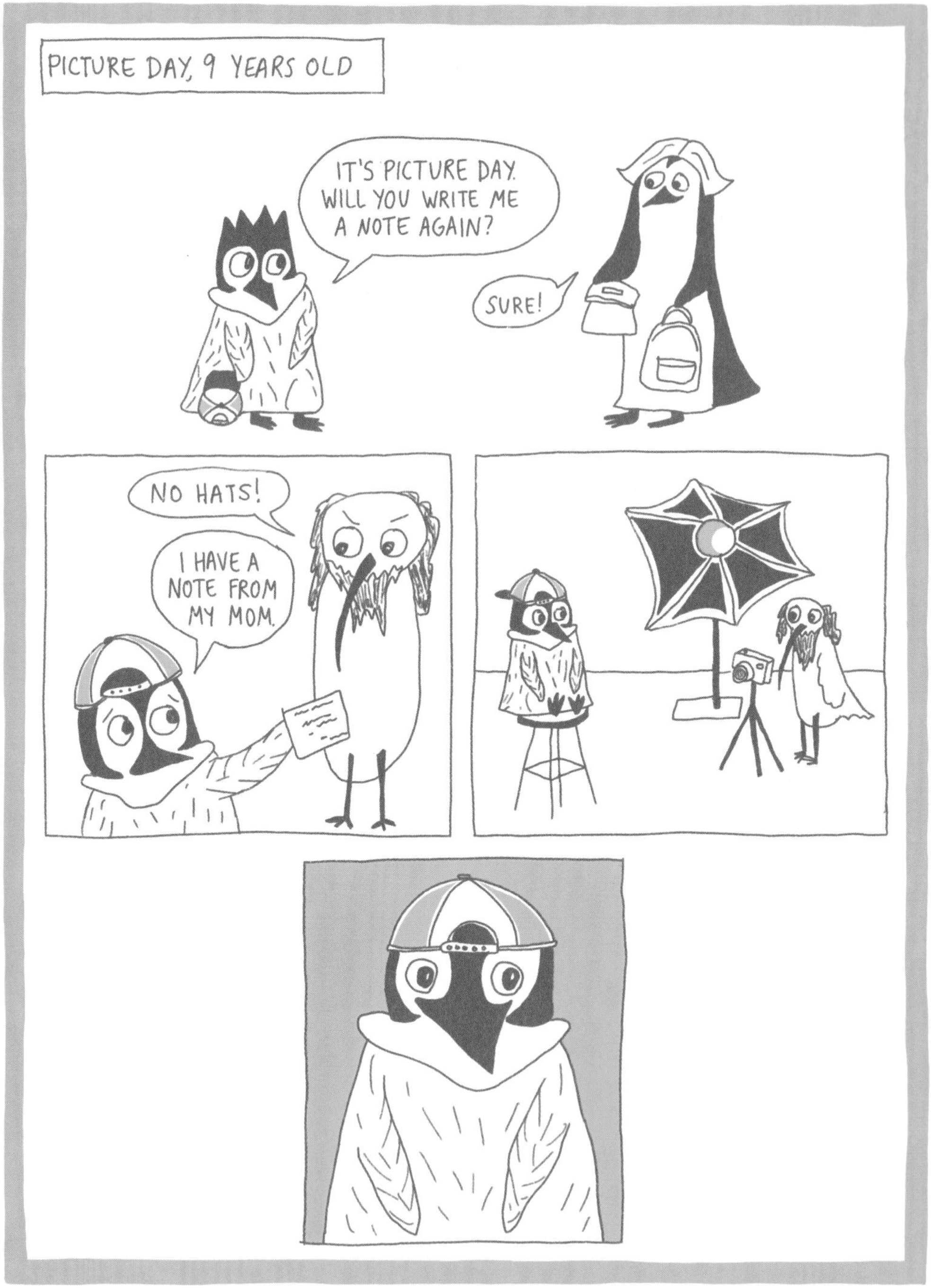
PICTURE DAY, 9 YEARS OLD
IT'S PICTURE DAY. WILL YOU WRITE ME A NOTE AGAIN?
SURE!
NO HATS!
I HAVE A NOTE FROM MY MOM.

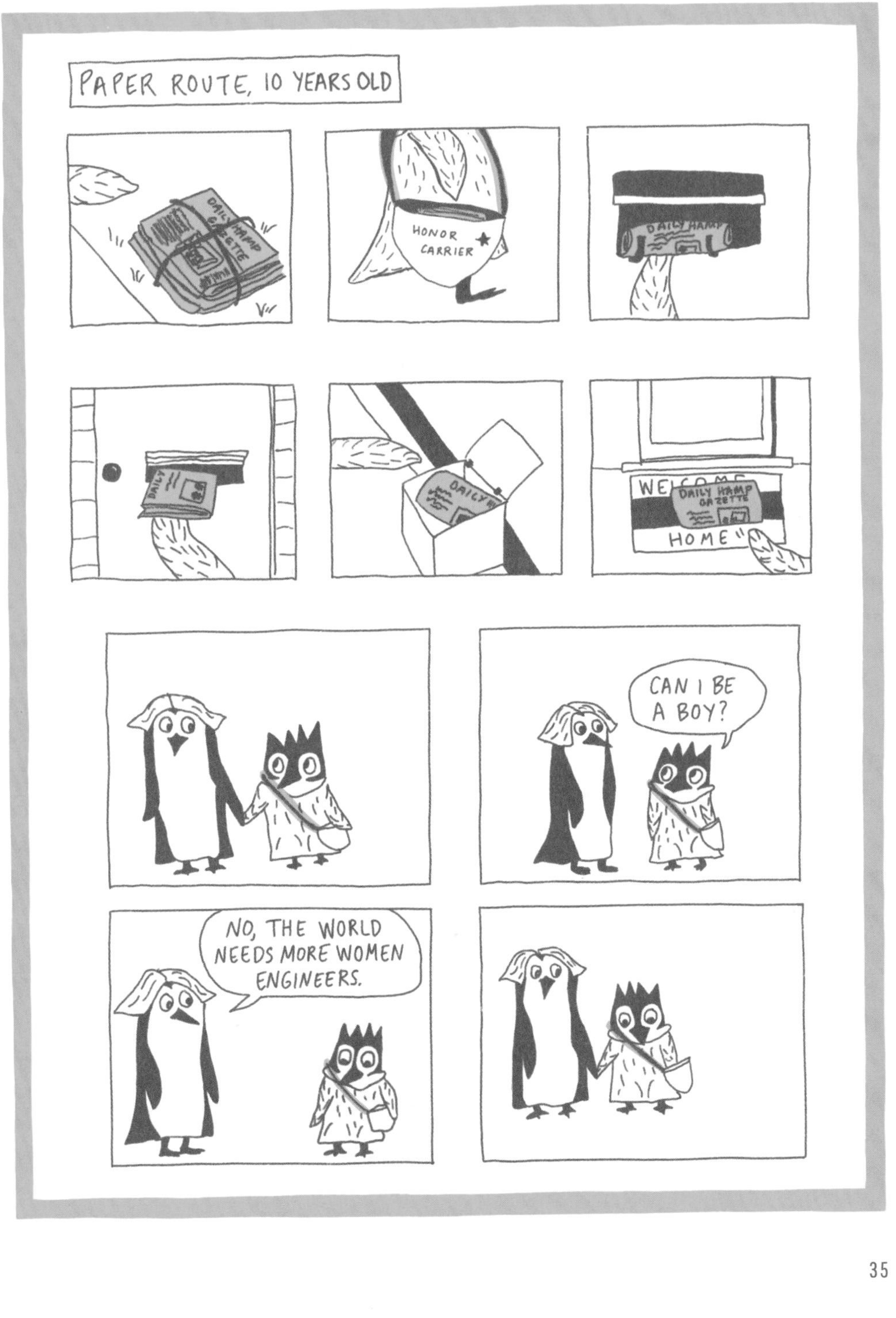
PAPER ROUTE, 10 YEARS OLD
DAILY HAMP GAZETTE
HONOR CARRIER
DAILY HAMP
DAILY
DAILY
DAILY HAMP GAZETTE
HOME
CAN I BE A BOY?
NO, THE WORLD NEEDS MORE WOMEN ENGINEERS.

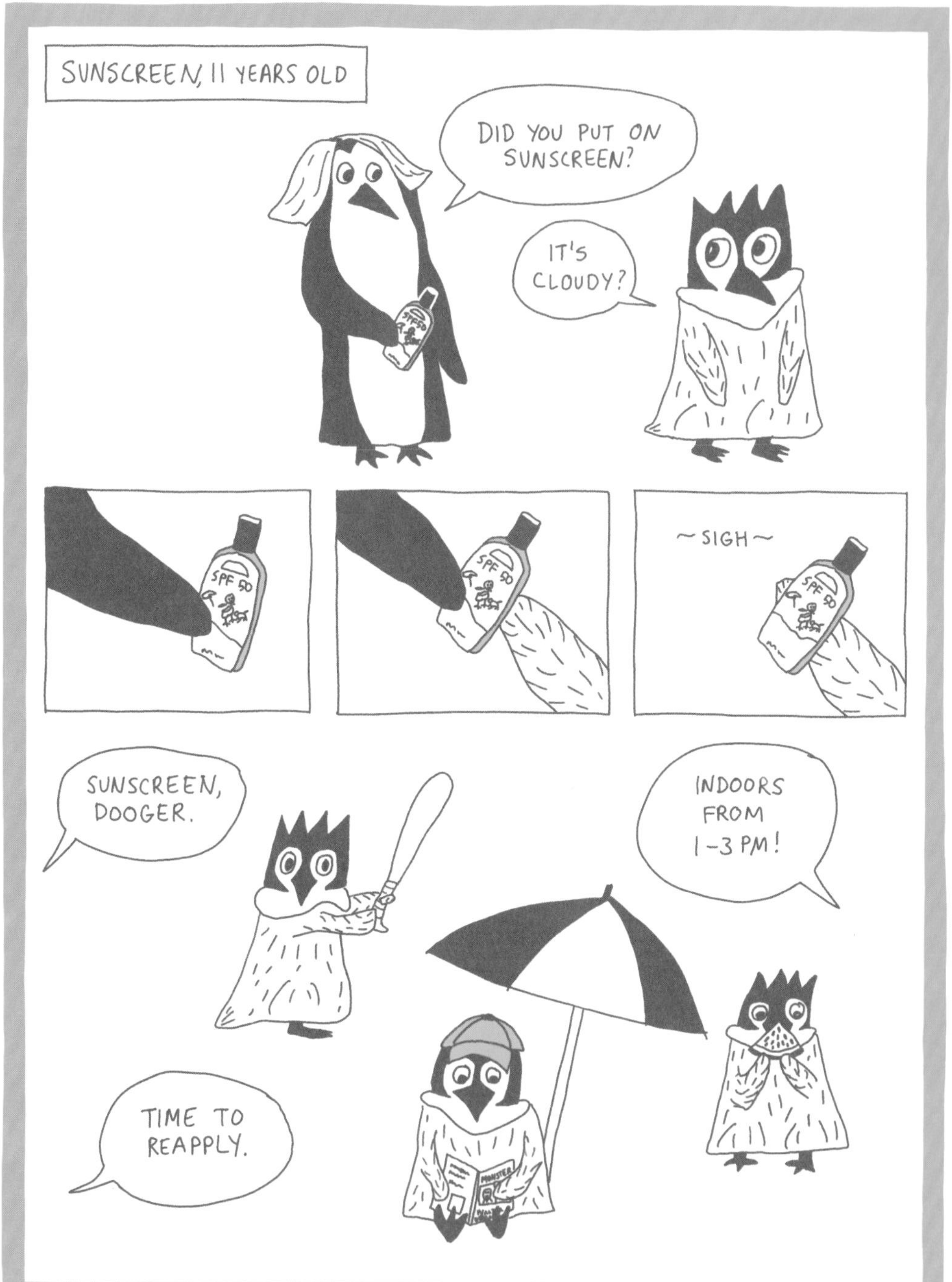
SUNSCREEN, 11 YEARS OLD
DID YOU PUT ON SUNSCREEN?
IT'S CLOUDY?
SPF 50
~SIGH~
SUNSCREEN, DOOGER.
INDOORS FROM 1-3 PM!
TIME TO REAPPLY.
MONSTER

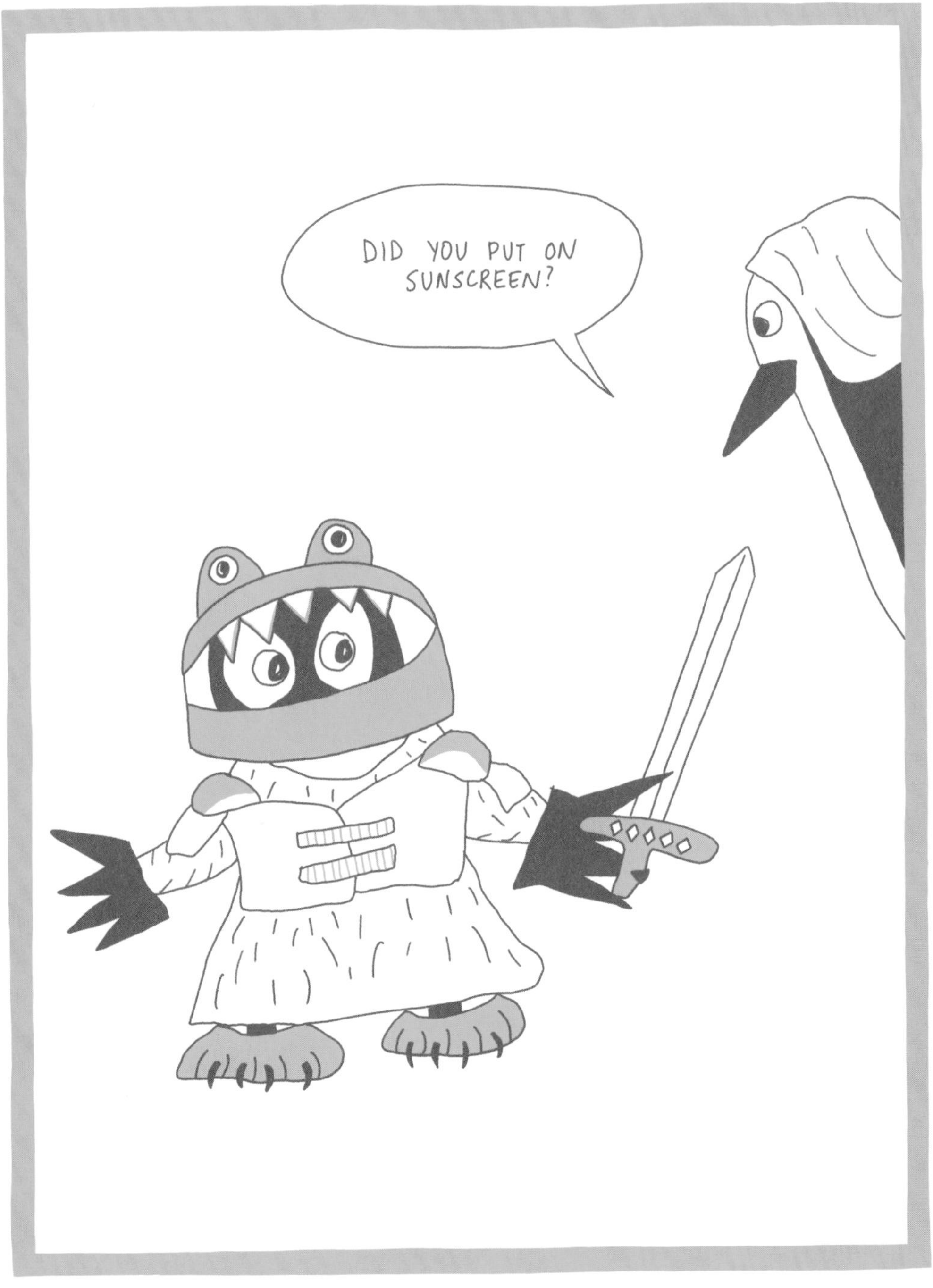
DID YOU PUT ON SUNSCREEN?

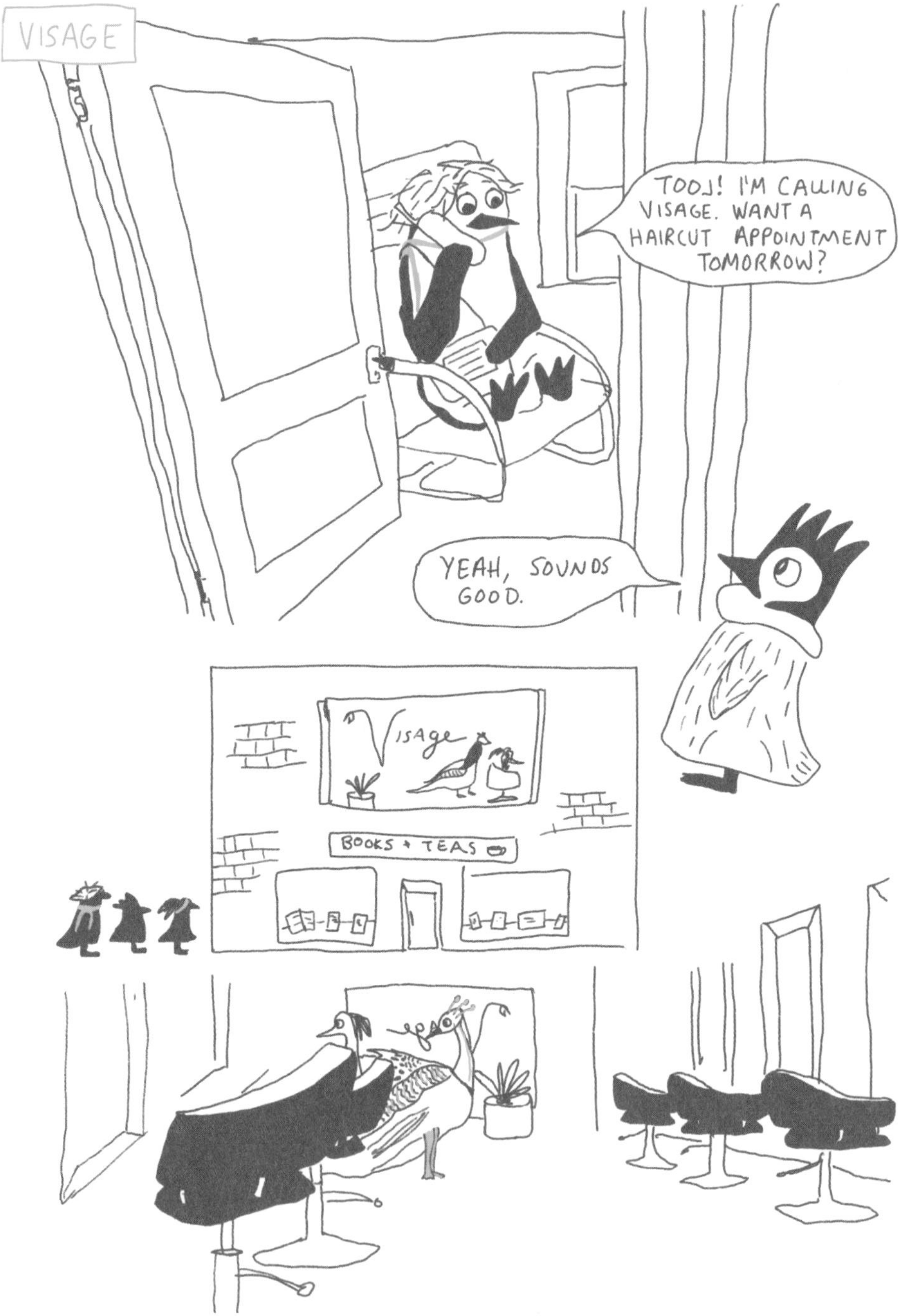
VISAGE
TOOJ! I'M CALLING VISAGE. WANT A HAIRCUT APPOINTMENT TOMORROW?
YEAH, SOUNDS GOOD.
Visage
BOOKS + TEAS

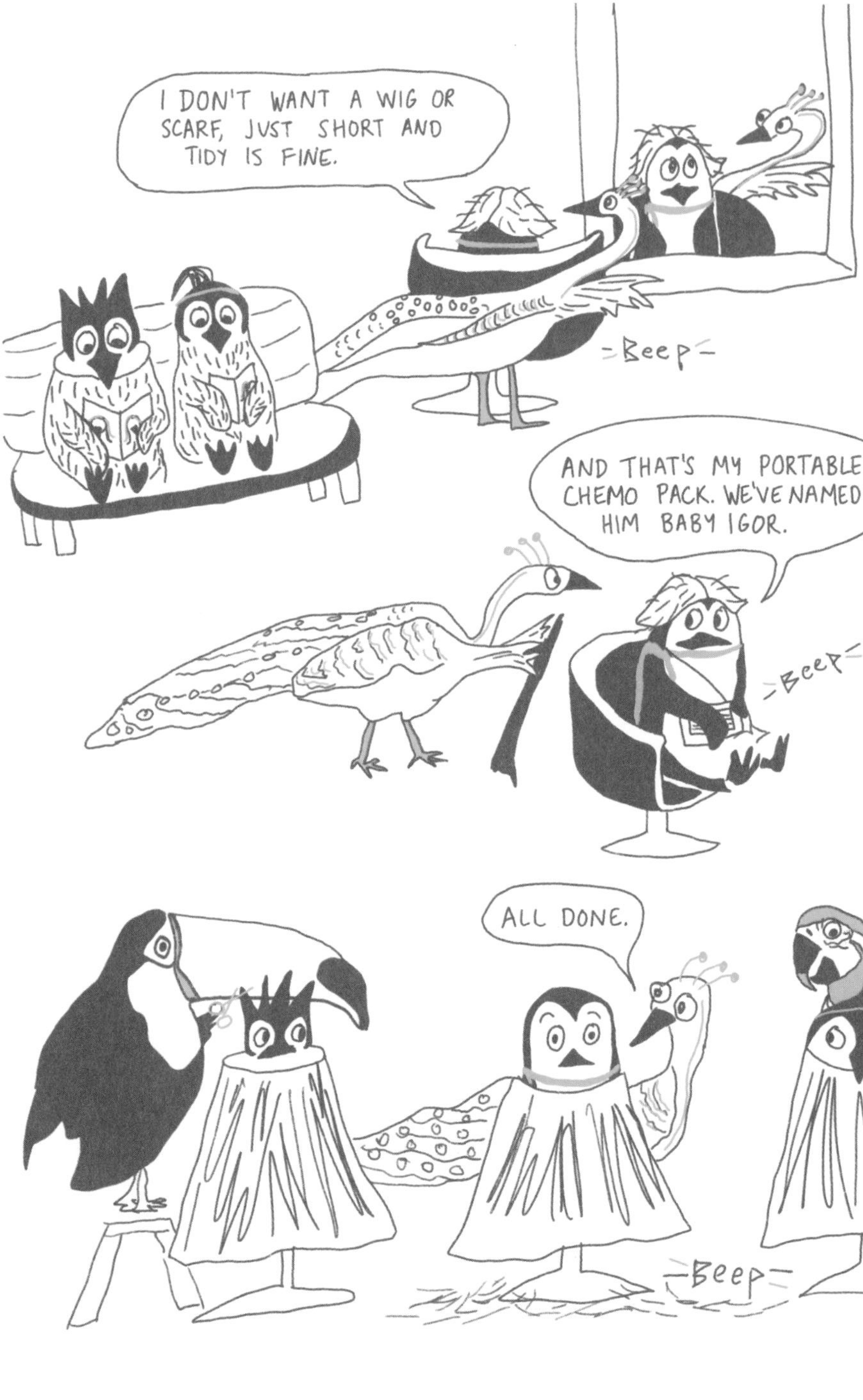
I DON'T WANT A WIG OR SCARF, JUST SHORT AND TIDY IS FINE.
Beep
AND THAT'S MY PORTABLE CHEMO PACK. WE'VE NAMED HIM BABY IGOR.
Beep
ALL DONE.
Beep

MOVING OUT

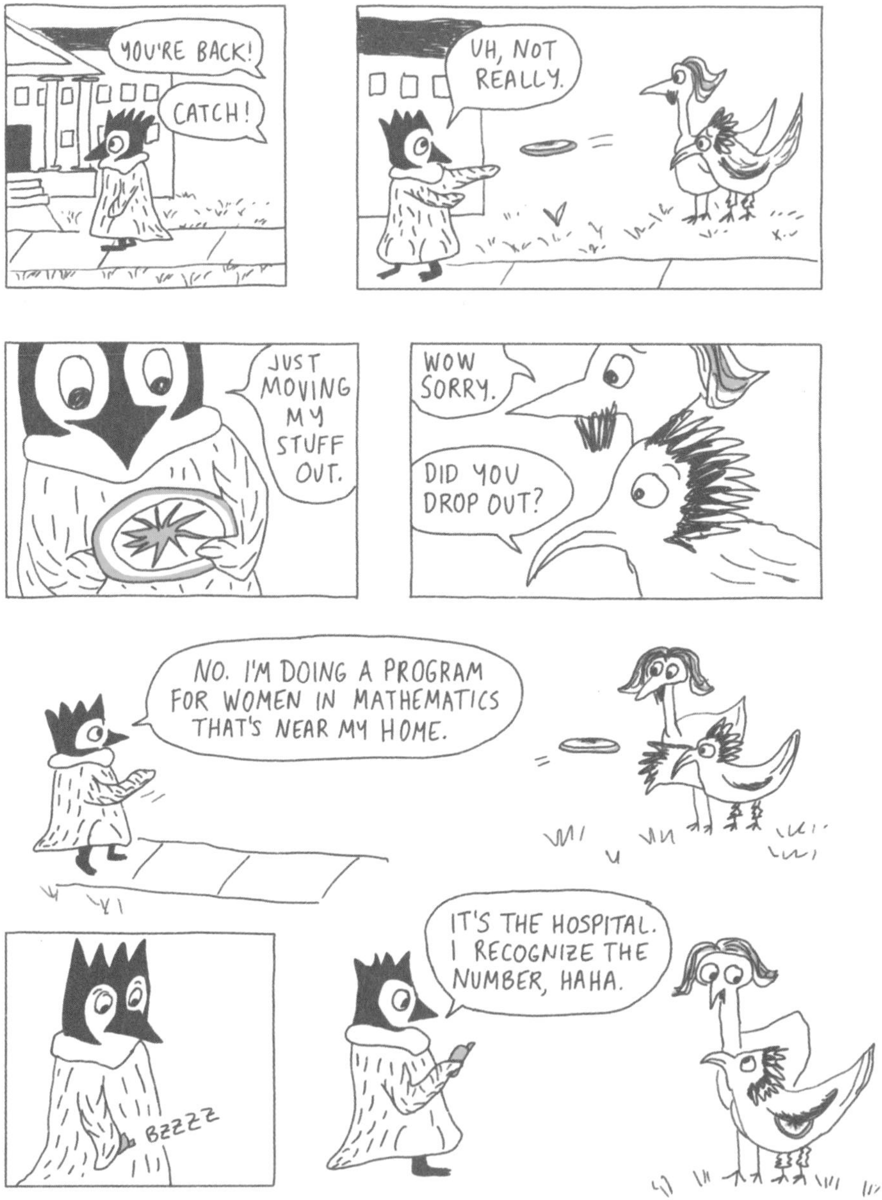
YOU'RE BACK!
CATCH!
UH, NOT REALLY.
JUST MOVING MY STUFF OUT.
WOW SORRY.
DID YOU DROP OUT?
NO. I'M DOING A PROGRAM FOR WOMEN IN MATHEMATICS THAT'S NEAR MY HOME.
BZZZZ
IT'S THE HOSPITAL. I RECOGNIZE THE NUMBER, HAHA.

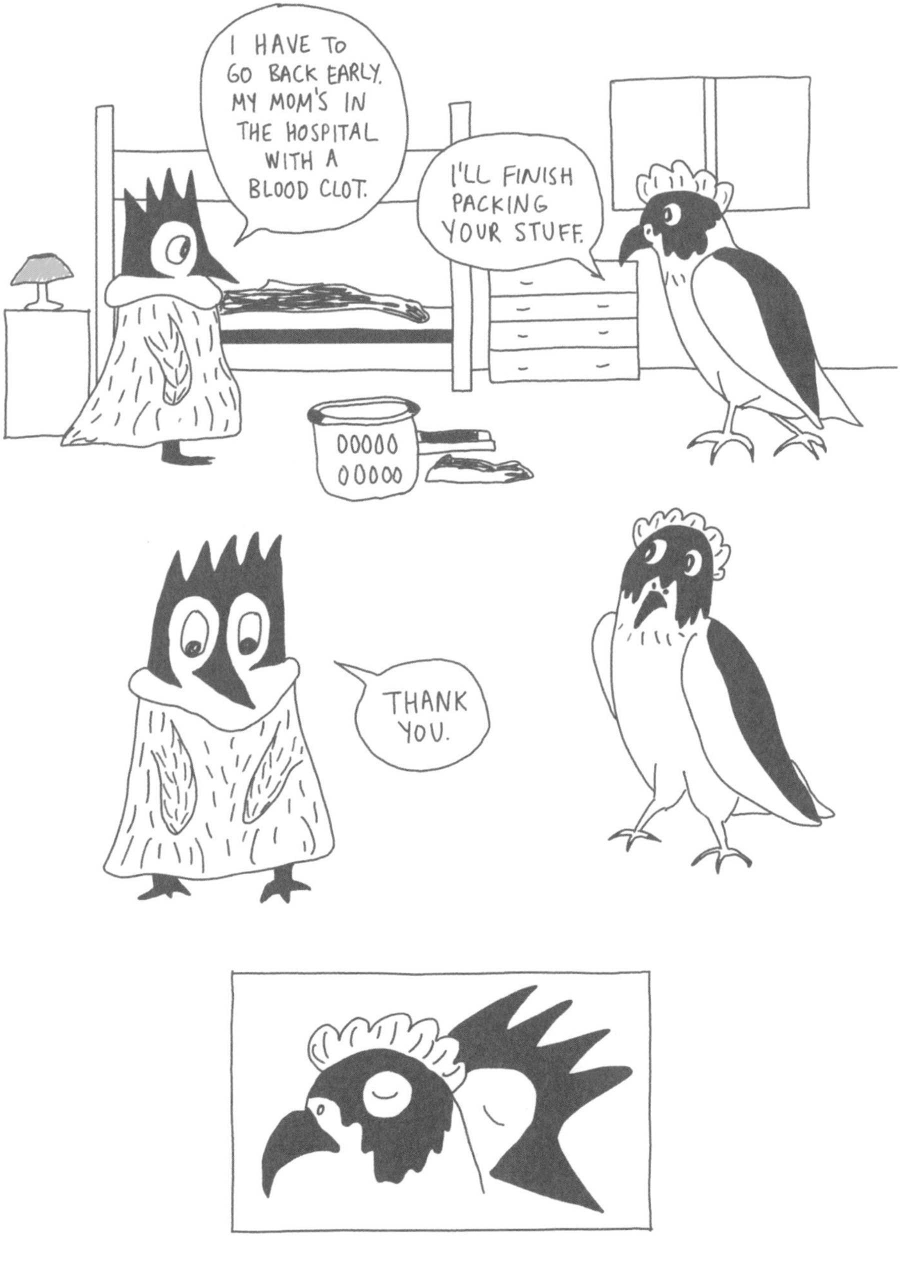
I HAVE TO GO BACK EARLY. MY MOM'S IN THE HOSPITAL WITH A BLOOD CLOT.
I'LL FINISH PACKING YOUR STUFF.
THANK YOU.

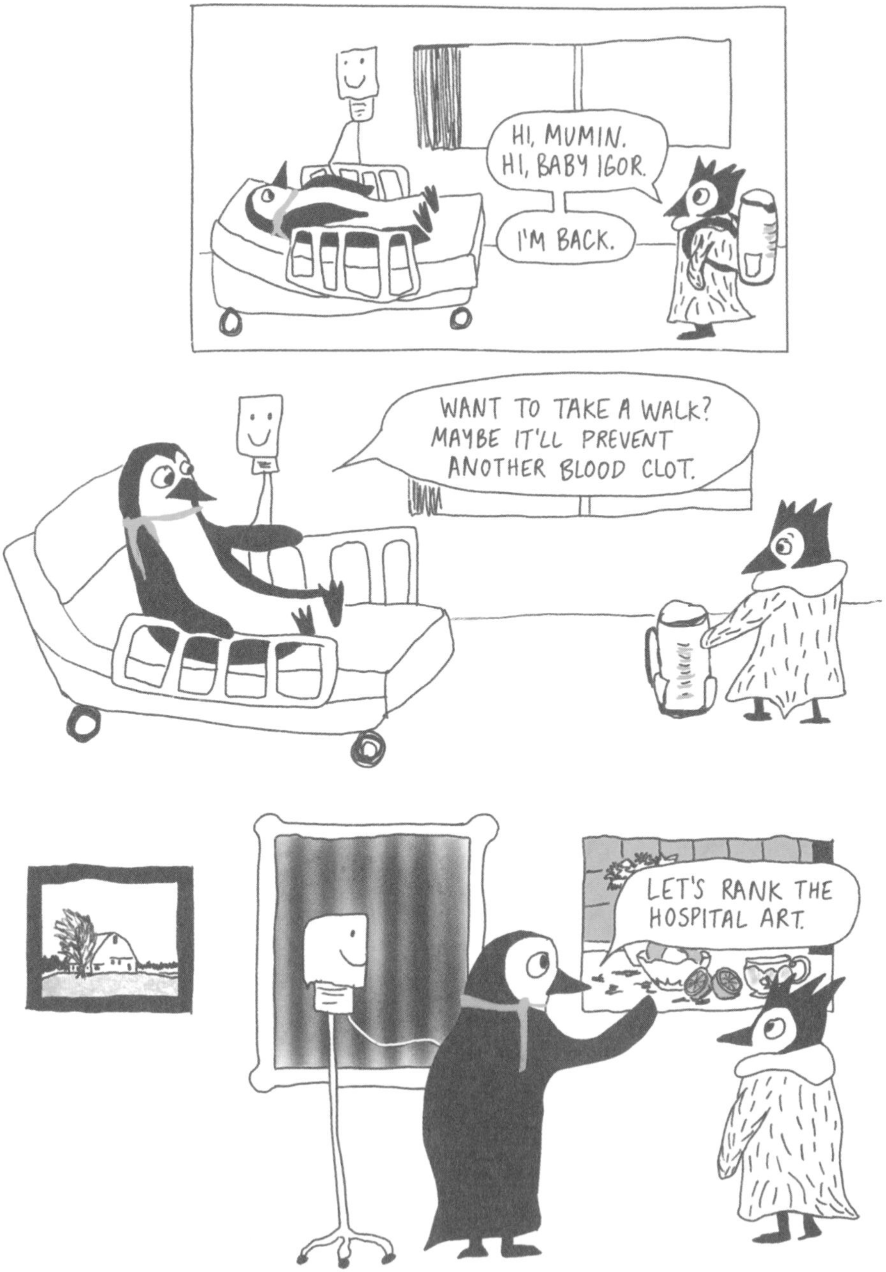
HI, MUMIN.
HI, BABY IGOR.
I'M BACK.
WANT TO TAKE A WALK? MAYBE IT'LL PREVENT ANOTHER BLOOD CLOT.
LET'S RANK THE HOSPITAL ART.

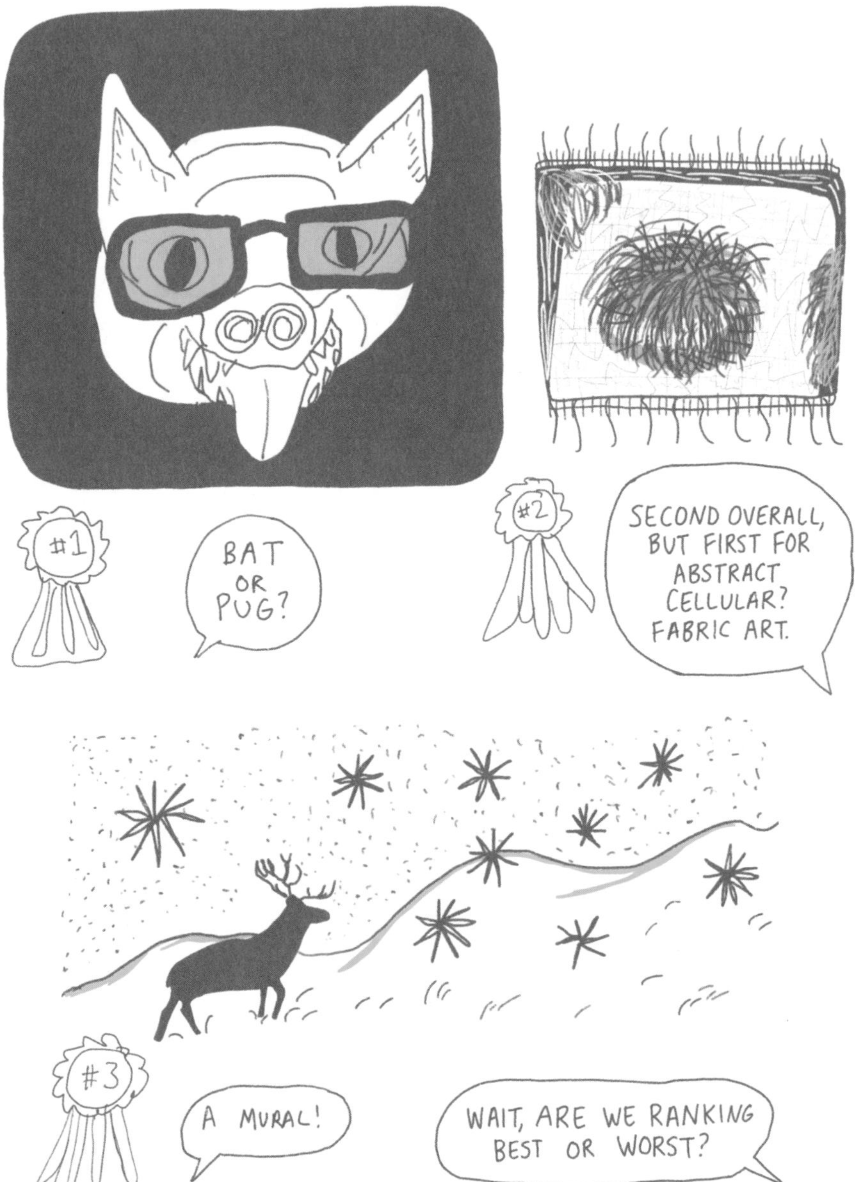
#1
BAT OR PUG?
#2
SECOND OVERALL, BUT FIRST FOR ABSTRACT CELLULAR? FABRIC ART.
#3
A MURAL!
WAIT, ARE WE RANKING BEST OR WORST?

GENDERQUEER

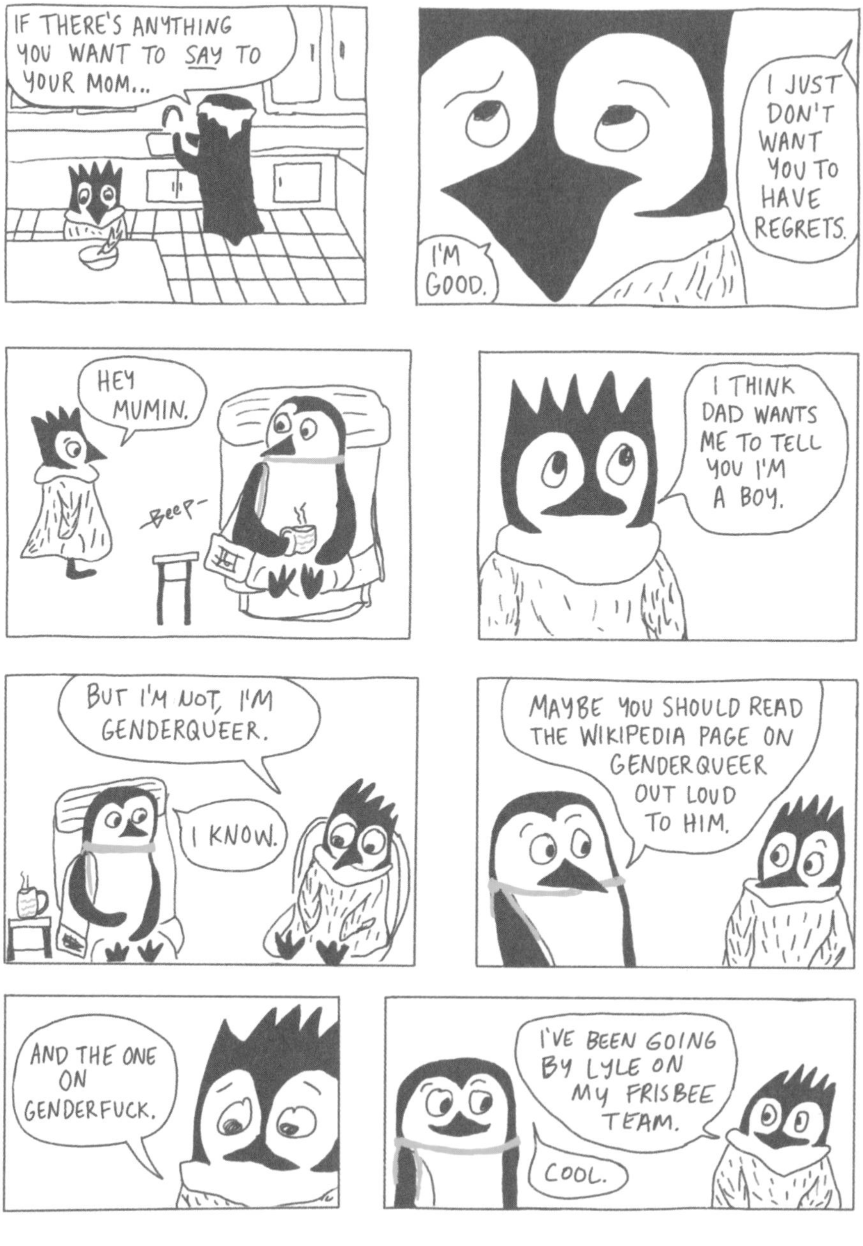
IF THERE'S ANYTHING YOU WANT TO SAY TO YOUR MOM...
I JUST DON'T WANT YOU TO HAVE REGRETS.
I'M GOOD.
HEY MUMIN.
-BEEP-
I THINK DAD WANTS ME TO TELL YOU I'M A BOY.
BUT I'M NOT, I'M GENDERQUEER.
I KNOW.
MAYBE YOU SHOULD READ THE WIKIPEDIA PAGE ON GENDERQUEER OUT LOUD TO HIM.
AND THE ONE ON GENDERFUCK.
I'VE BEEN GOING BY LYLE ON MY FRISBEE TEAM.
COOL.

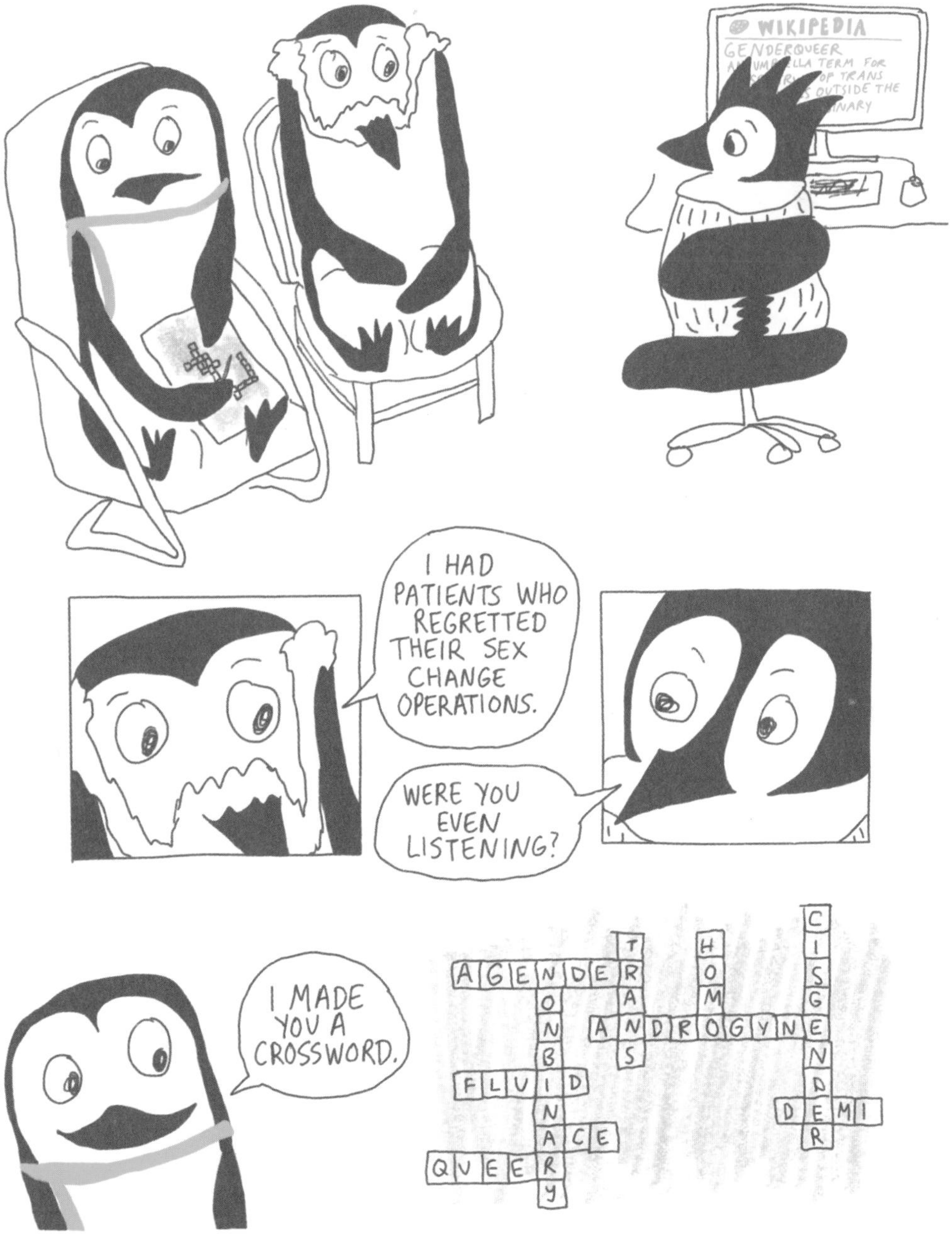
WIKIPEDIA
GENDERQUEER
I HAD PATIENTS WHO REGRETTED THEIR SEX CHANGE OPERATIONS.
WERE YOU EVEN LISTENING?
I MADE YOU A CROSSWORD.
AGENDER
TRANS
HOM
CISGENDER
NONBINARY
ANDROGYNE
FLUID
DEMI
ACE
QUEER

JUNE

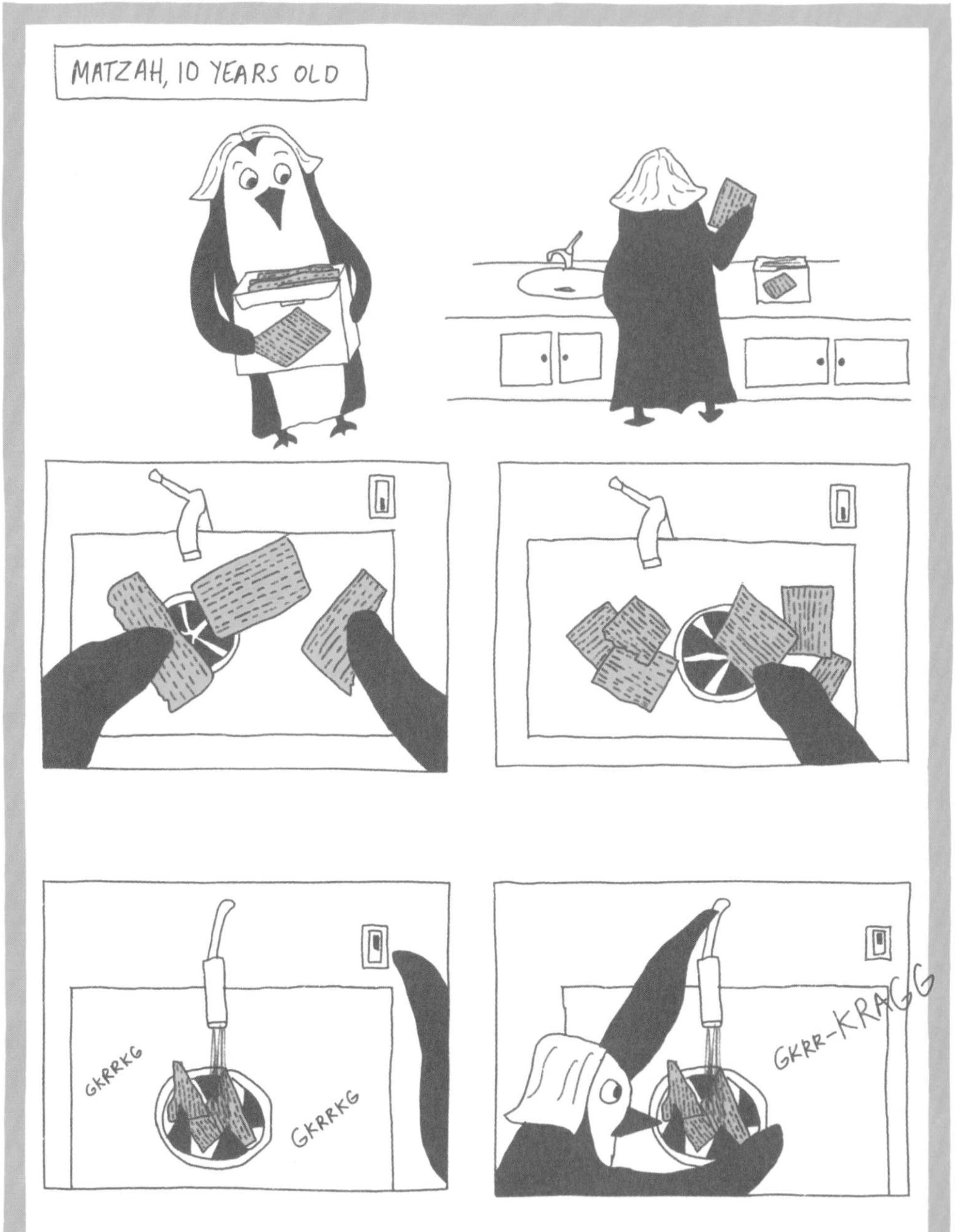
MATZAH, 10 YEARS OLD
GKRRKG
GKRRKG
GKRR-KRAGG

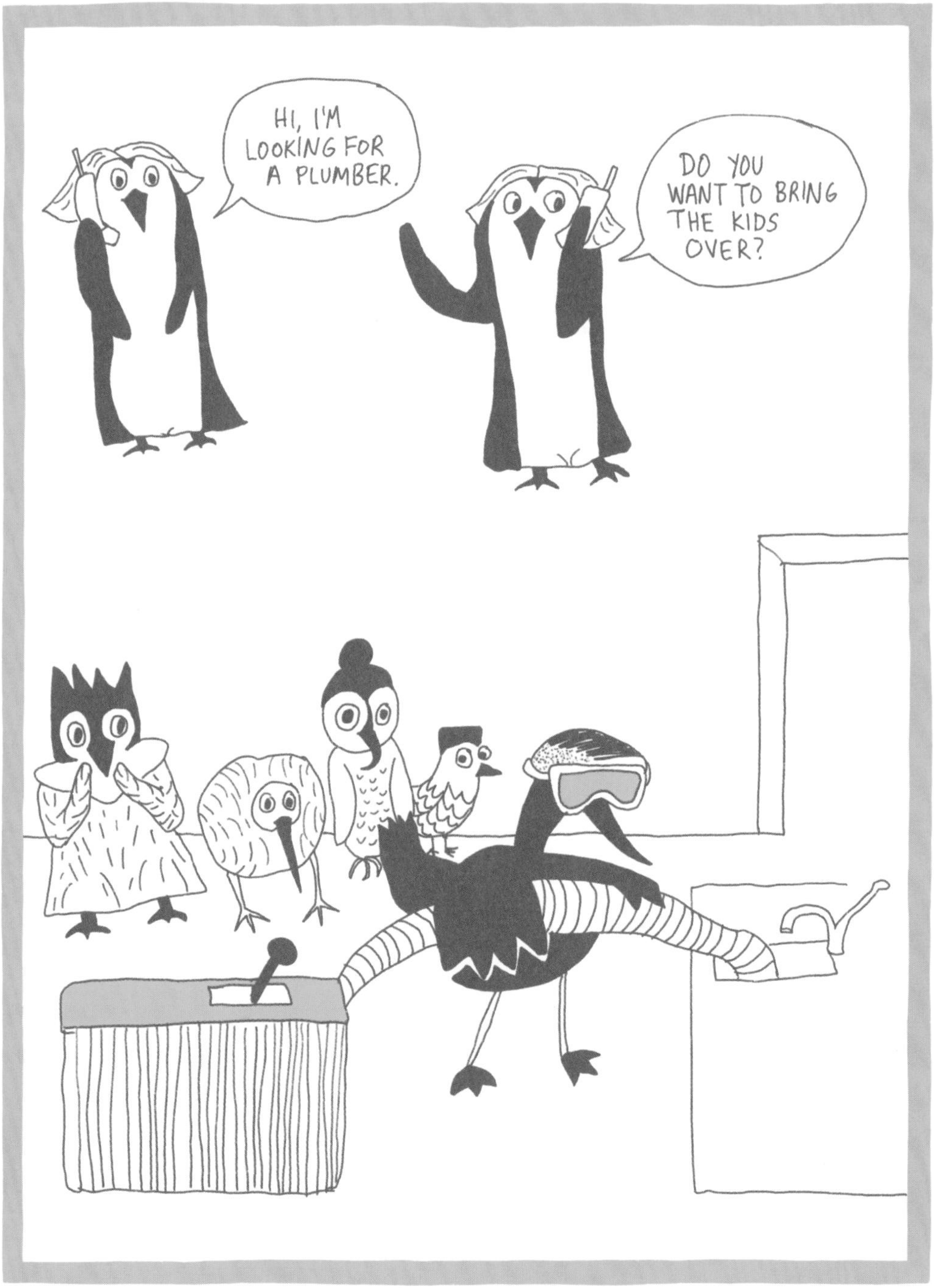
HI, I'M LOOKING FOR A PLUMBER.
DO YOU WANT TO BRING THE KIDS OVER?

SMOOTHIES

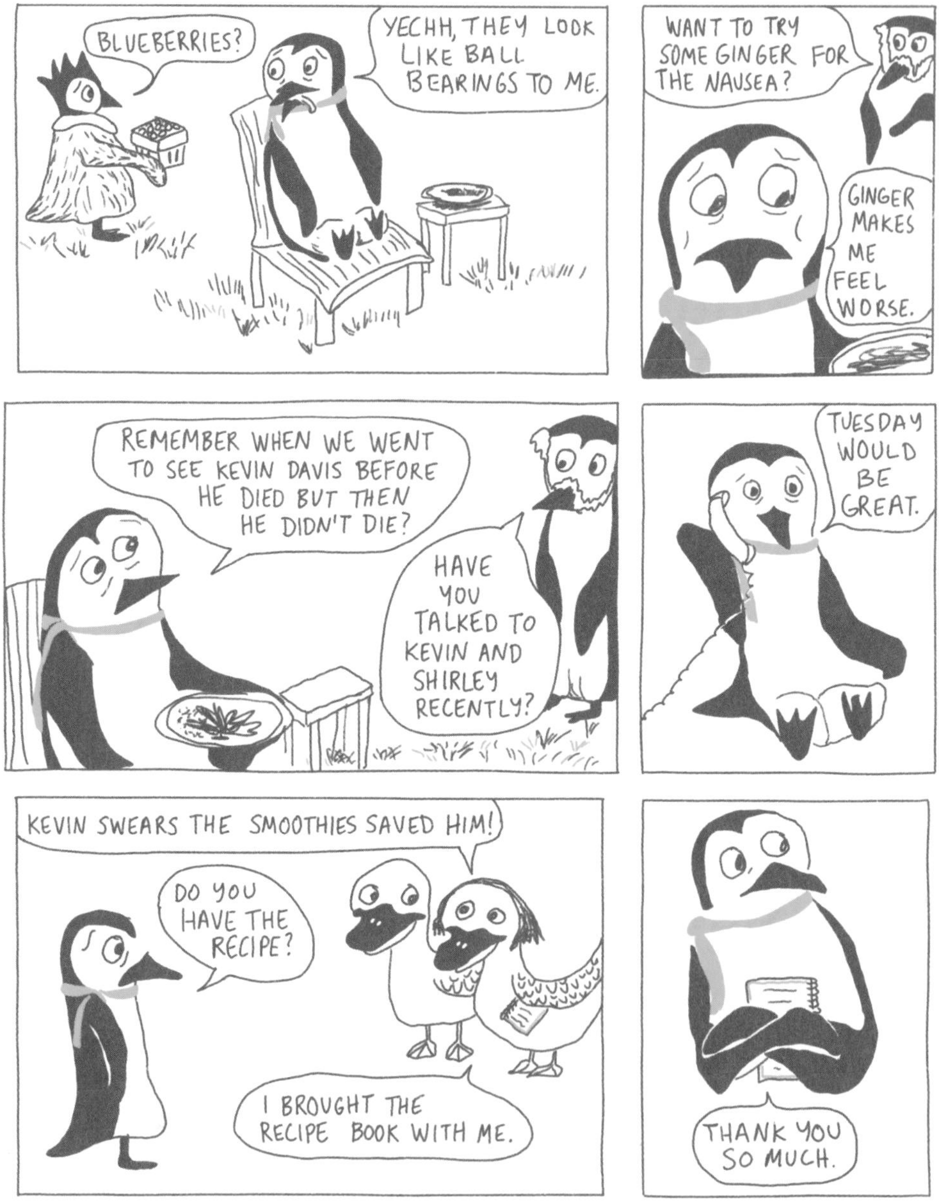

BLUEBERRIES?
YECHH, THEY LOOK LIKE BALL BEARINGS TO ME.
WANT TO TRY SOME GINGER FOR THE NAUSEA?
GINGER MAKES ME FEEL WORSE.
REMEMBER WHEN WE WENT TO SEE KEVIN DAVIS BEFORE HE DIED BUT THEN HE DIDN'T DIE?
HAVE YOU TALKED TO KEVIN AND SHIRLEY RECENTLY?
TUESDAY WOULD BE GREAT.
KEVIN SWEARS THE SMOOTHIES SAVED HIM!
DO YOU HAVE THE RECIPE?
I BROUGHT THE RECIPE BOOK WITH ME.
THANK YOU SO MUCH.

MAGIC MOMENTS WITH MARCI

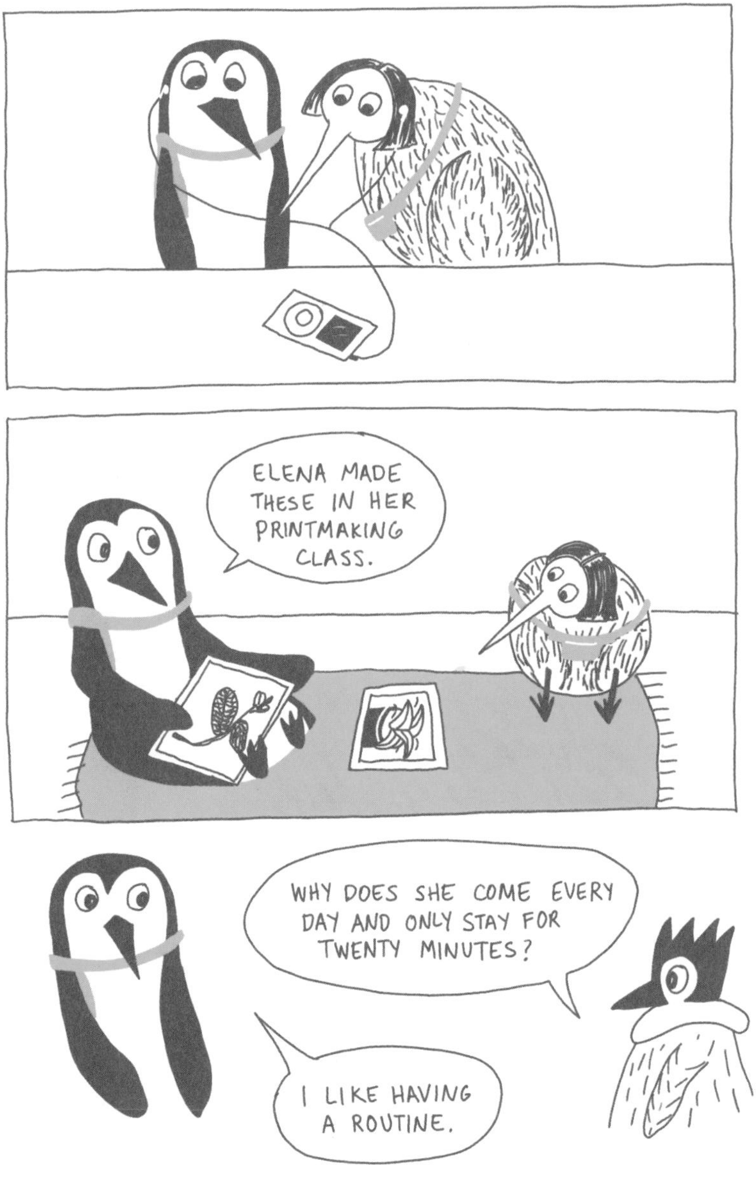
ELENA MADE THESE IN HER PRINTMAKING CLASS.
WHY DOES SHE COME EVERY DAY AND ONLY STAY FOR TWENTY MINUTES?
I LIKE HAVING A ROUTINE.

WEED

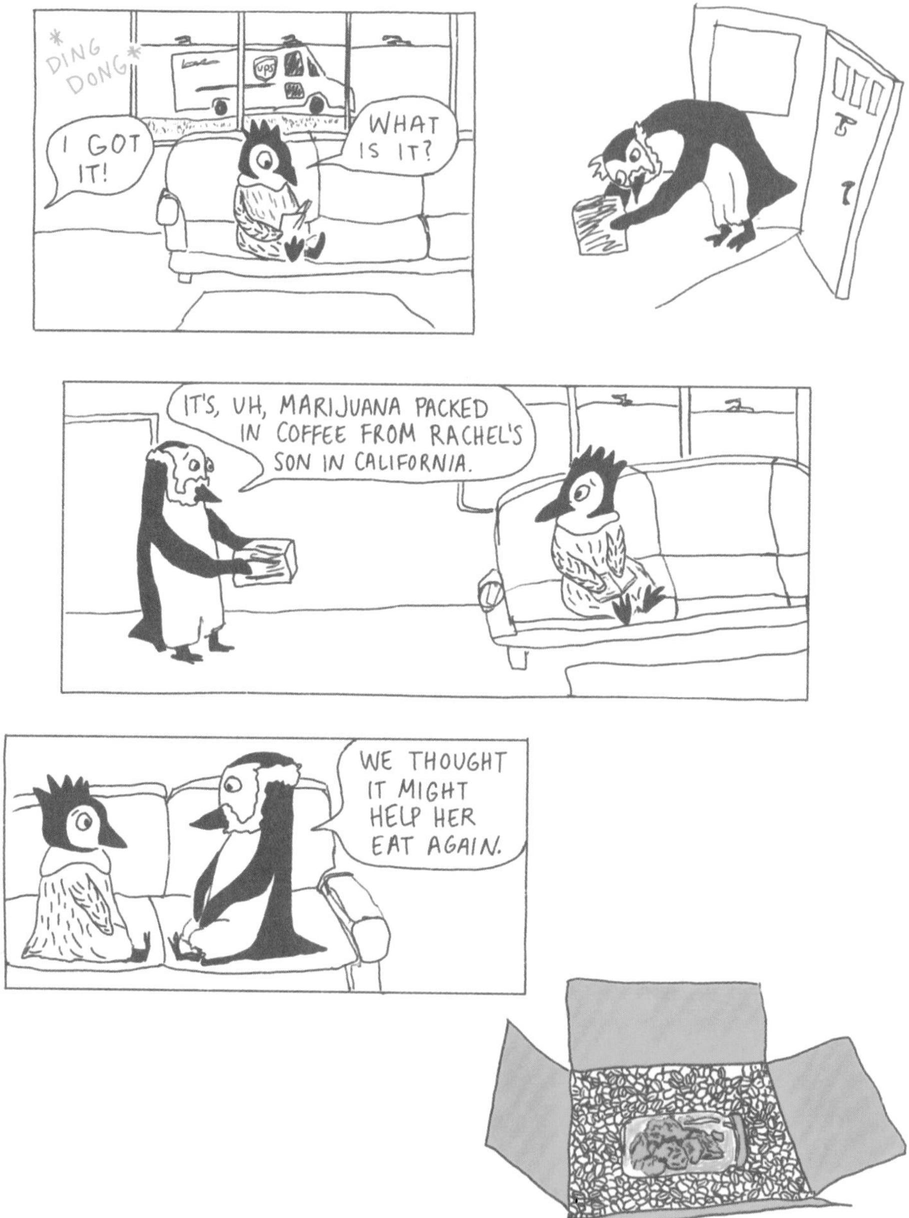

DING DONG
I GOT IT!
WHAT IS IT?
IT'S, UH, MARIJUANA PACKED IN COFFEE FROM RACHEL'S SON IN CALIFORNIA.
WE THOUGHT IT MIGHT HELP HER EAT AGAIN.

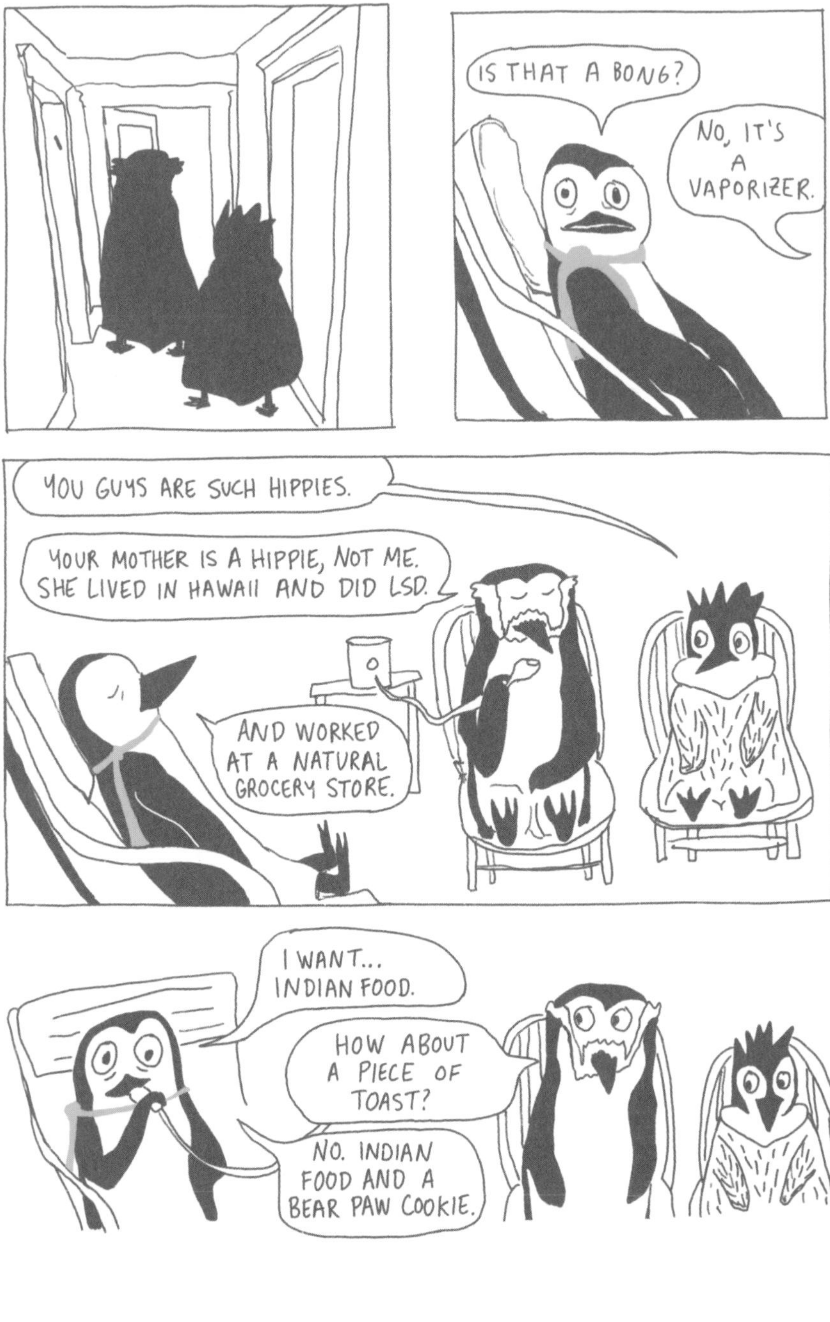
IS THAT A BONG?
NO, IT'S A VAPORIZER.
YOU GUYS ARE SUCH HIPPIES.
YOUR MOTHER IS A HIPPIE, NOT ME. SHE LIVED IN HAWAII AND DID LSD.
AND WORKED AT A NATURAL GROCERY STORE.
I WANT... INDIAN FOOD.
HOW ABOUT A PIECE OF TOAST?
NO. INDIAN FOOD AND A BEAR PAW COOKIE.

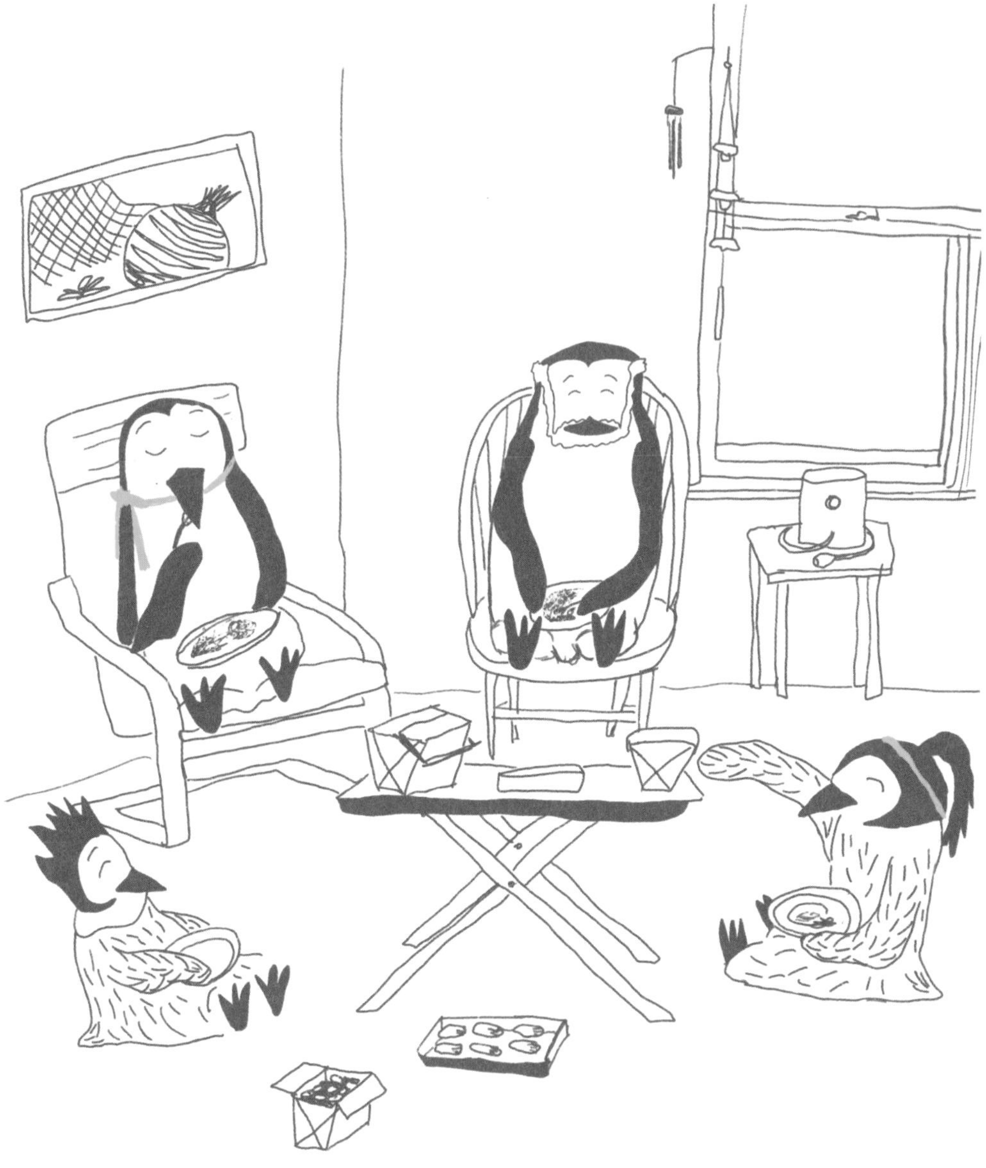

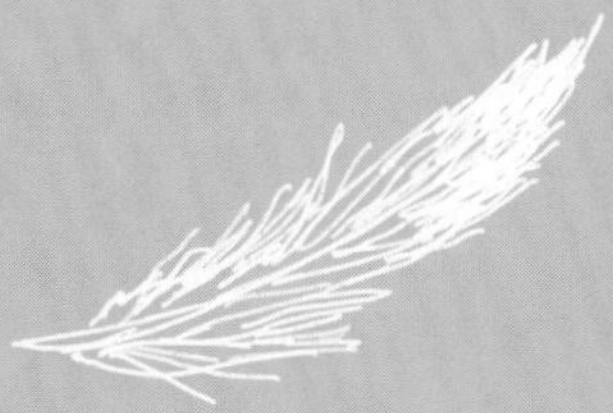

JULY

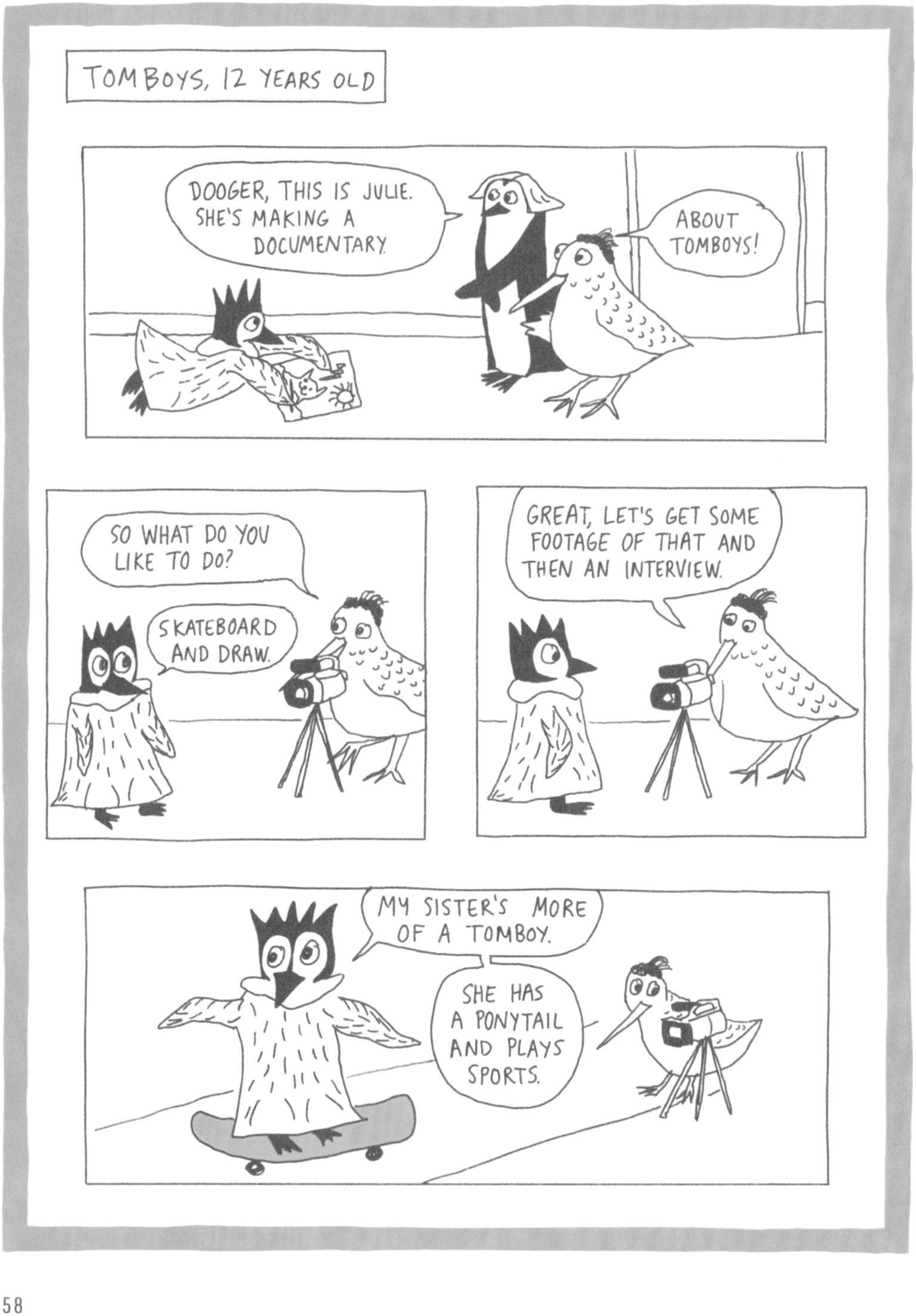
TOMBOYS, 12 YEARS OLD
DOOGER, THIS IS JULIE. SHE'S MAKING A DOCUMENTARY.
ABOUT TOMBOYS!
SO WHAT DO YOU LIKE TO DO?
SKATEBOARD AND DRAW.
GREAT, LET'S GET SOME FOOTAGE OF THAT AND THEN AN INTERVIEW.
MY SISTER'S MORE OF A TOMBOY.
SHE HAS A PONYTAIL AND PLAYS SPORTS.

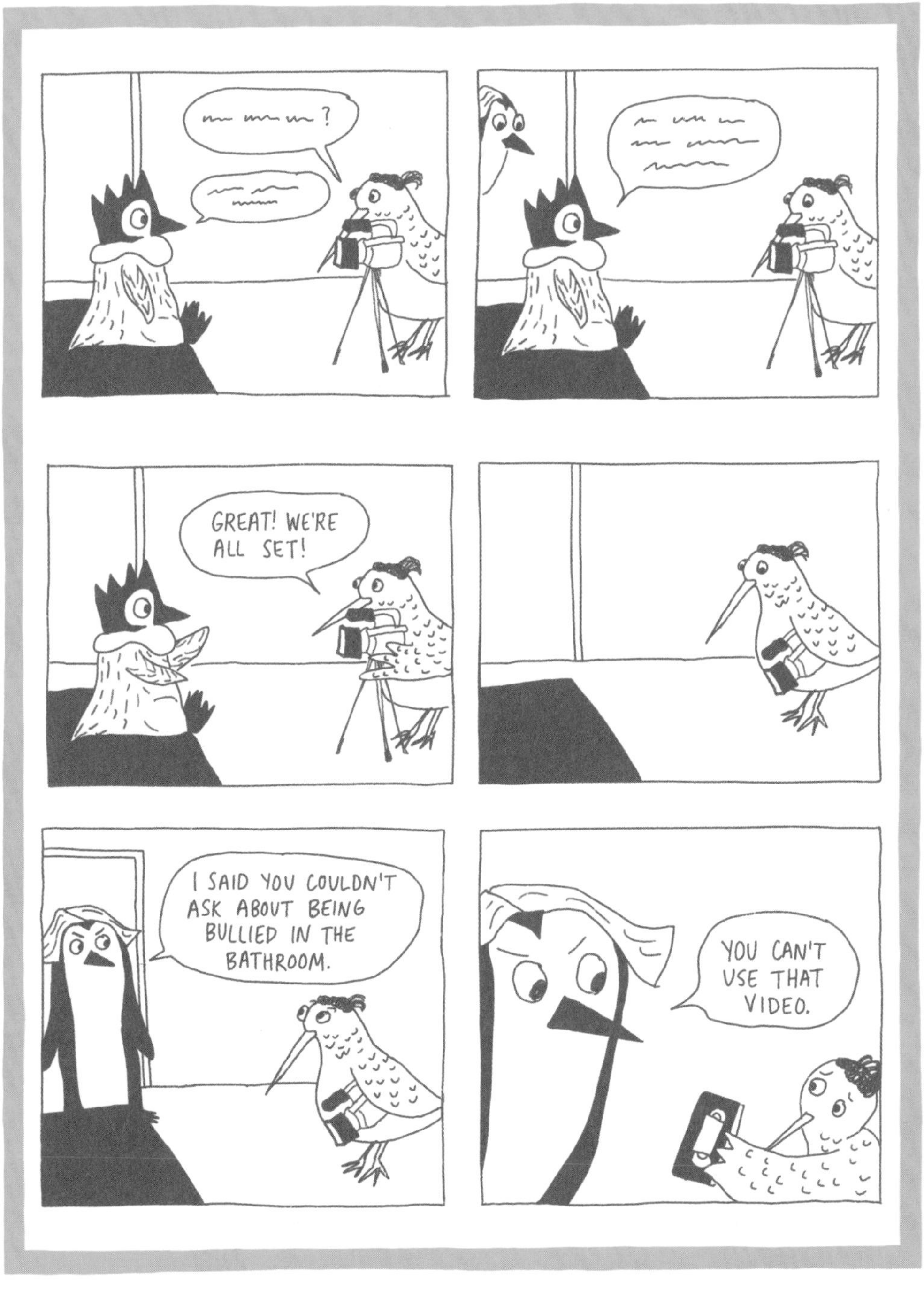
GREAT! WE'RE ALL SET!
I SAID YOU COULDN'T ASK ABOUT BEING BULLIED IN THE BATHROOM.
YOU CAN'T USE THAT VIDEO.

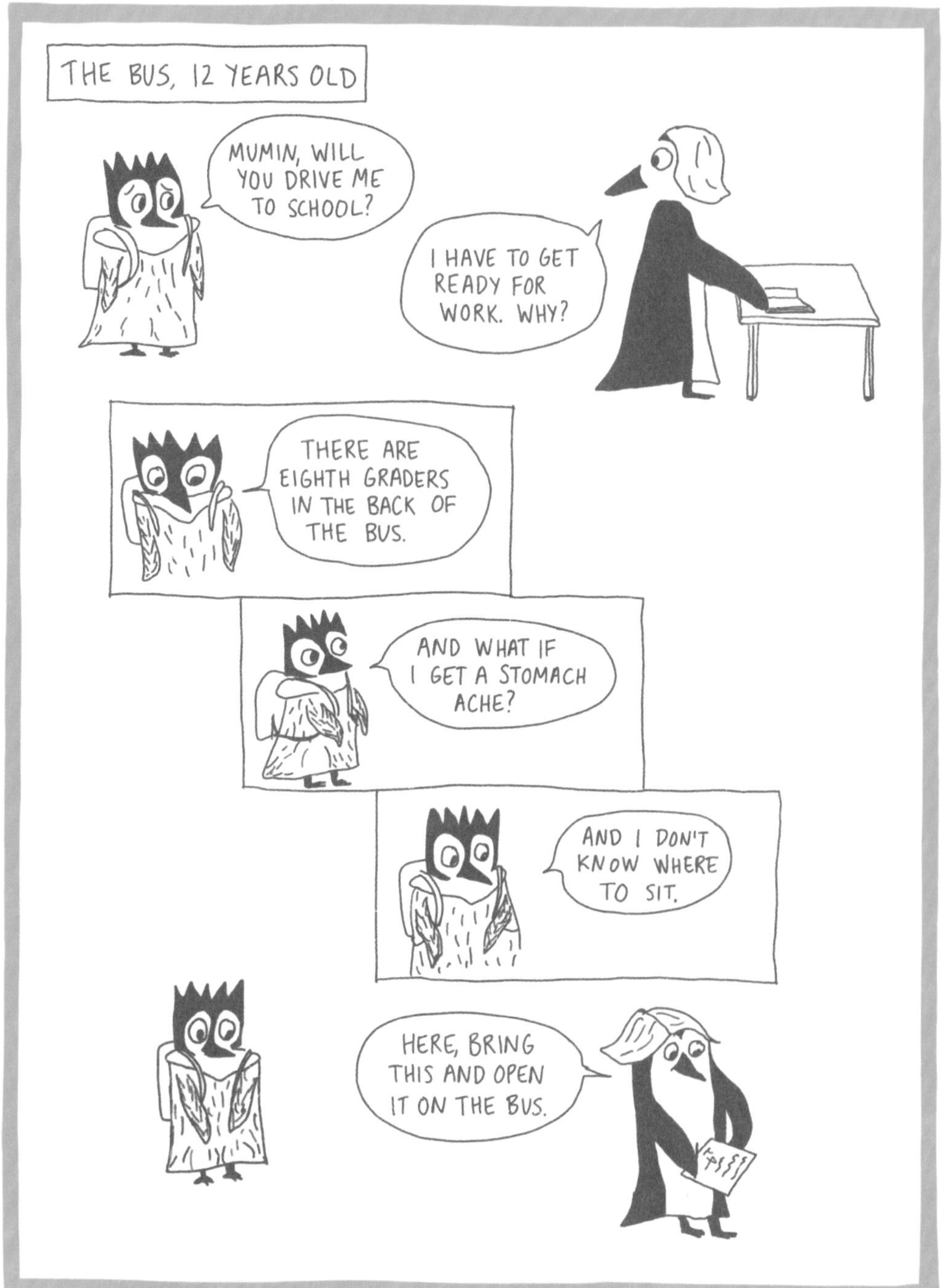
THE BUS, 12 YEARS OLD
MUMIN, WILL YOU DRIVE ME TO SCHOOL?
I HAVE TO GET READY FOR WORK. WHY?
THERE ARE EIGHTH GRADERS IN THE BACK OF THE BUS.
AND WHAT IF I GET A STOMACH ACHE?
AND I DON'T KNOW WHERE TO SIT.
HERE, BRING THIS AND OPEN IT ON THE BUS.

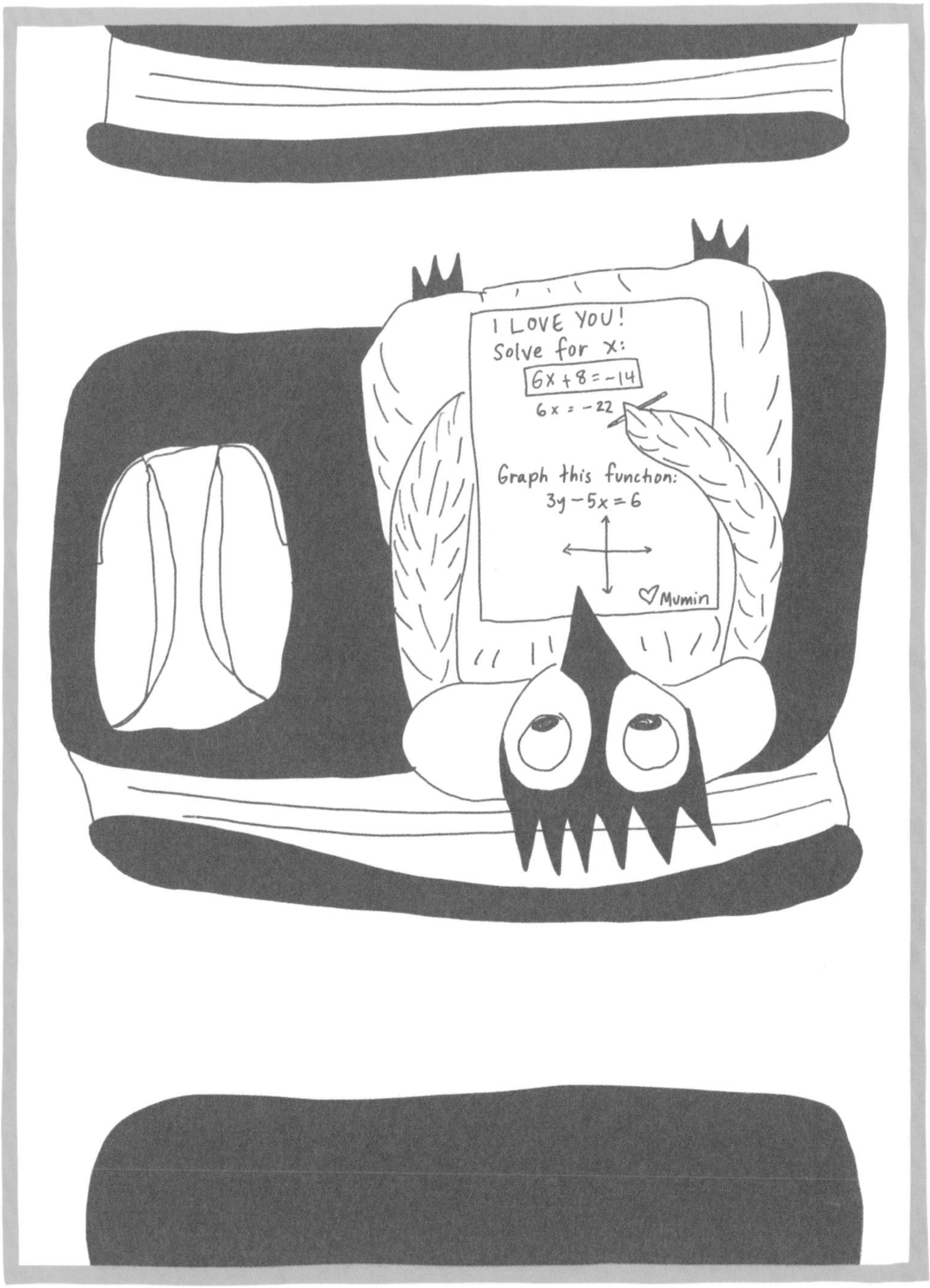
I LOVE YOU!
Solve for x:
6x + 8 = -14
6x = -22
Graph this function:
3y - 5x = 6
♡Mumin

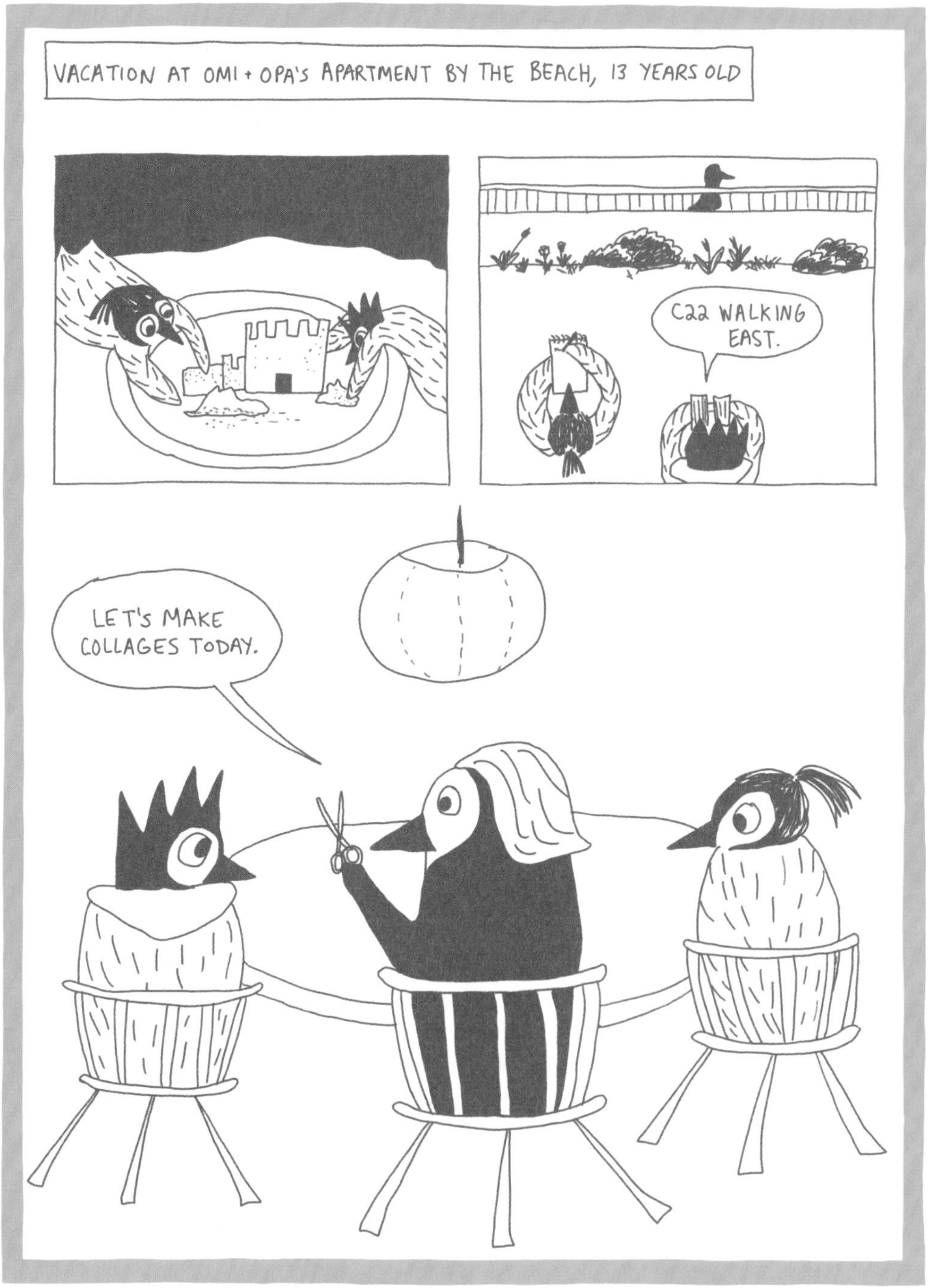
VACATION AT OMI + OPA'S APARTMENT BY THE BEACH, 13 YEARS OLD
C22 WALKING EAST.
LET'S MAKE COLLAGES TODAY.

POSTMODERN ART CAMP

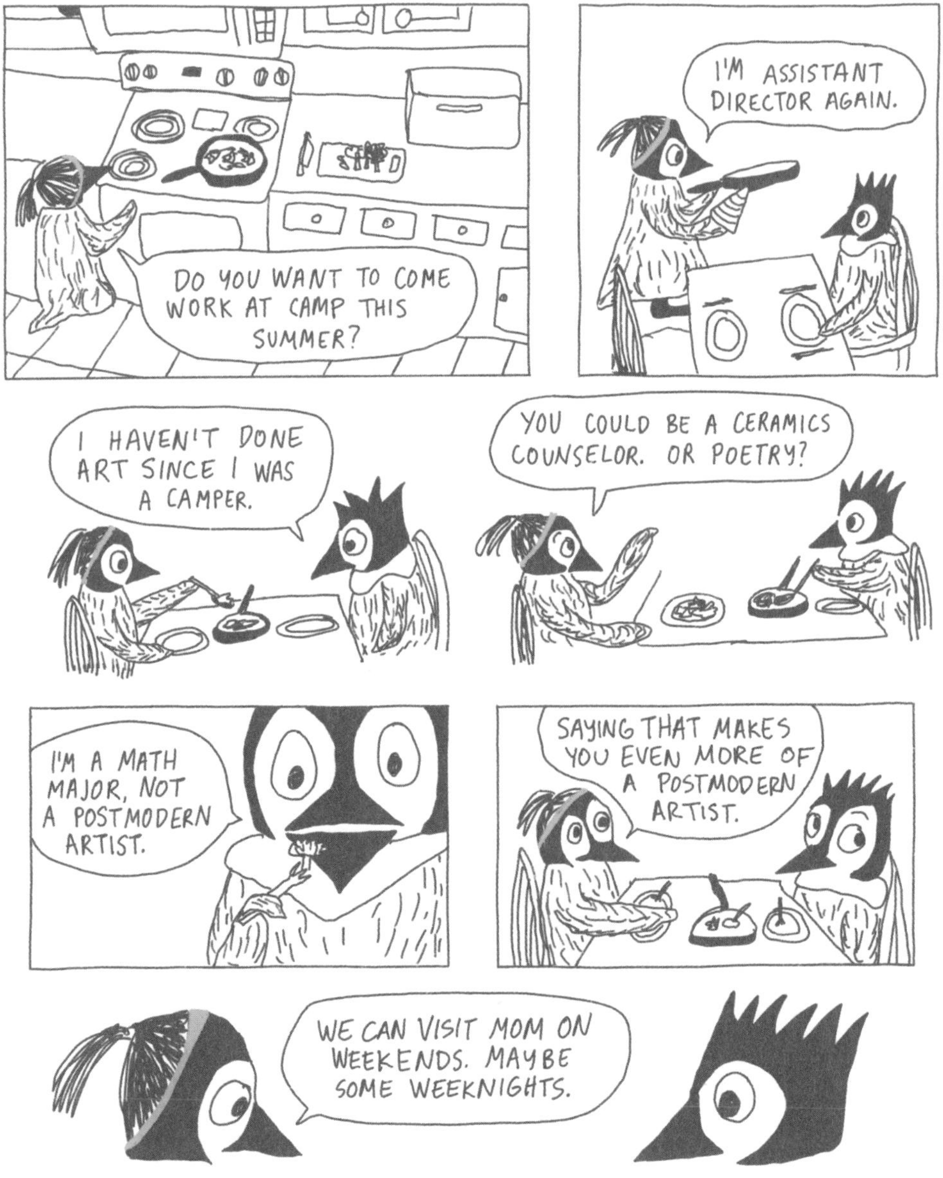
DO YOU WANT TO COME WORK AT CAMP THIS SUMMER?
I'M ASSISTANT DIRECTOR AGAIN.
I HAVEN'T DONE ART SINCE I WAS A CAMPER.
YOU COULD BE A CERAMICS COUNSELOR. OR POETRY?
I'M A MATH MAJOR, NOT A POSTMODERN ARTIST.
SAYING THAT MAKES YOU EVEN MORE OF A POSTMODERN ARTIST.
WE CAN VISIT MOM ON WEEKENDS. MAYBE SOME WEEKNIGHTS.

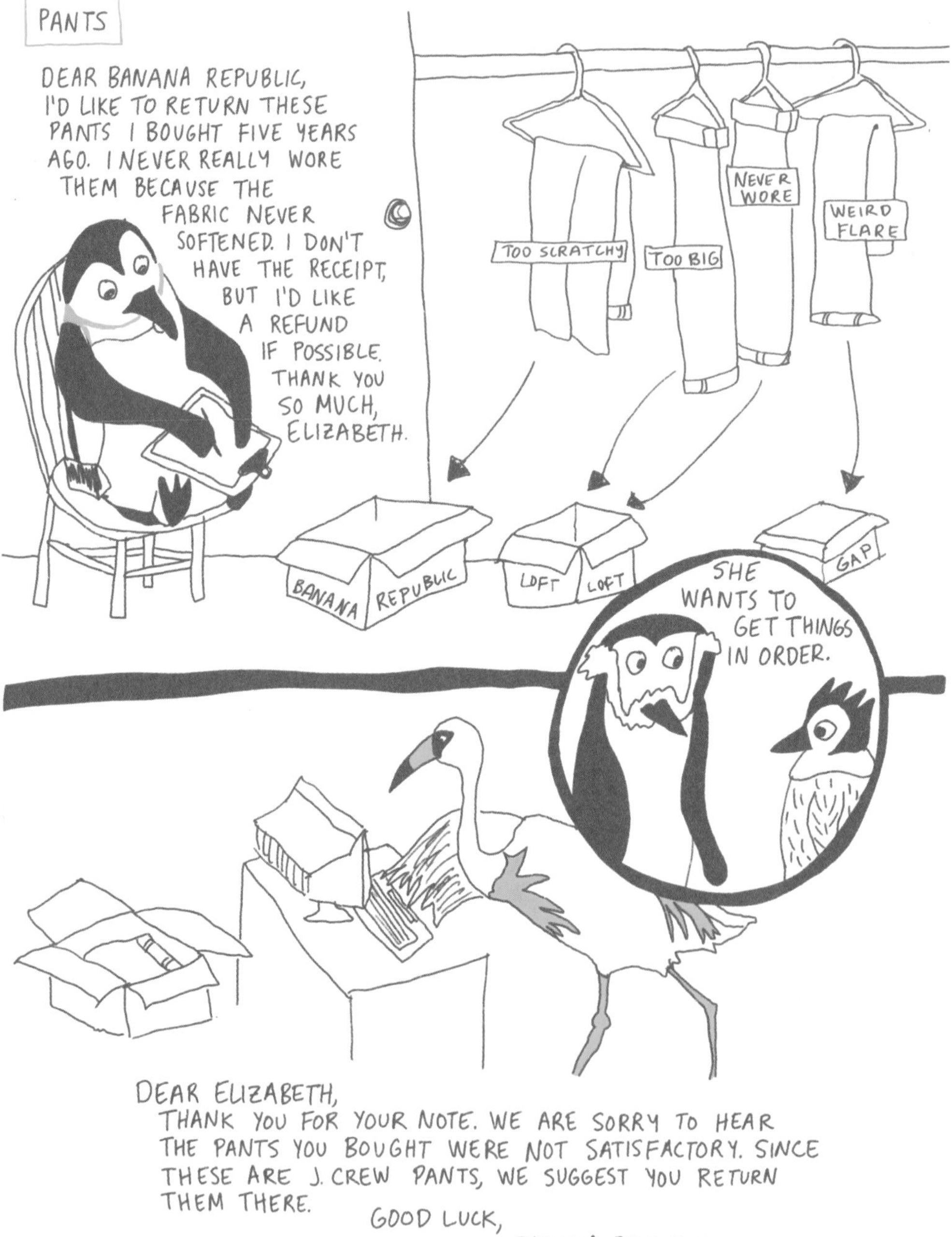
PANTS
DEAR BANANA REPUBLIC, I'D LIKE TO RETURN THESE PANTS I BOUGHT FIVE YEARS AGO. I NEVER REALLY WORE THEM BECAUSE THE FABRIC NEVER SOFTENED. I DON'T HAVE THE RECEIPT, BUT I'D LIKE A REFUND IF POSSIBLE. THANK YOU SO MUCH, ELIZABETH.
TOO SCRATCHY
TOO BIG
NEVER WORE
WEIRD FLARE
BANANA REPUBLIC
LOFT LOFT
GAP
SHE WANTS TO GET THINGS IN ORDER.
DEAR ELIZABETH,
THANK YOU FOR YOUR NOTE. WE ARE SORRY TO HEAR THE PANTS YOU BOUGHT WERE NOT SATISFACTORY. SINCE THESE ARE J. CREW PANTS, WE SUGGEST YOU RETURN THEM THERE.
GOOD LUCK,
BANANA REPUBLIC

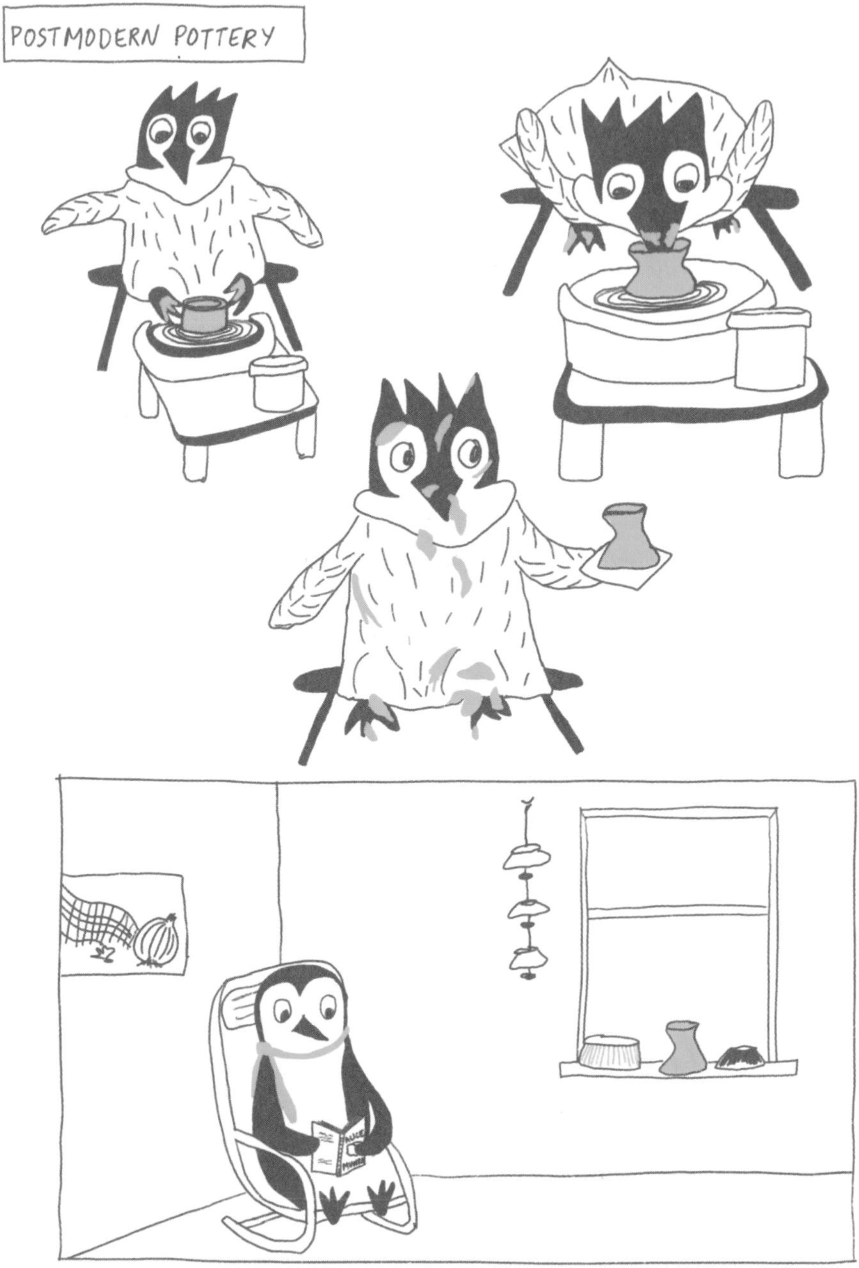
POSTMODERN POTTERY

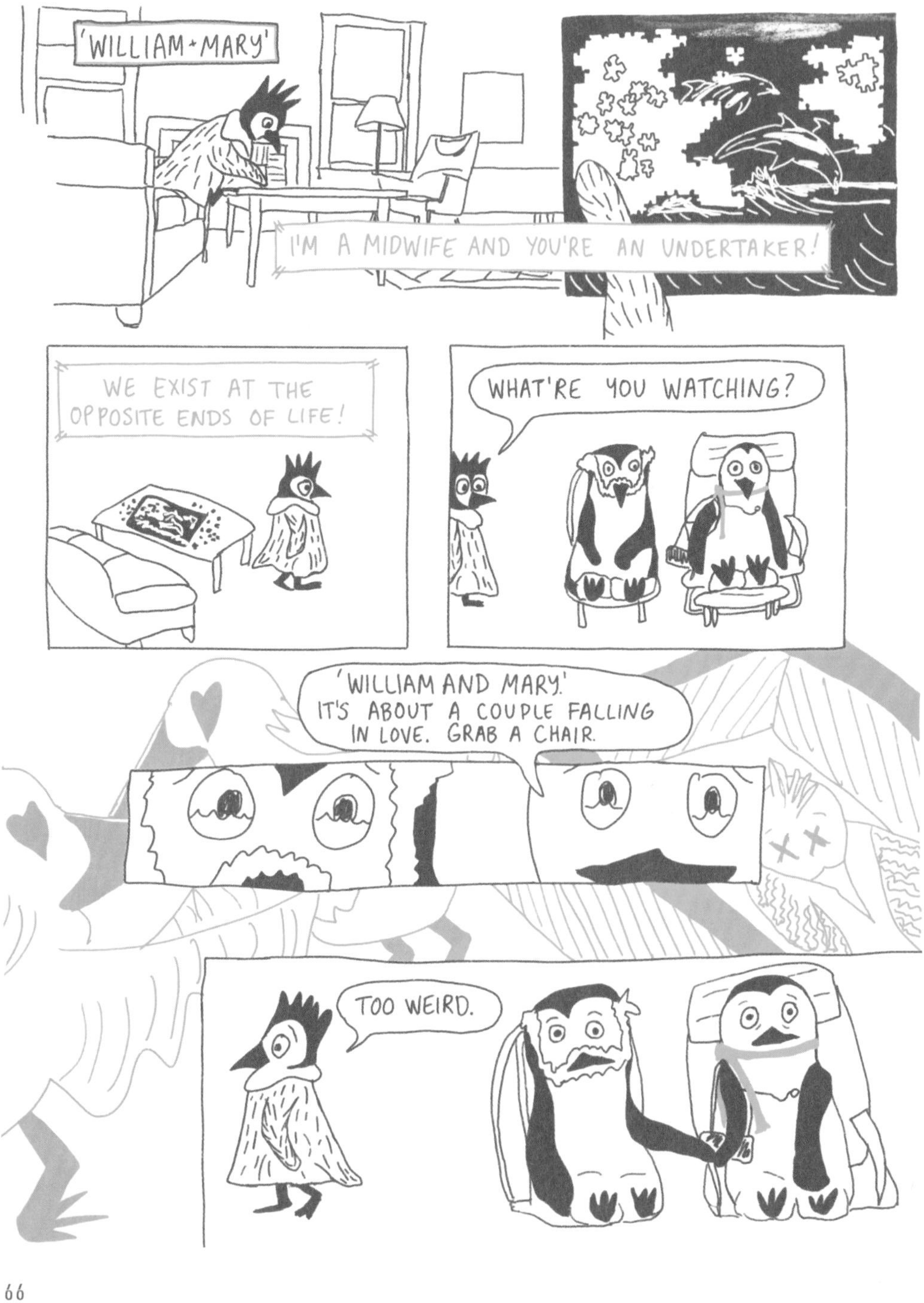

'WILLIAM + MARY'
I'M A MIDWIFE AND YOU'RE AN UNDERTAKER!
WE EXIST AT THE OPPOSITE ENDS OF LIFE!
WHAT'RE YOU WATCHING?
'WILLIAM AND MARY.' IT'S ABOUT A COUPLE FALLING IN LOVE. GRAB A CHAIR.
TOO WEIRD.

IN THE FRIDGE

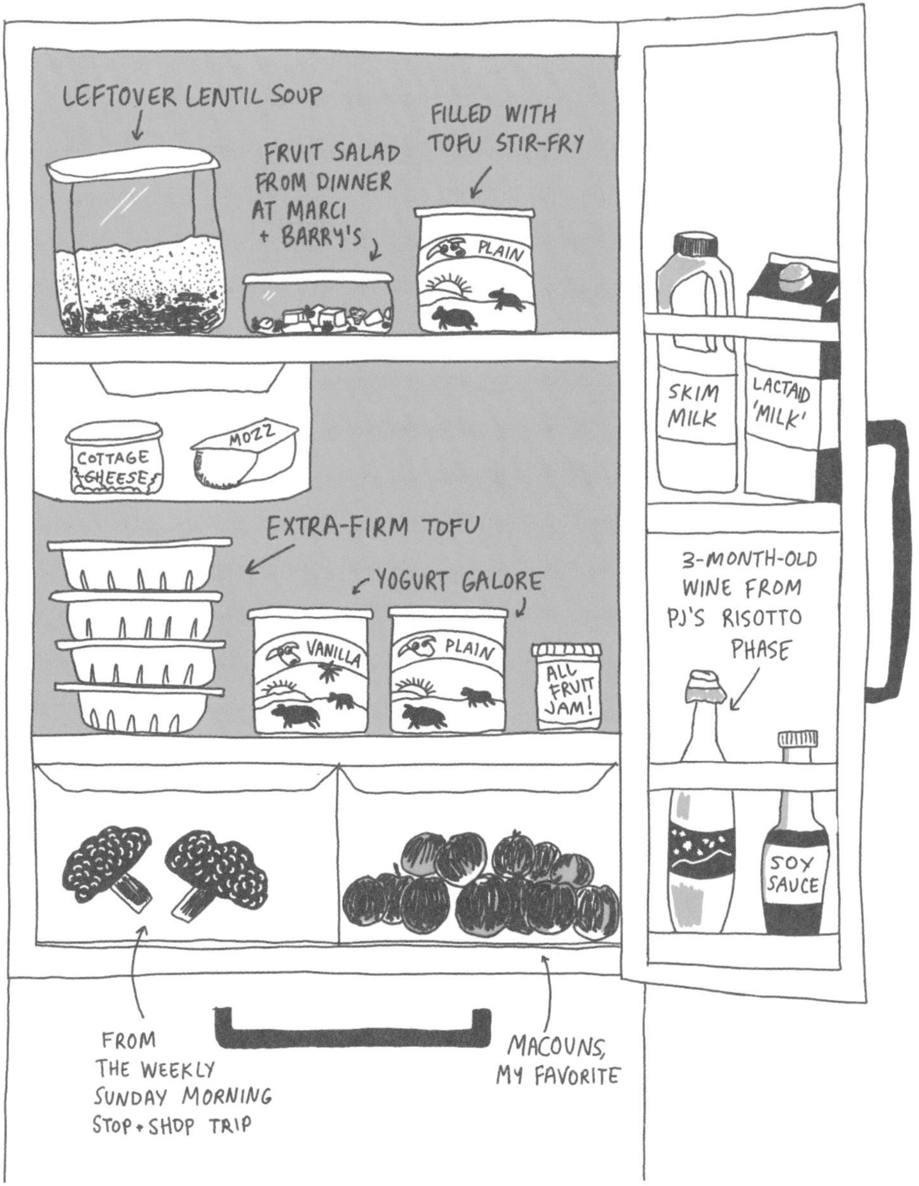
LEFTOVER LENTIL SOUP
FRUIT SALAD FROM DINNER AT MARCI + BARRY'S
FILLED WITH TOFU STIR-FRY
PLAIN
SKIM MILK
LACTAID 'MILK'
COTTAGE CHEESE
MOZZ
EXTRA-FIRM TOFU
YOGURT GALORE
VANILLA
PLAIN
ALL FRUIT JAM!
3-MONTH-OLD WINE FROM PJ'S RISOTTO PHASE
SOY SAUCE
FROM THE WEEKLY SUNDAY MORNING STOP + SHOP TRIP
MACOUNS, MY FAVORITE

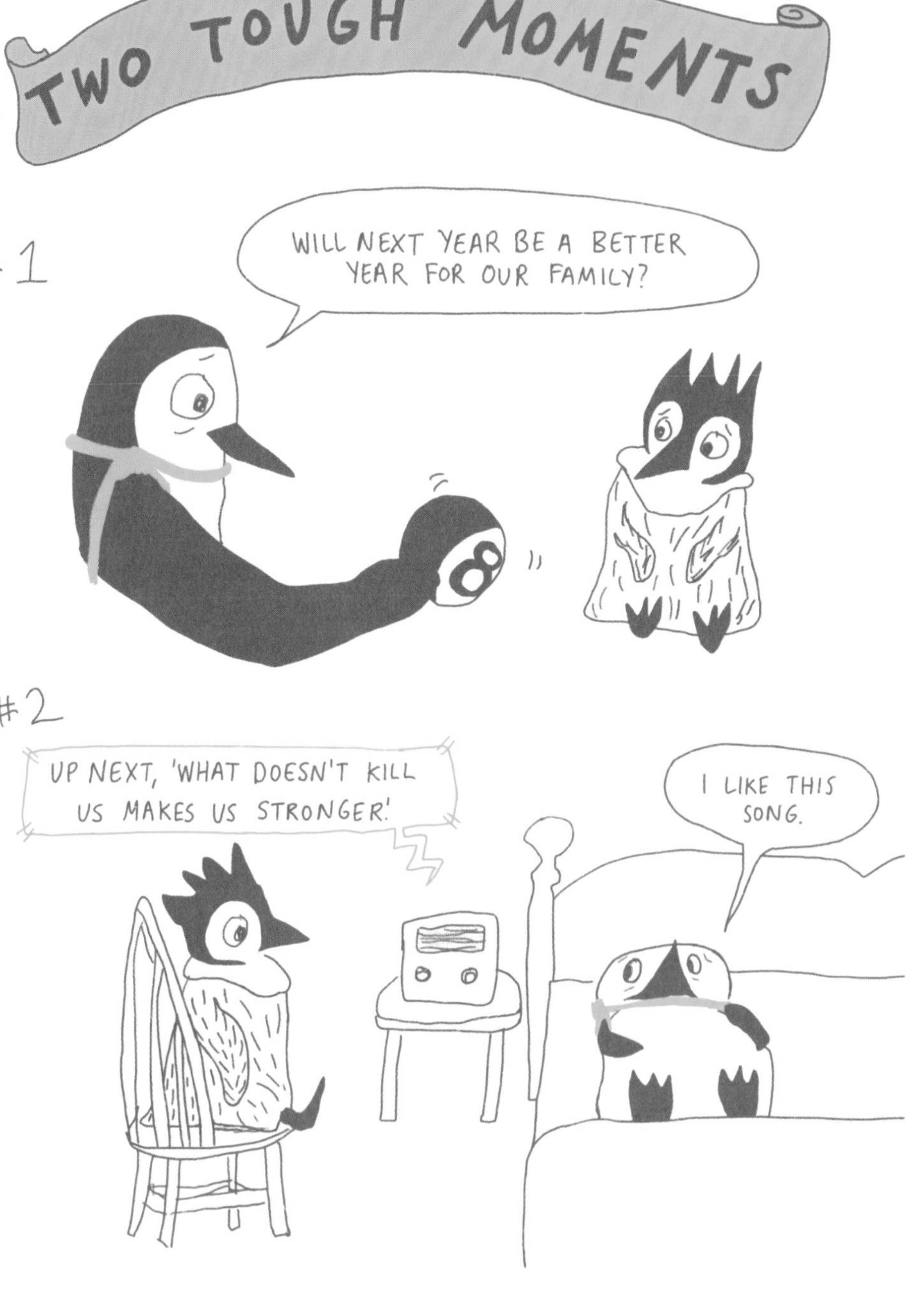
TWO TOUGH MOMENTS
#1
WILL NEXT YEAR BE A BETTER YEAR FOR OUR FAMILY?
#2
UP NEXT, 'WHAT DOESN'T KILL US MAKES US STRONGER.'
I LIKE THIS SONG.

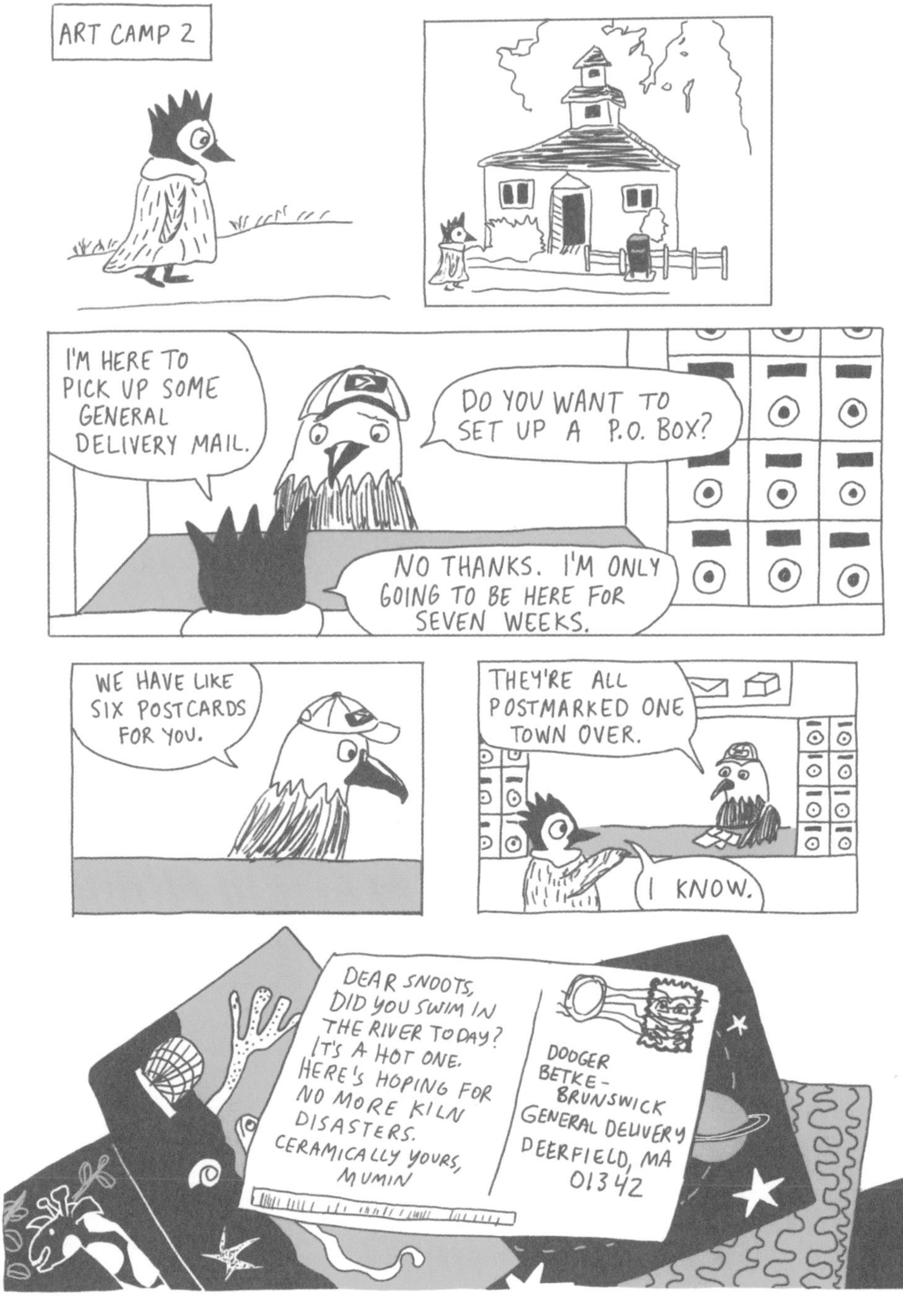
ART CAMP 2
I'M HERE TO PICK UP SOME GENERAL DELIVERY MAIL.
DO YOU WANT TO SET UP A P.O. BOX?
NO THANKS. I'M ONLY GOING TO BE HERE FOR SEVEN WEEKS.
WE HAVE LIKE SIX POSTCARDS FOR YOU.
THEY'RE ALL POSTMARKED ONE TOWN OVER.
I KNOW.
DEAR SNOOTS, DID YOU SWIM IN THE RIVER TODAY? IT'S A HOT ONE. HERE'S HOPING FOR NO MORE KILN DISASTERS. CERAMICALLY YOURS, MUMIN
DODGER BETKE-BRUNSWICK GENERAL DELIVERY DEERFIELD, MA 01342

AUGUST

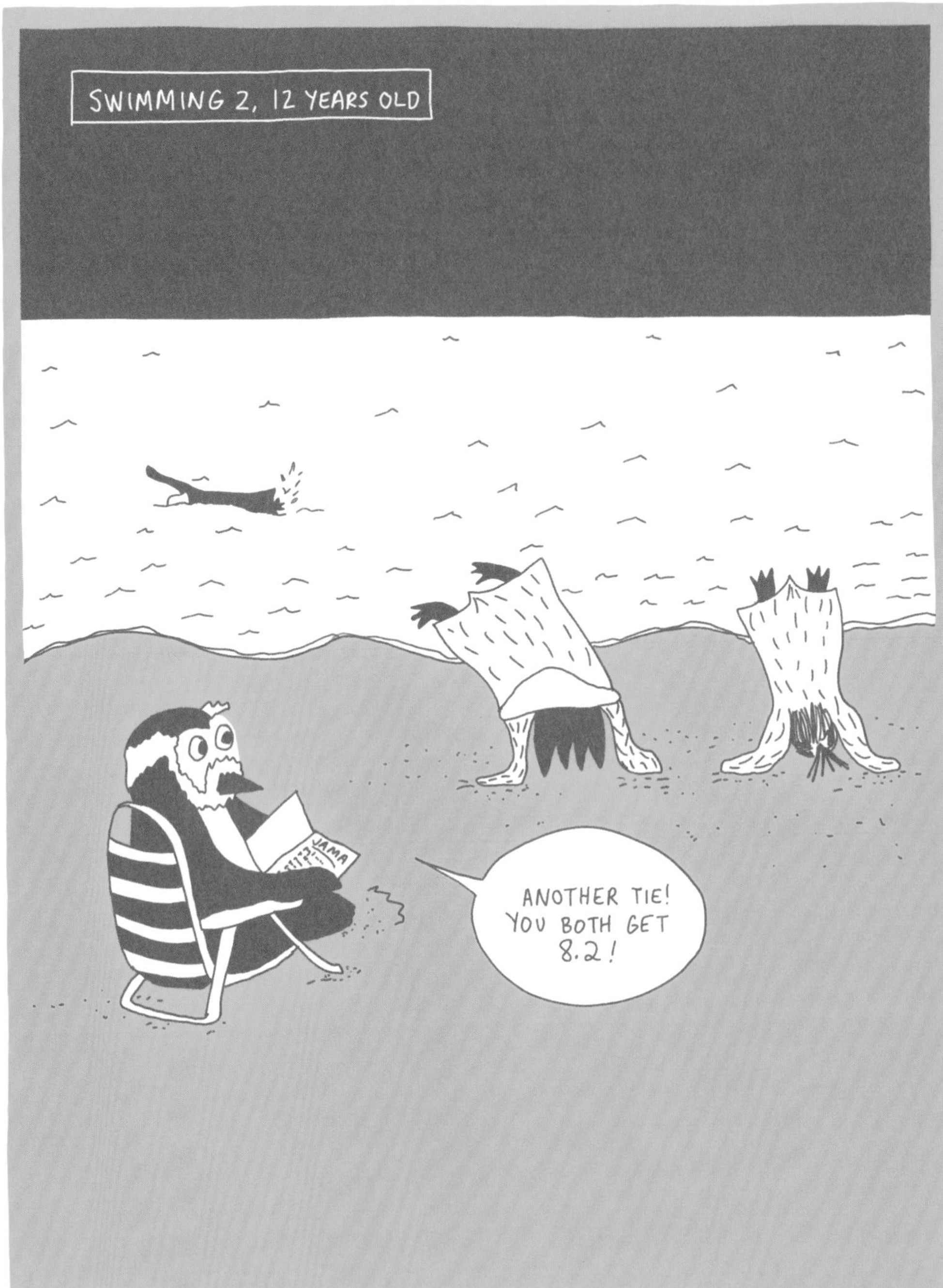
SWIMMING 2, 12 YEARS OLD
JAMA
ANOTHER TIE! YOU BOTH GET 8.2!

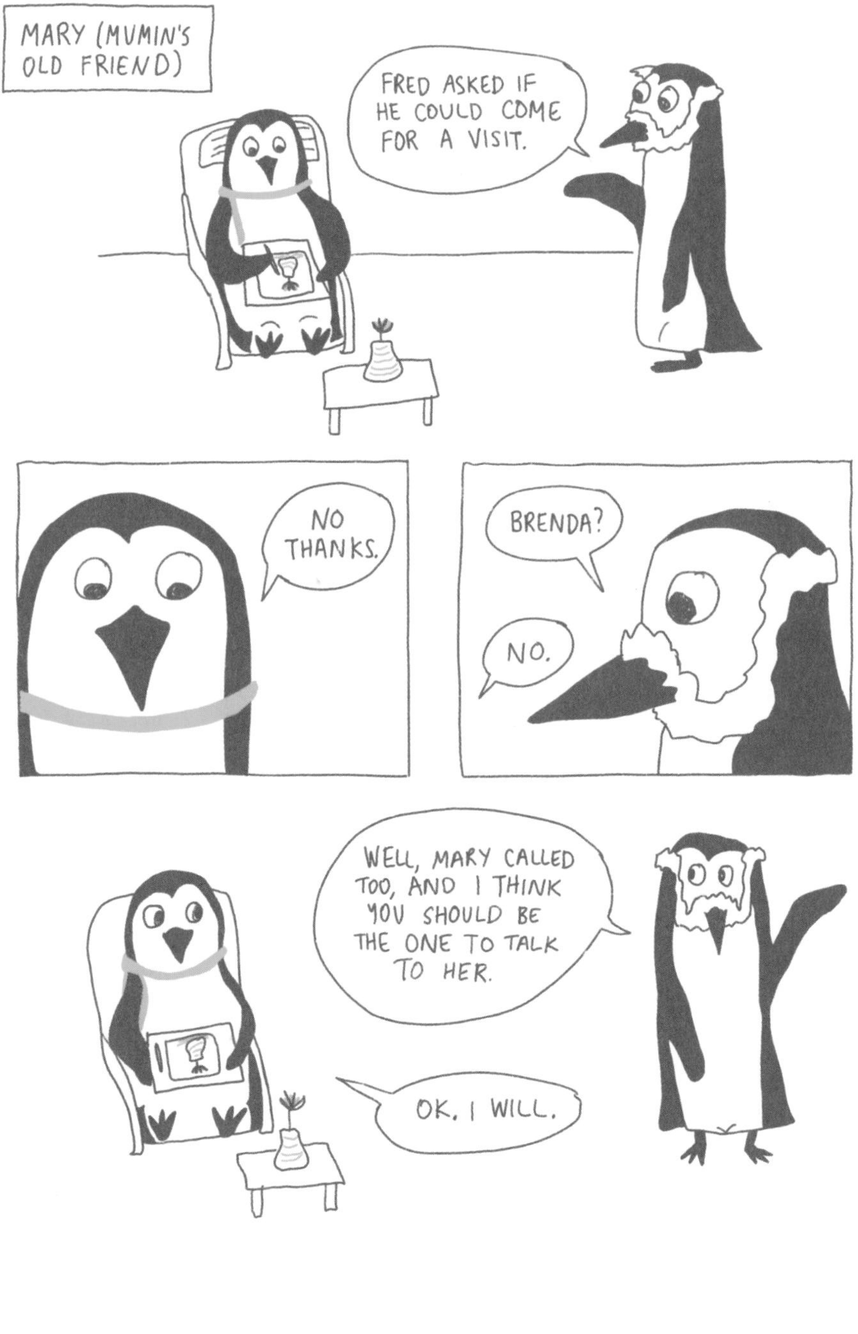
MARY (MUMIN'S OLD FRIEND)
FRED ASKED IF HE COULD COME FOR A VISIT.
NO THANKS.
BRENDA?
NO.
WELL, MARY CALLED TOO, AND I THINK YOU SHOULD BE THE ONE TO TALK TO HER.
OK. I WILL.

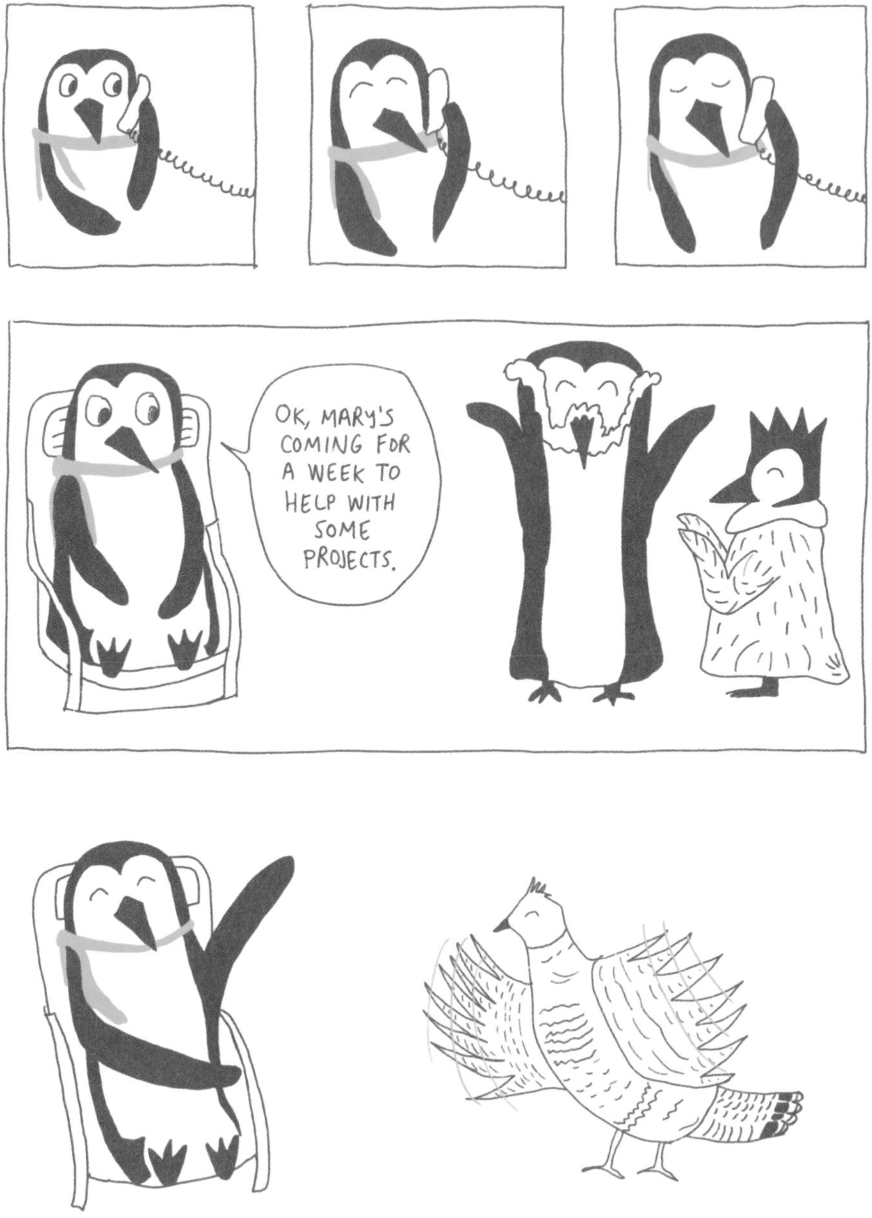
OK, MARY'S COMING FOR A WEEK TO HELP WITH SOME PROJECTS.

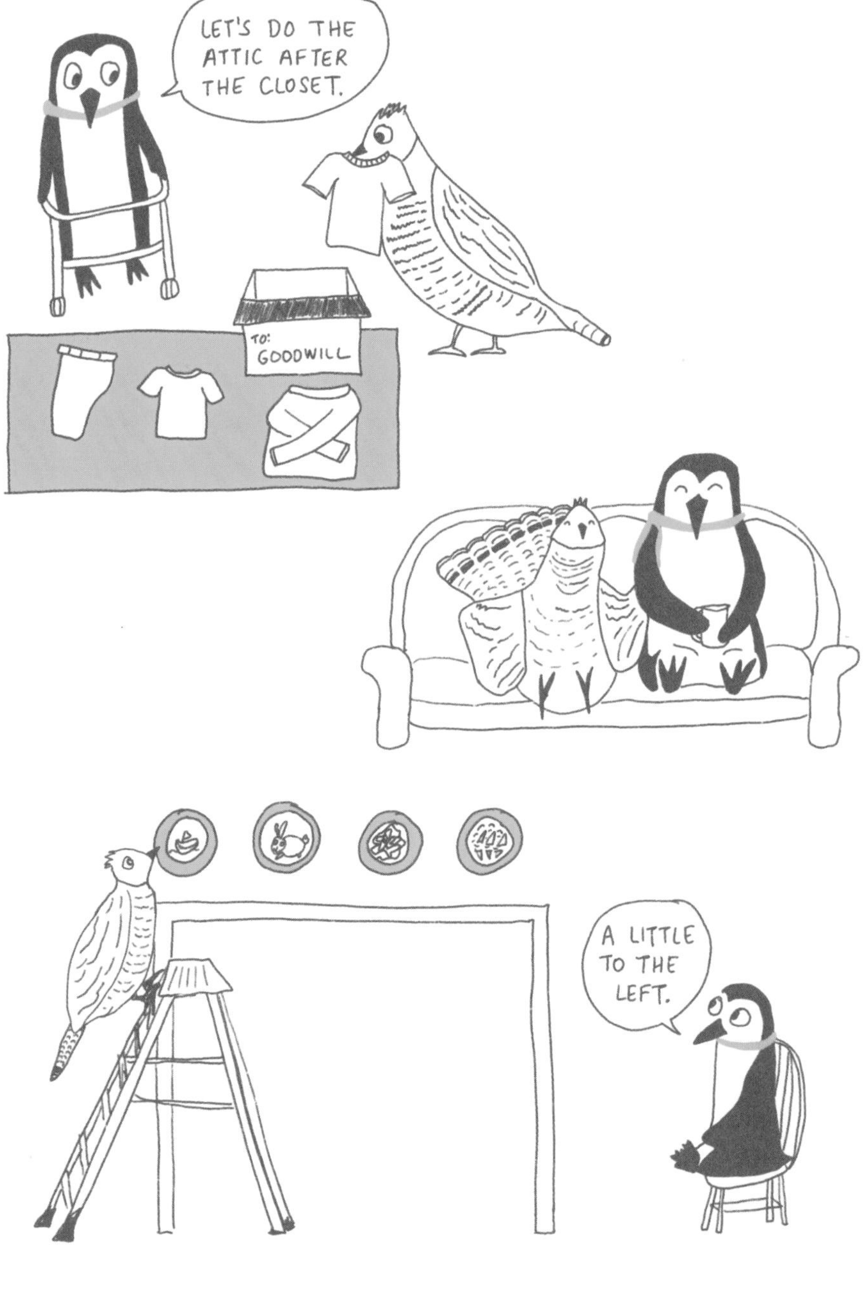
LET'S DO THE ATTIC AFTER THE CLOSET.
TO: GOODWILL
A LITTLE TO THE LEFT.

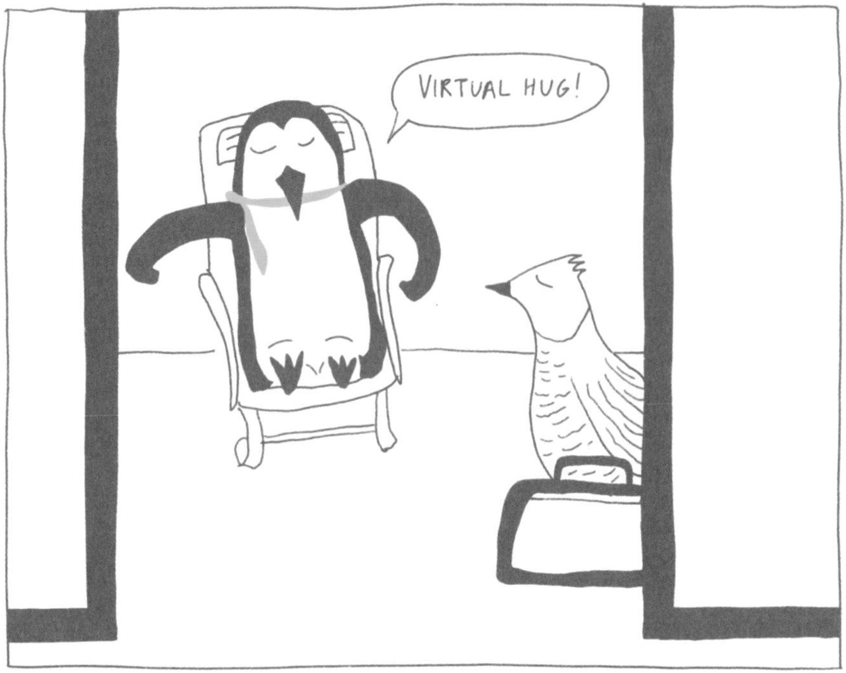
VIRTUAL HUG!

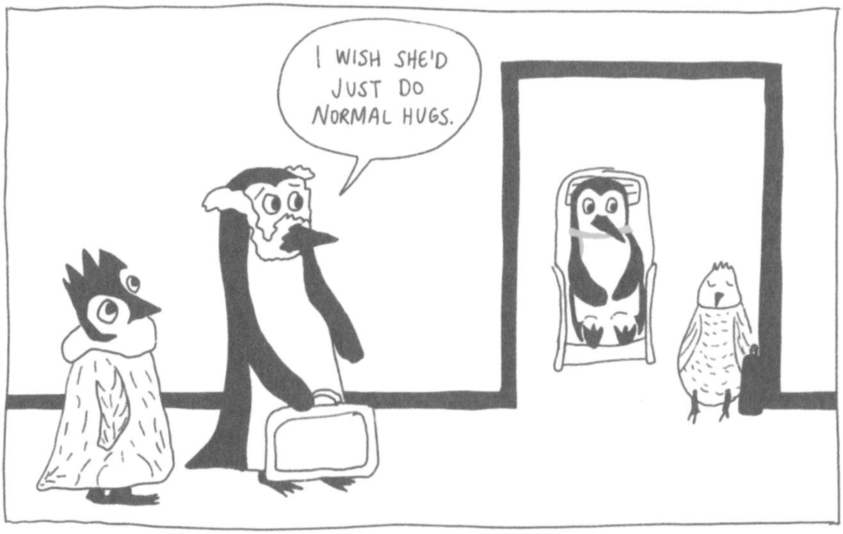
I WISH SHE'D JUST DO NORMAL HUGS.

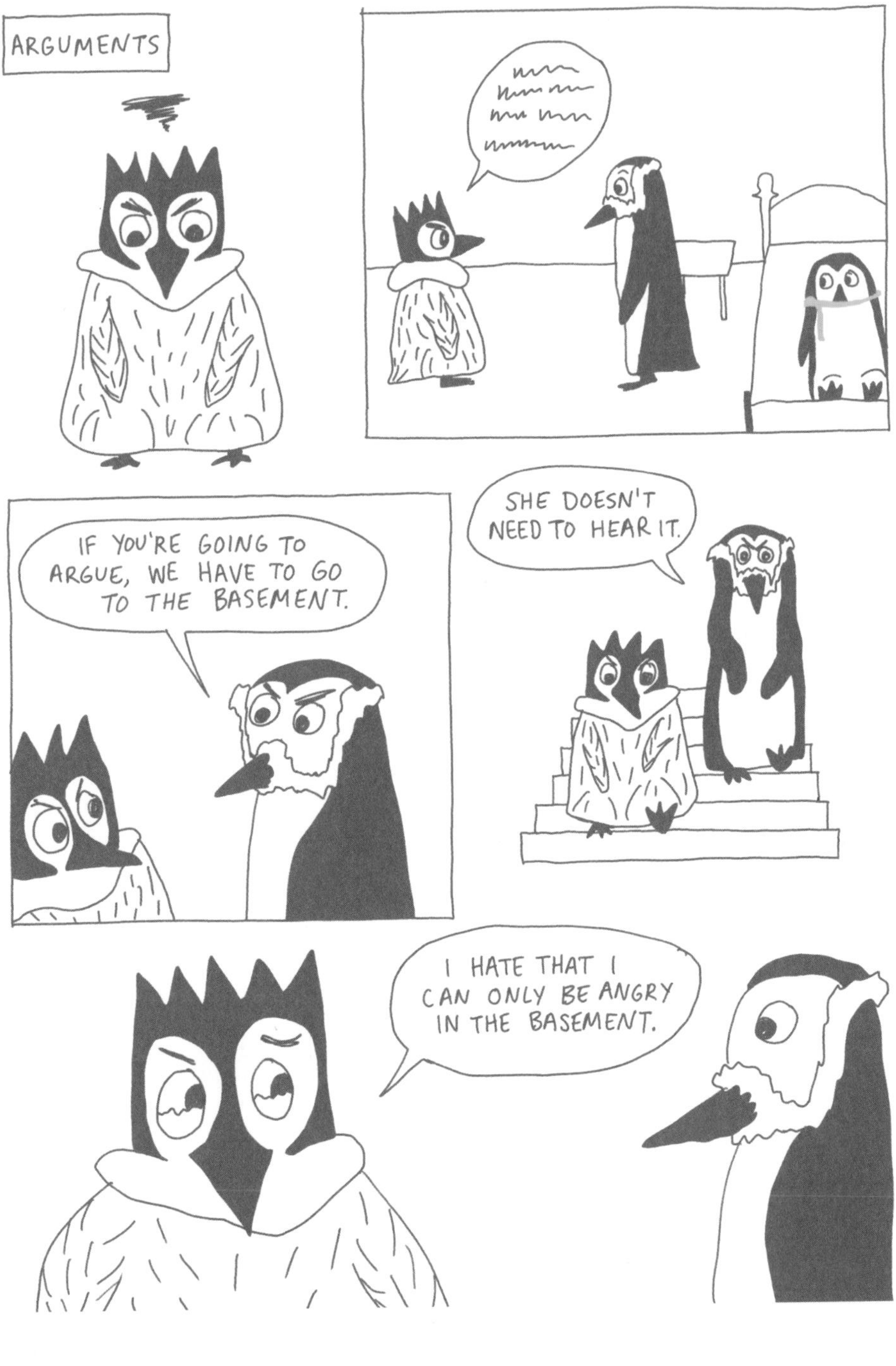
ARGUMENTS
IF YOU'RE GOING TO ARGUE, WE HAVE TO GO TO THE BASEMENT.
SHE DOESN'T NEED TO HEAR IT.
I HATE THAT I CAN ONLY BE ANGRY IN THE BASEMENT.

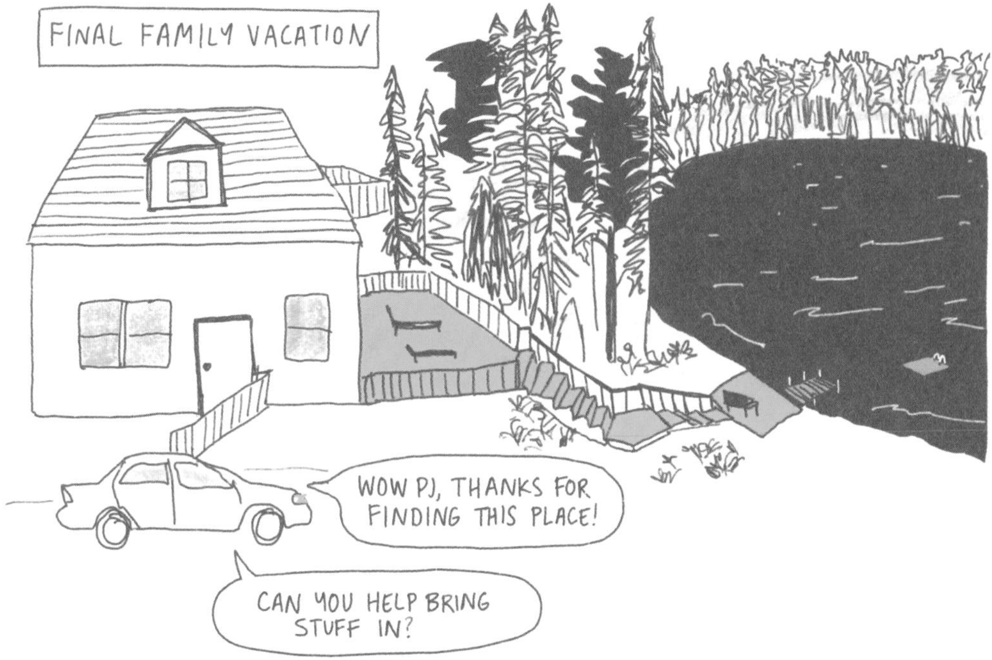
FINAL FAMILY VACATION
WOW PJ, THANKS FOR FINDING THIS PLACE!
CAN YOU HELP BRING STUFF IN?

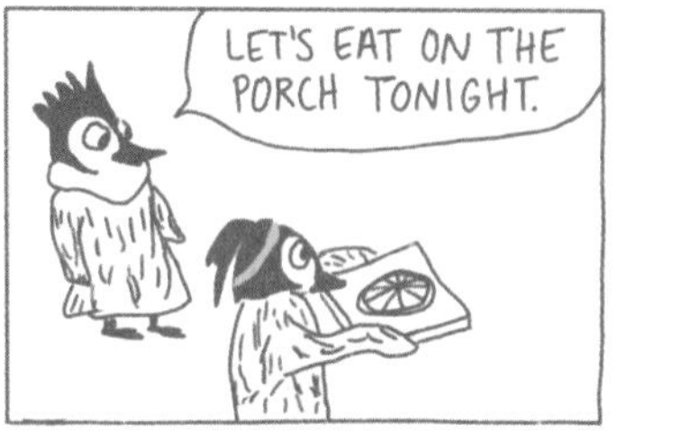
LET'S EAT ON THE PORCH TONIGHT.

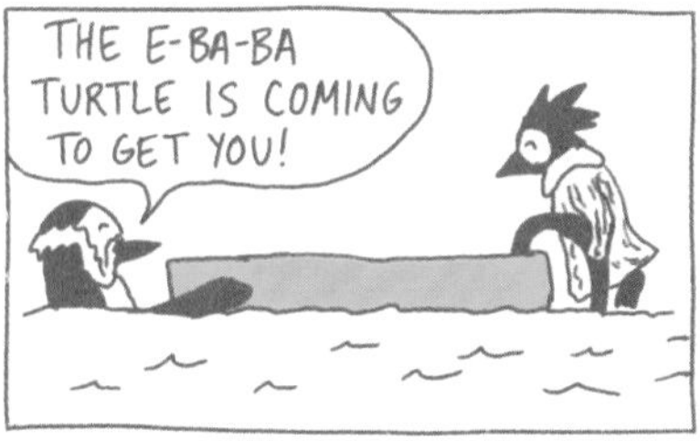
THE E-BA-BA TURTLE IS COMING TO GET YOU!

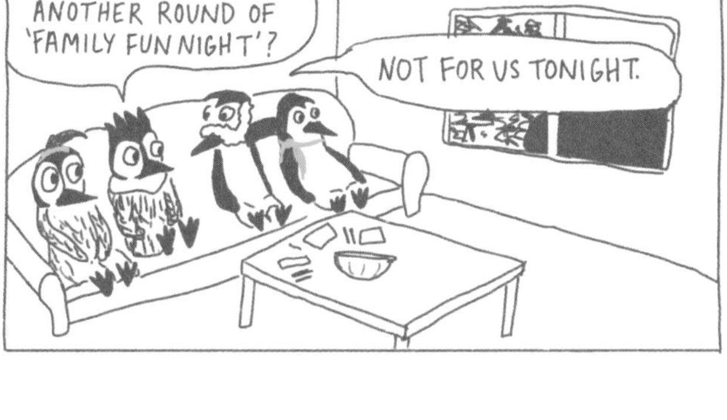
ANOTHER ROUND OF 'FAMILY FUN NIGHT'?
NOT FOR US TONIGHT.

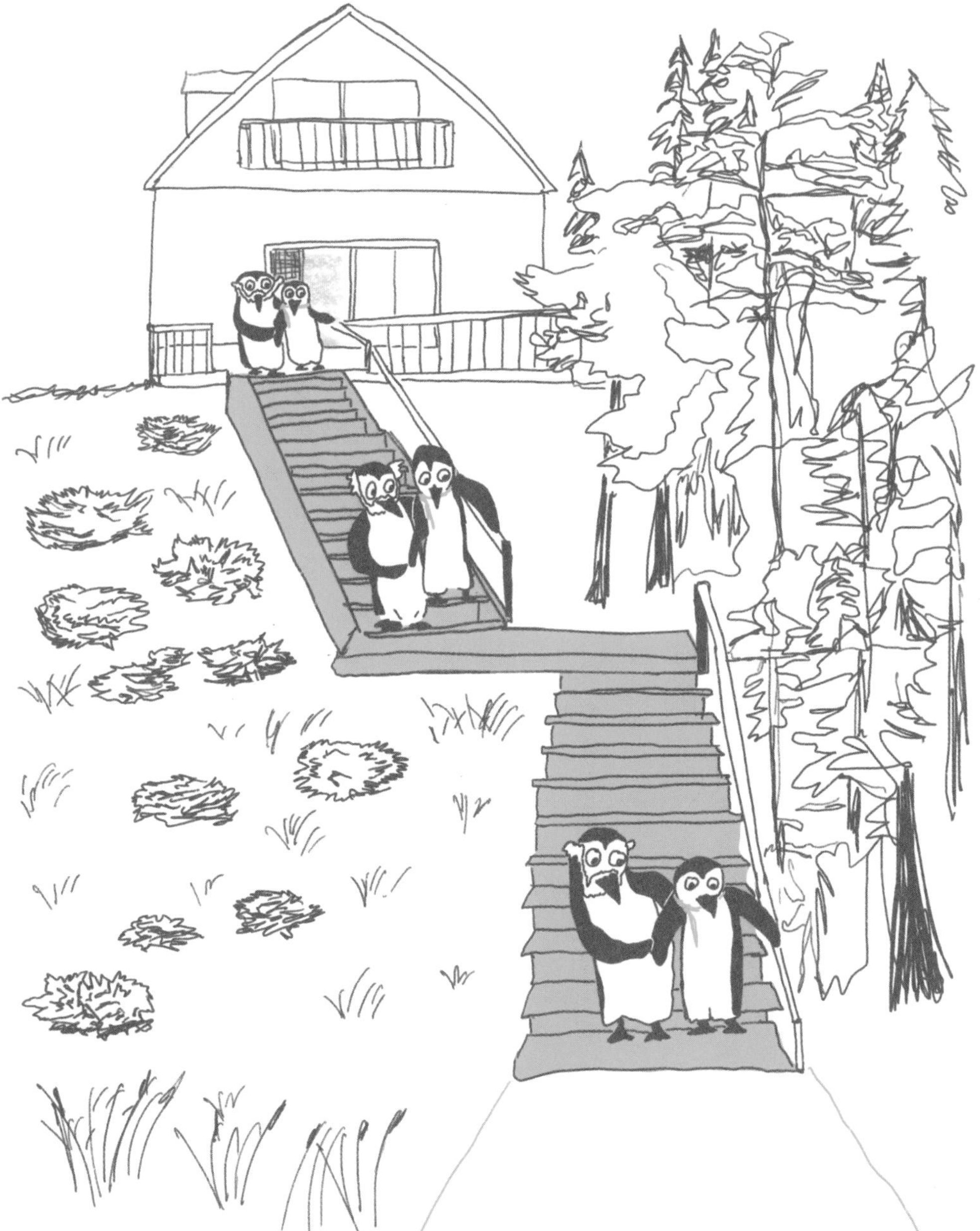

SEPTEMBER

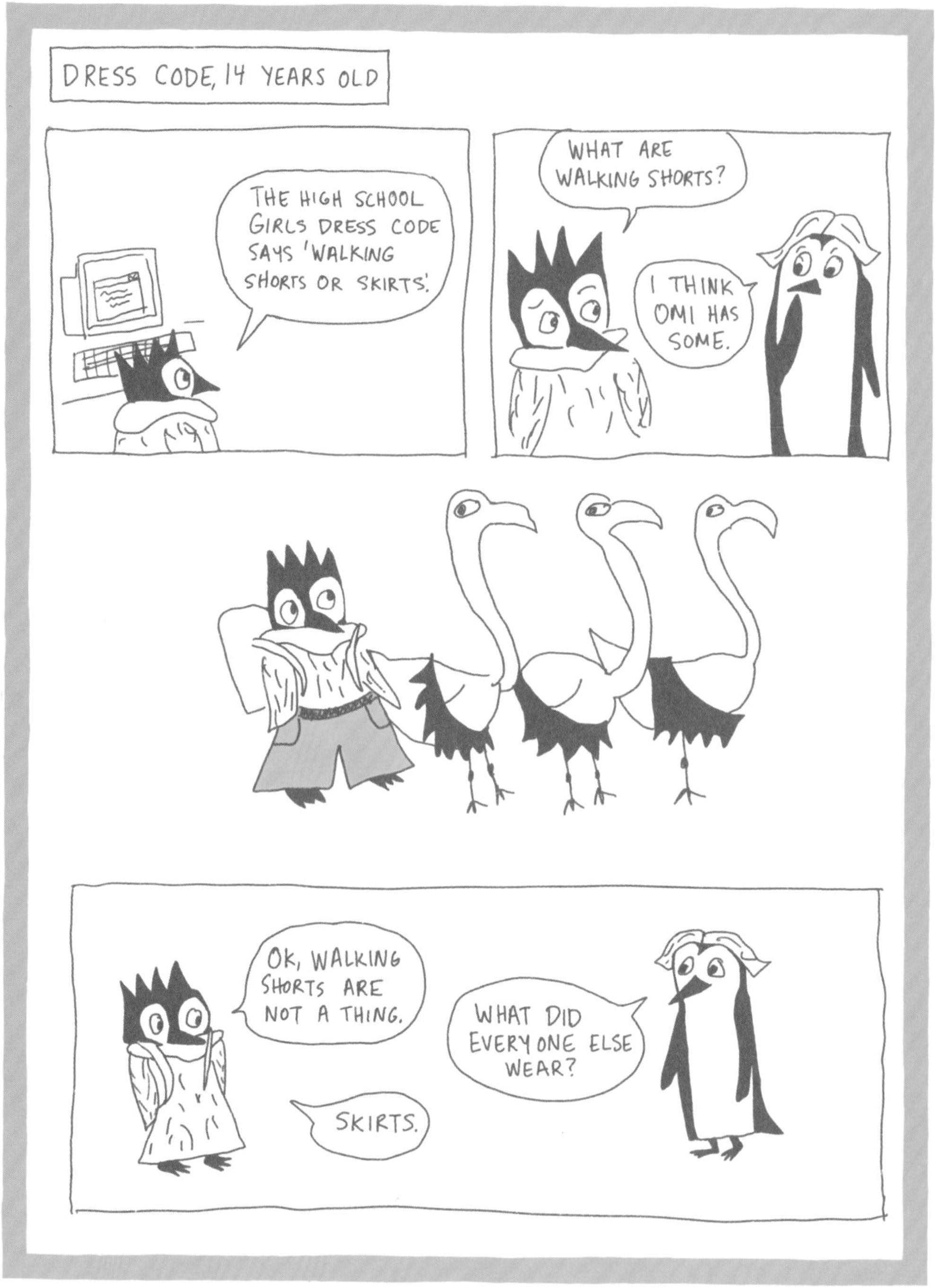
DRESS CODE, 14 YEARS OLD
THE HIGH SCHOOL GIRLS DRESS CODE SAYS 'WALKING SHORTS OR SKIRTS.'
WHAT ARE WALKING SHORTS?
I THINK OMI HAS SOME.
OK, WALKING SHORTS ARE NOT A THING.
WHAT DID EVERYONE ELSE WEAR?
SKIRTS.

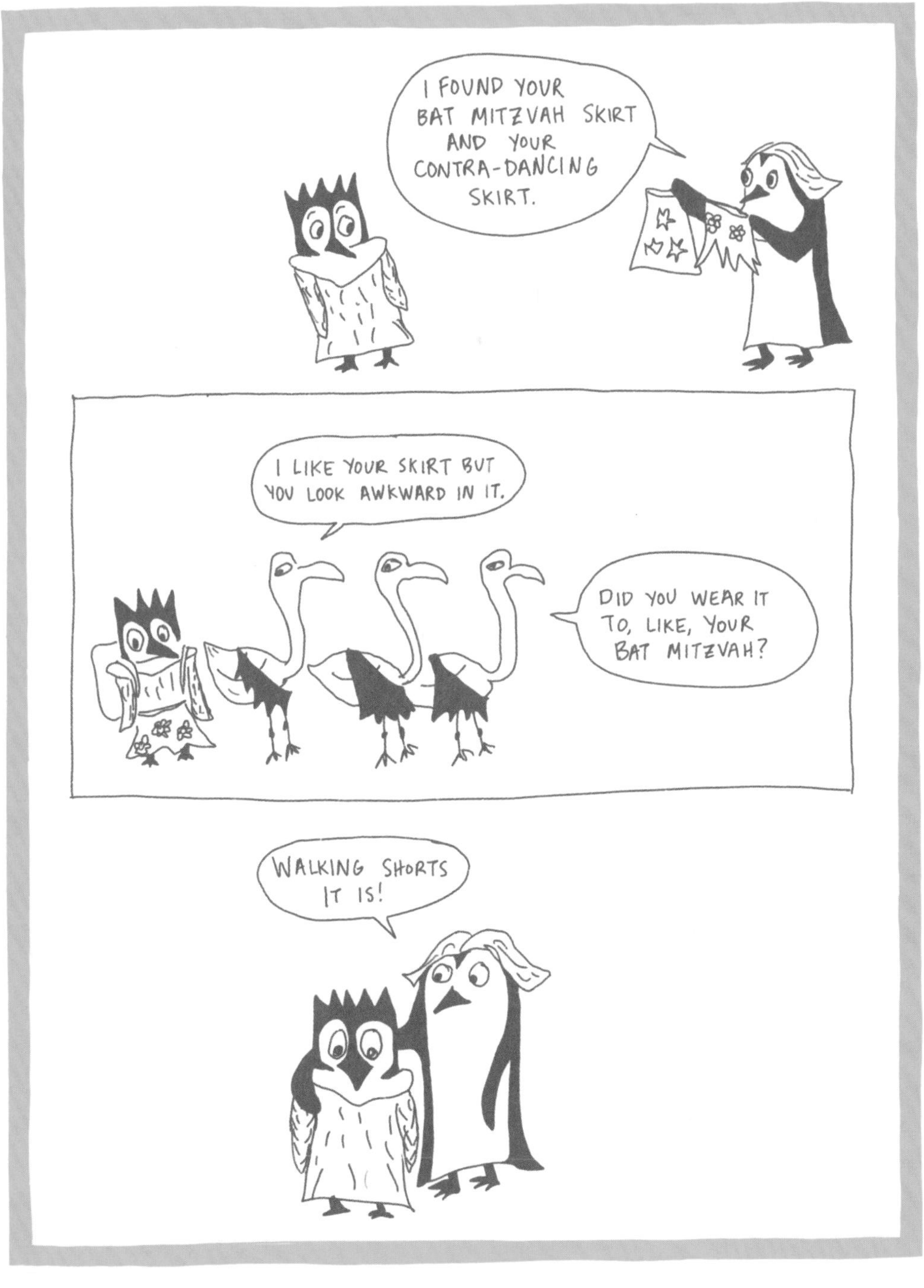
I FOUND YOUR BAT MITZVAH SKIRT AND YOUR CONTRA-DANCING SKIRT.
I LIKE YOUR SKIRT BUT YOU LOOK AWKWARD IN IT.
DID YOU WEAR IT TO, LIKE, YOUR BAT MITZVAH?
WALKING SHORTS IT IS!

MARIA

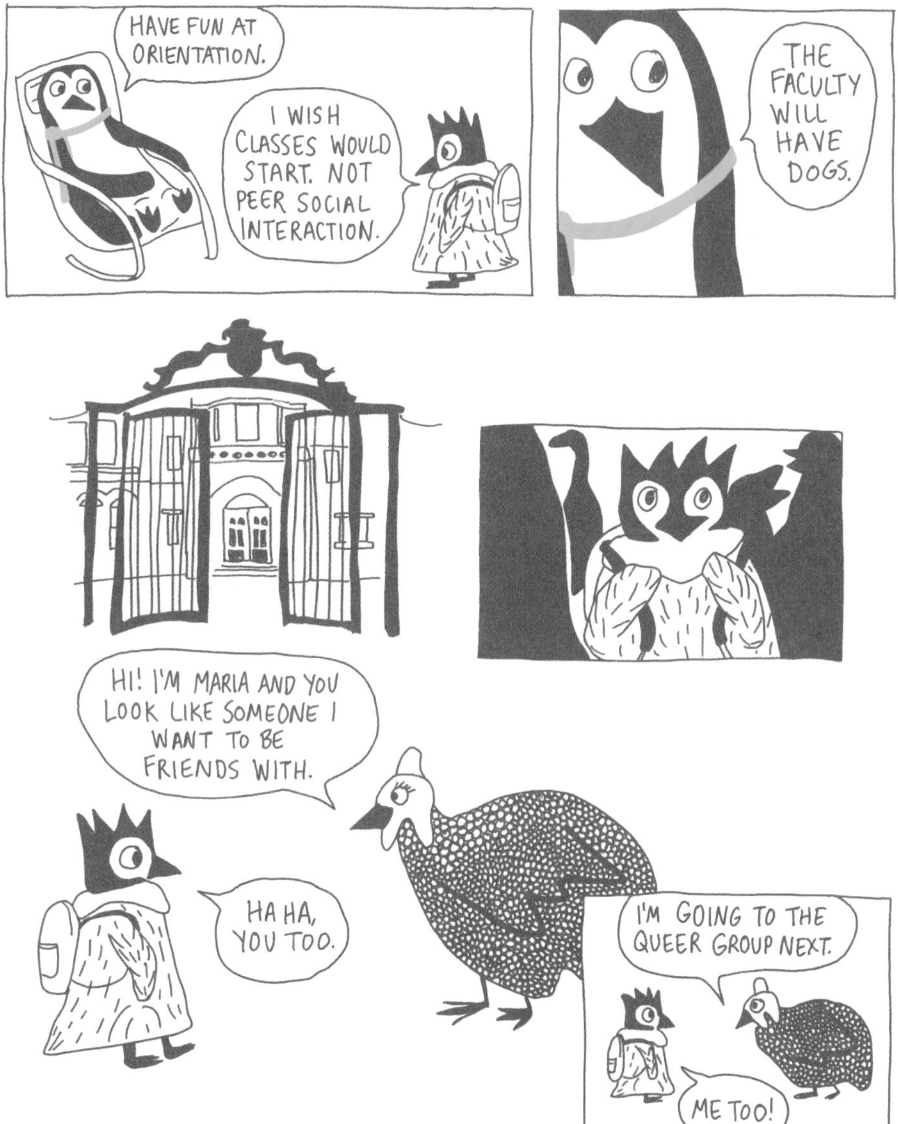
HAVE FUN AT ORIENTATION.
I WISH CLASSES WOULD START. NOT PEER SOCIAL INTERACTION.
THE FACULTY WILL HAVE DOGS.
HI! I'M MARIA AND YOU LOOK LIKE SOMEONE I WANT TO BE FRIENDS WITH.
HA HA, YOU TOO.
I'M GOING TO THE QUEER GROUP NEXT.
ME TOO!

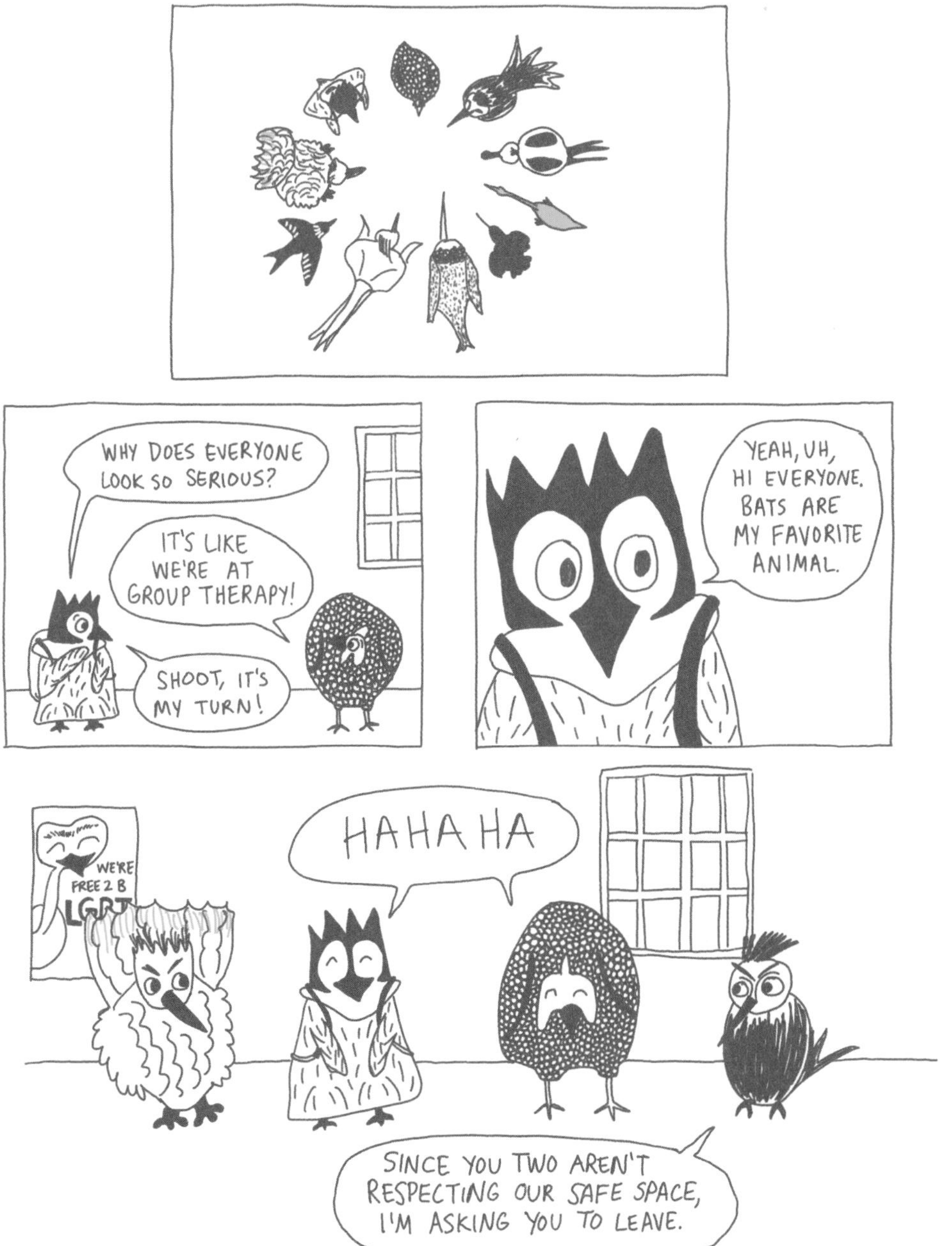
WHY DOES EVERYONE LOOK SO SERIOUS?
IT'S LIKE WE'RE AT GROUP THERAPY!
SHOOT, IT'S MY TURN!
YEAH, UH, HI EVERYONE. BATS ARE MY FAVORITE ANIMAL.
WE'RE FREE 2 B LGBT
HAHAHA
SINCE YOU TWO AREN'T RESPECTING OUR SAFE SPACE, I'M ASKING YOU TO LEAVE.

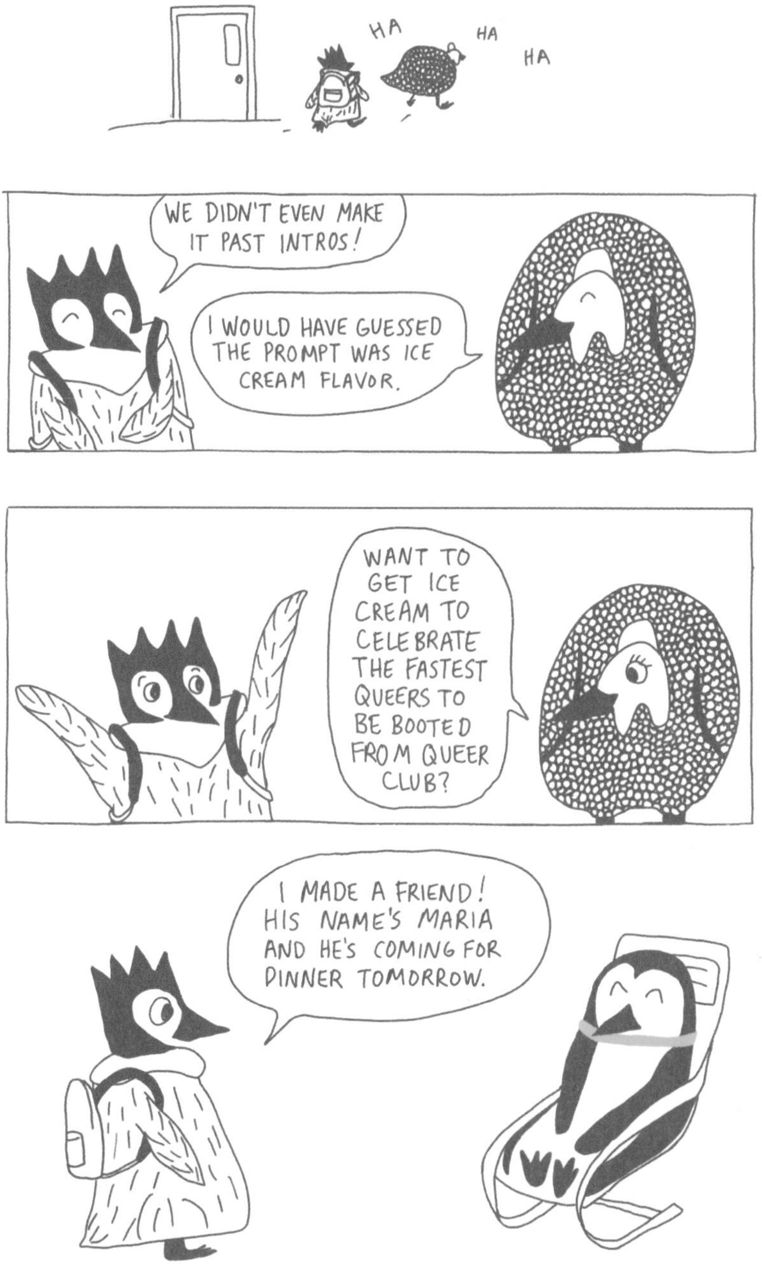
HA
HA
HA
WE DIDN'T EVEN MAKE IT PAST INTROS!
I WOULD HAVE GUESSED THE PROMPT WAS ICE CREAM FLAVOR.
WANT TO GET ICE CREAM TO CELEBRATE THE FASTEST QUEERS TO BE BOOTED FROM QUEER CLUB?
I MADE A FRIEND! HIS NAME'S MARIA AND HE'S COMING FOR DINNER TOMORROW.

THERAPY?

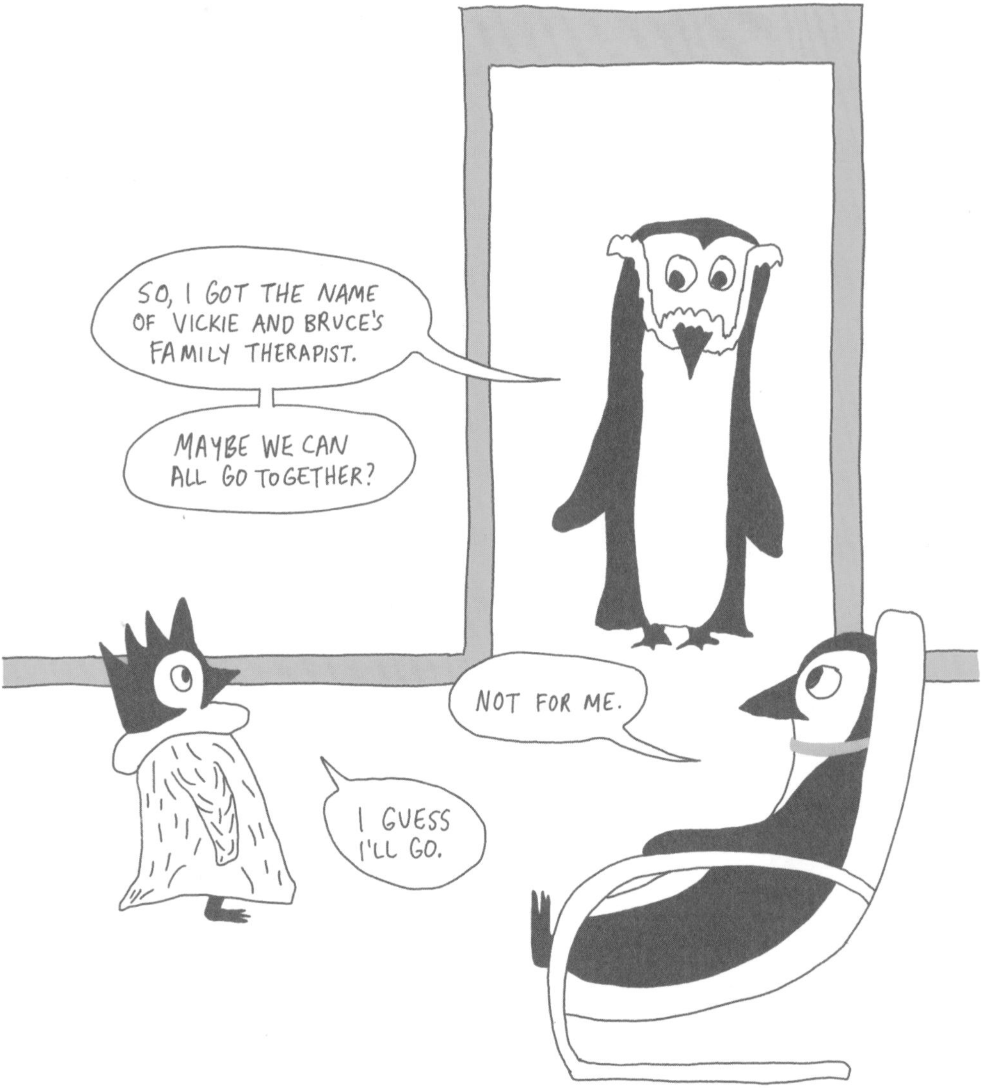
SO, I GOT THE NAME OF VICKIE AND BRUCE'S FAMILY THERAPIST.
MAYBE WE CAN ALL GO TOGETHER?
NOT FOR ME.
I GUESS I'LL GO.

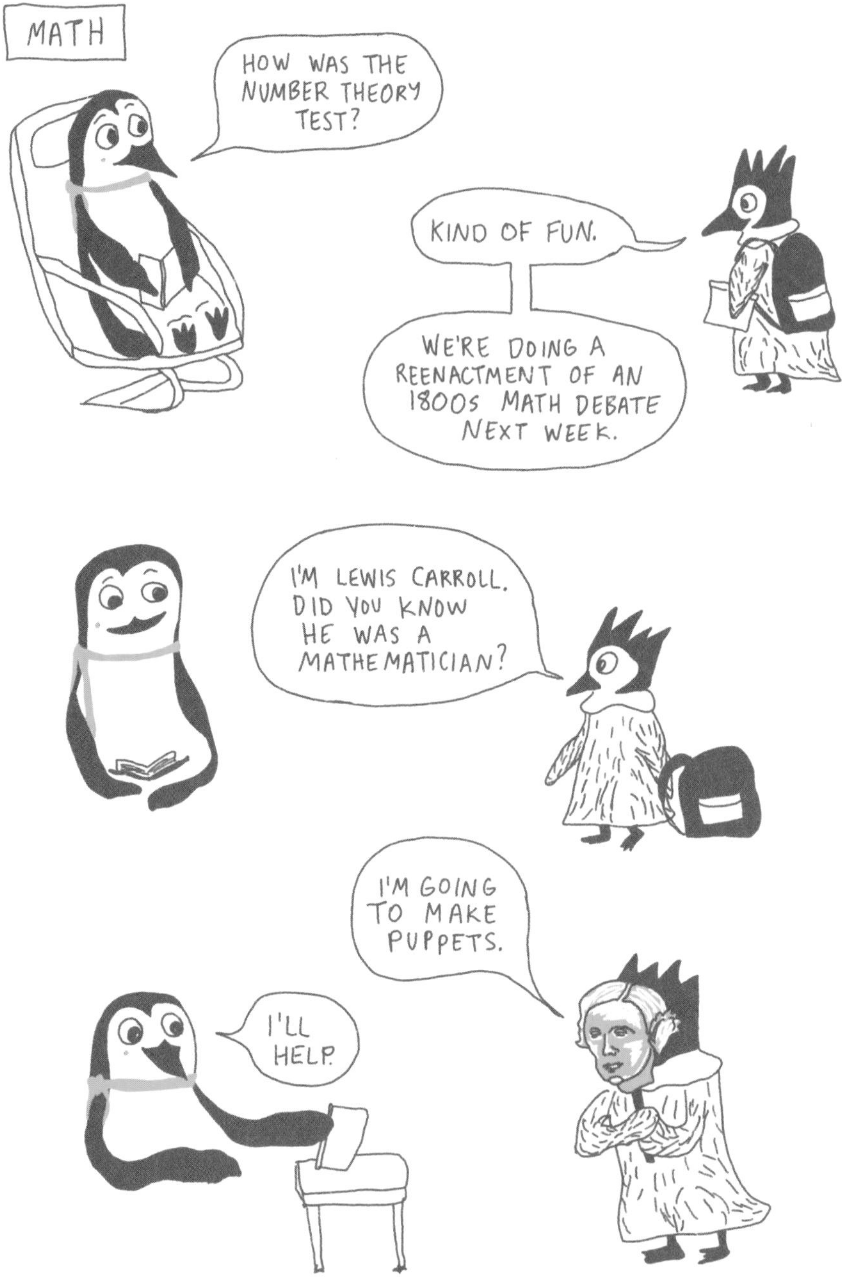
MATH
HOW WAS THE NUMBER THEORY TEST?
KIND OF FUN.
WE'RE DOING A REENACTMENT OF AN 1800s MATH DEBATE NEXT WEEK.
I'M LEWIS CARROLL. DID YOU KNOW HE WAS A MATHEMATICIAN?
I'M GOING TO MAKE PUPPETS.
I'LL HELP.

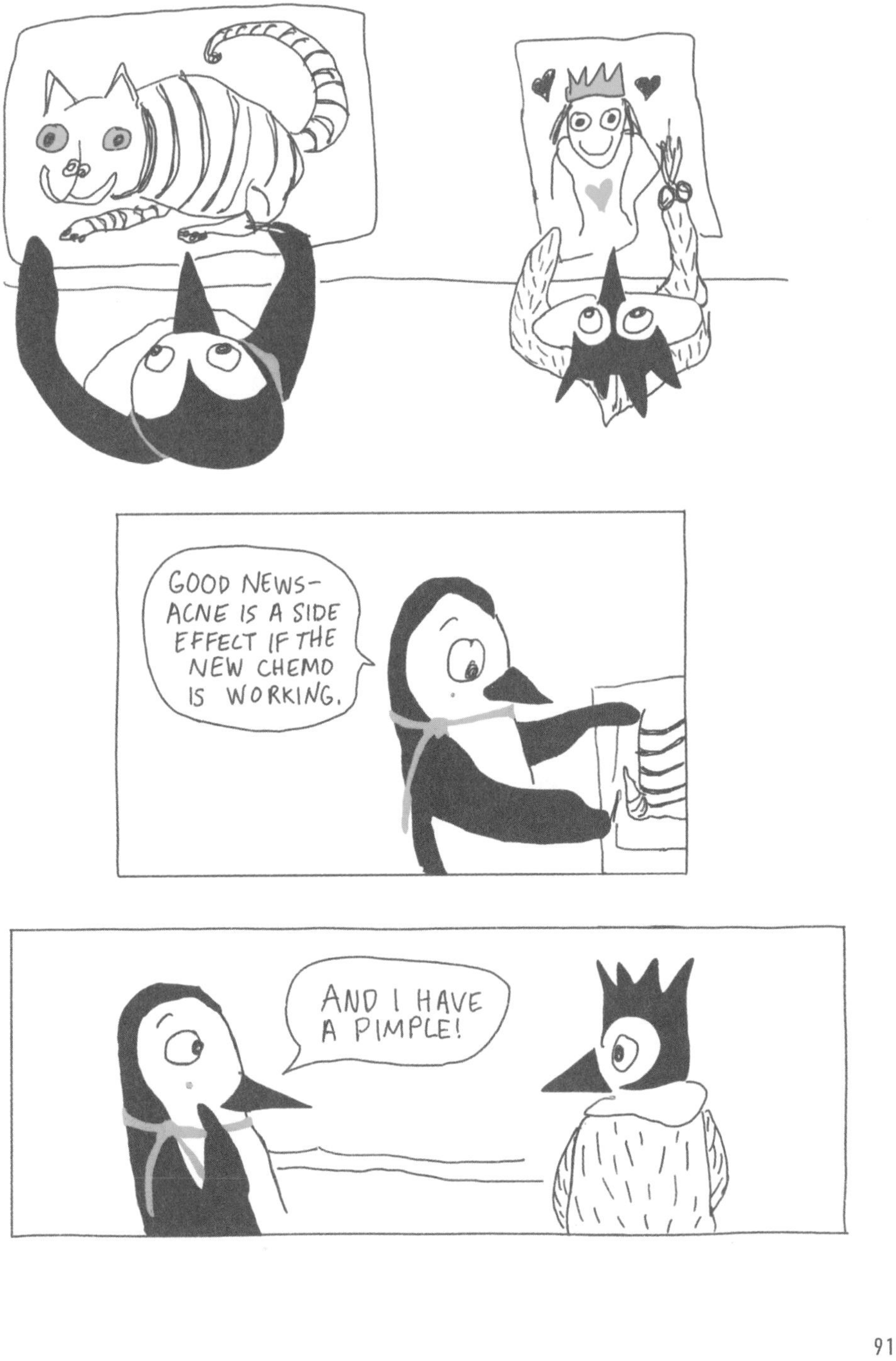
GOOD NEWS-
ACNE IS A SIDE
EFFECT IF THE
NEW CHEMO
IS WORKING.
AND I HAVE
A PIMPLE!

READING OUT LOUD

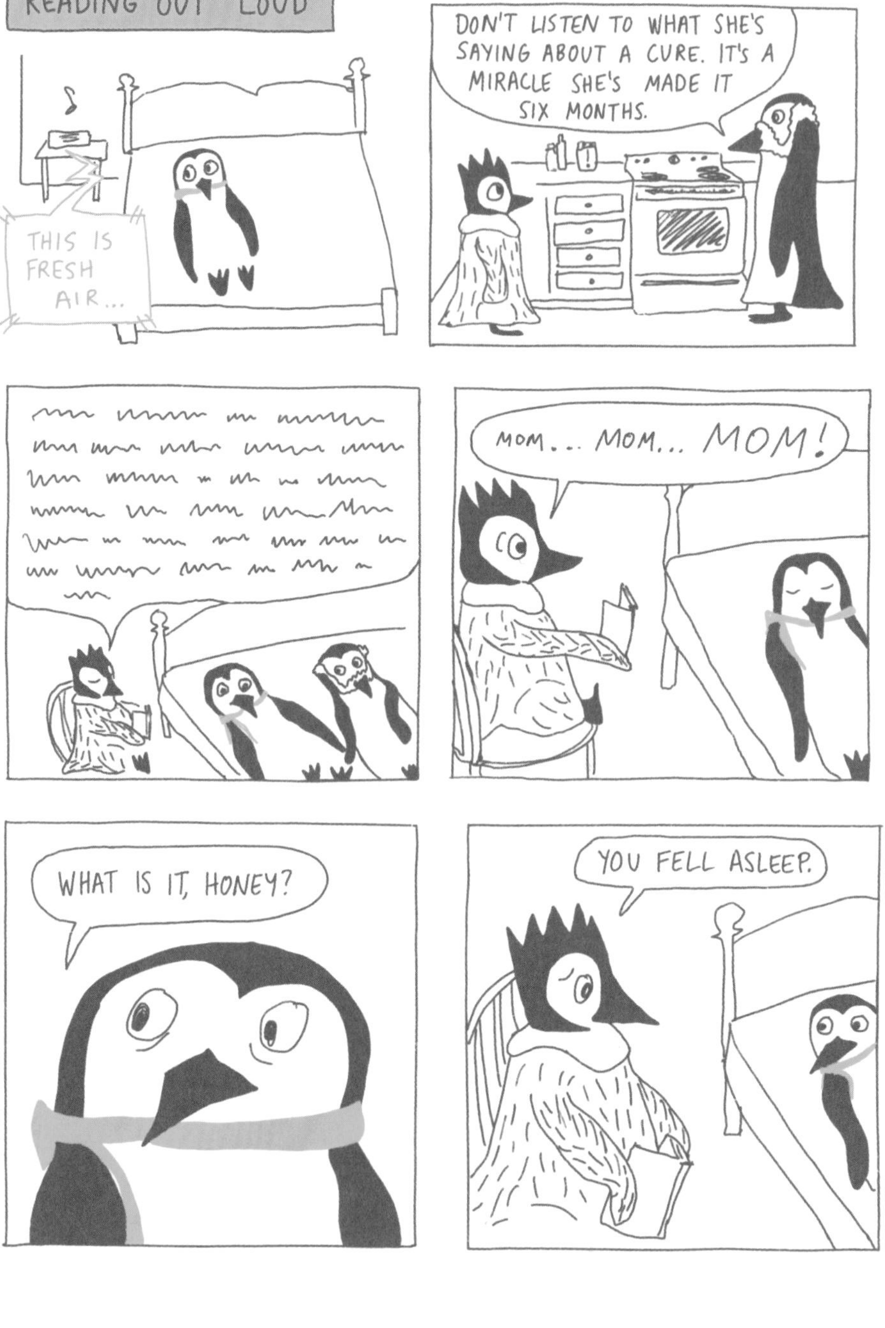

THIS IS FRESH AIR...
DON'T LISTEN TO WHAT SHE'S SAYING ABOUT A CURE. IT'S A MIRACLE SHE'S MADE IT SIX MONTHS.
MOM... MOM... MOM!
WHAT IS IT, HONEY?
YOU FELL ASLEEP.

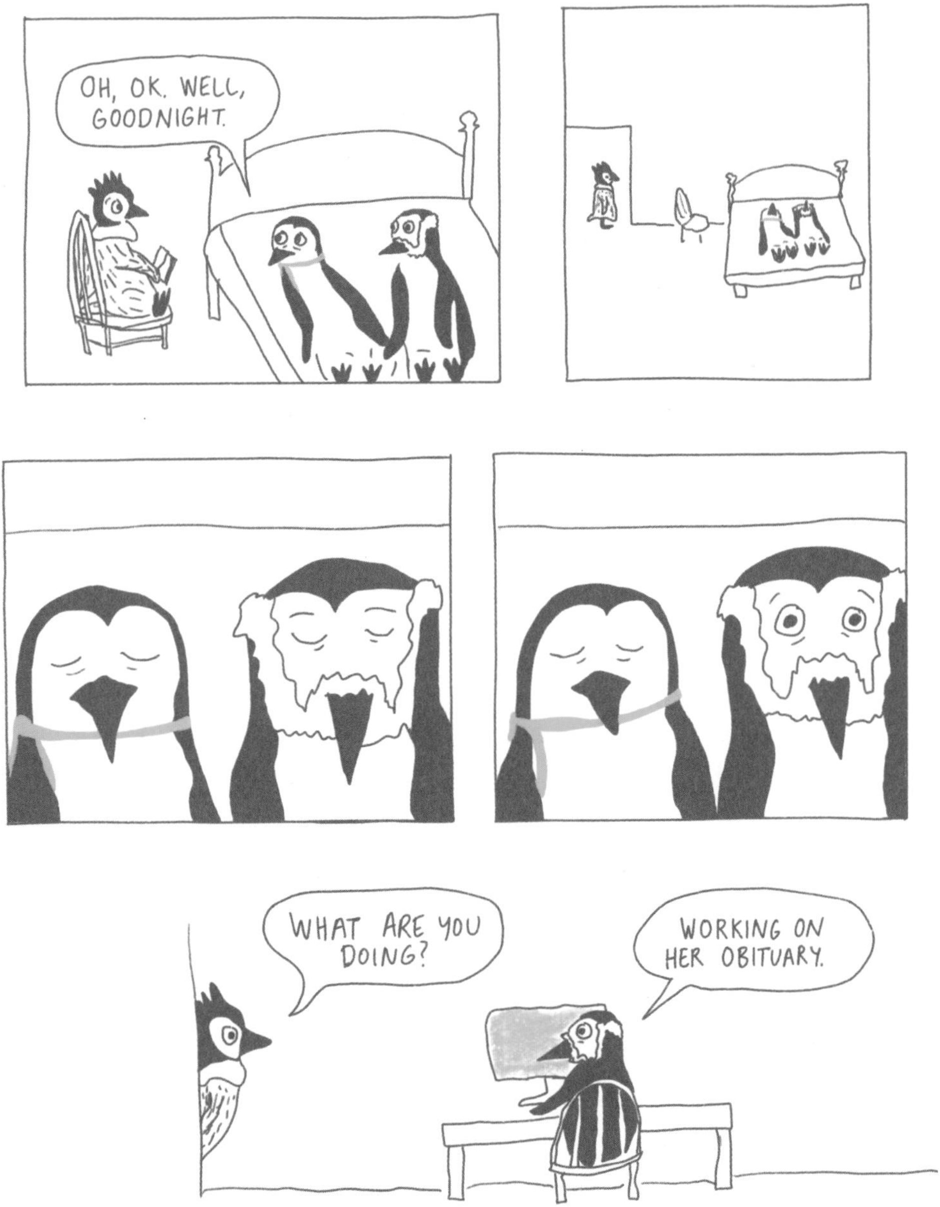

OH, OK. WELL, GOODNIGHT.
WHAT ARE YOU DOING?
WORKING ON HER OBITUARY.

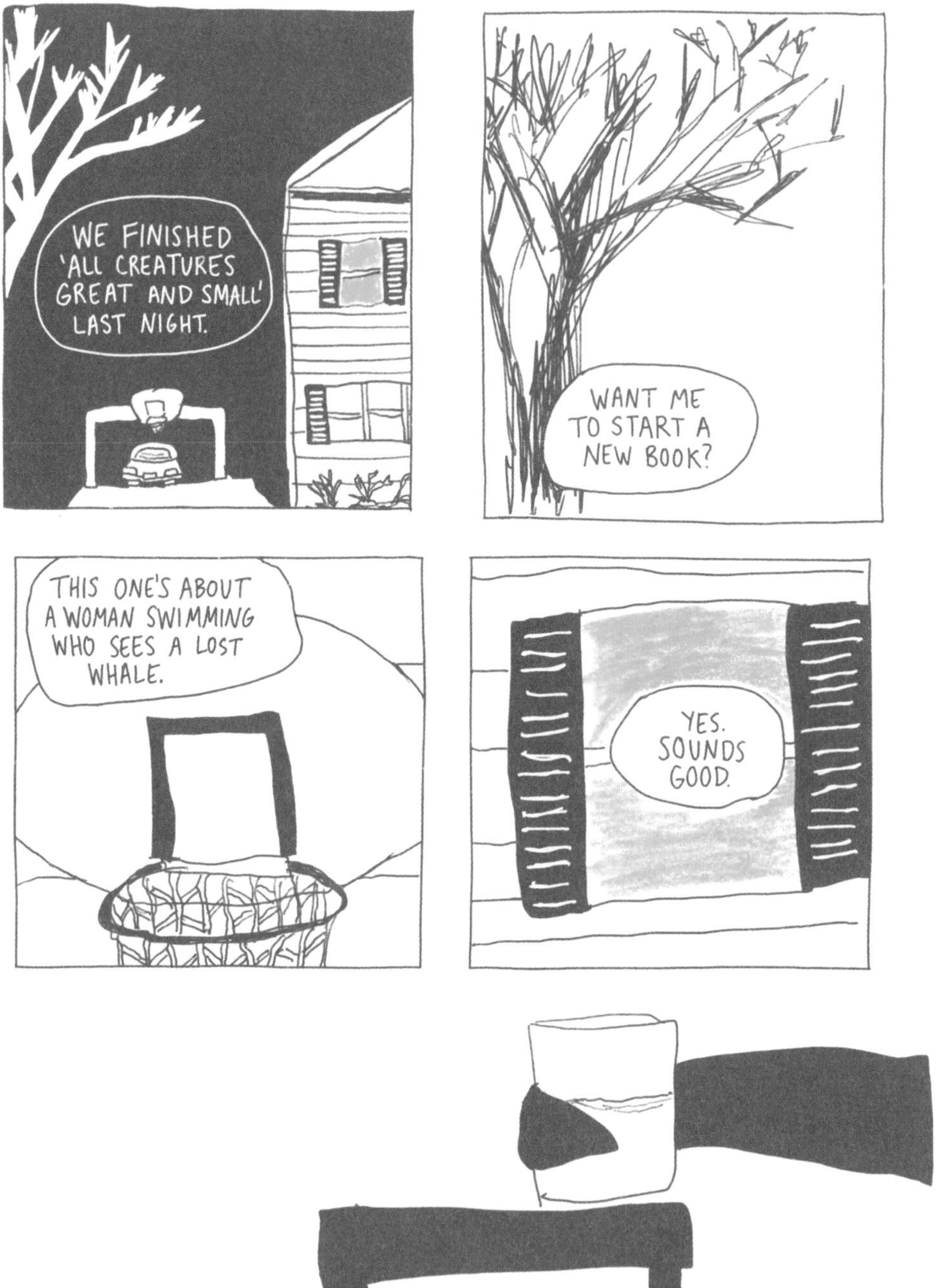
WE FINISHED 'ALL CREATURES GREAT AND SMALL' LAST NIGHT.
WANT ME TO START A NEW BOOK?
THIS ONE'S ABOUT A WOMAN SWIMMING WHO SEES A LOST WHALE.
YES. SOUNDS GOOD.

CLICK

WHAT ARE YOU WORKING ON TONIGHT?
FOUND A COUPLE IN VERMONT WHO DO FAMILY DIRECT CREMATION.
ONLY AN HOUR AWAY.

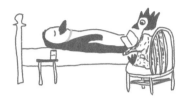

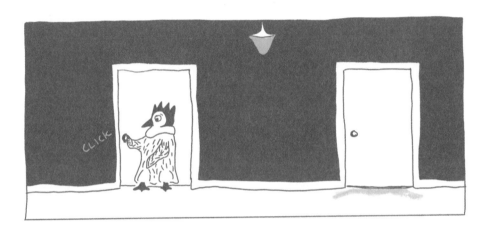

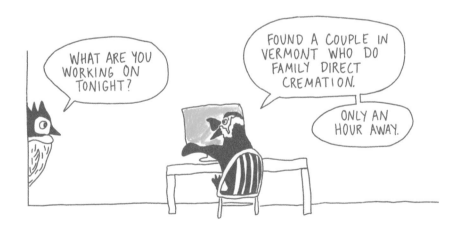

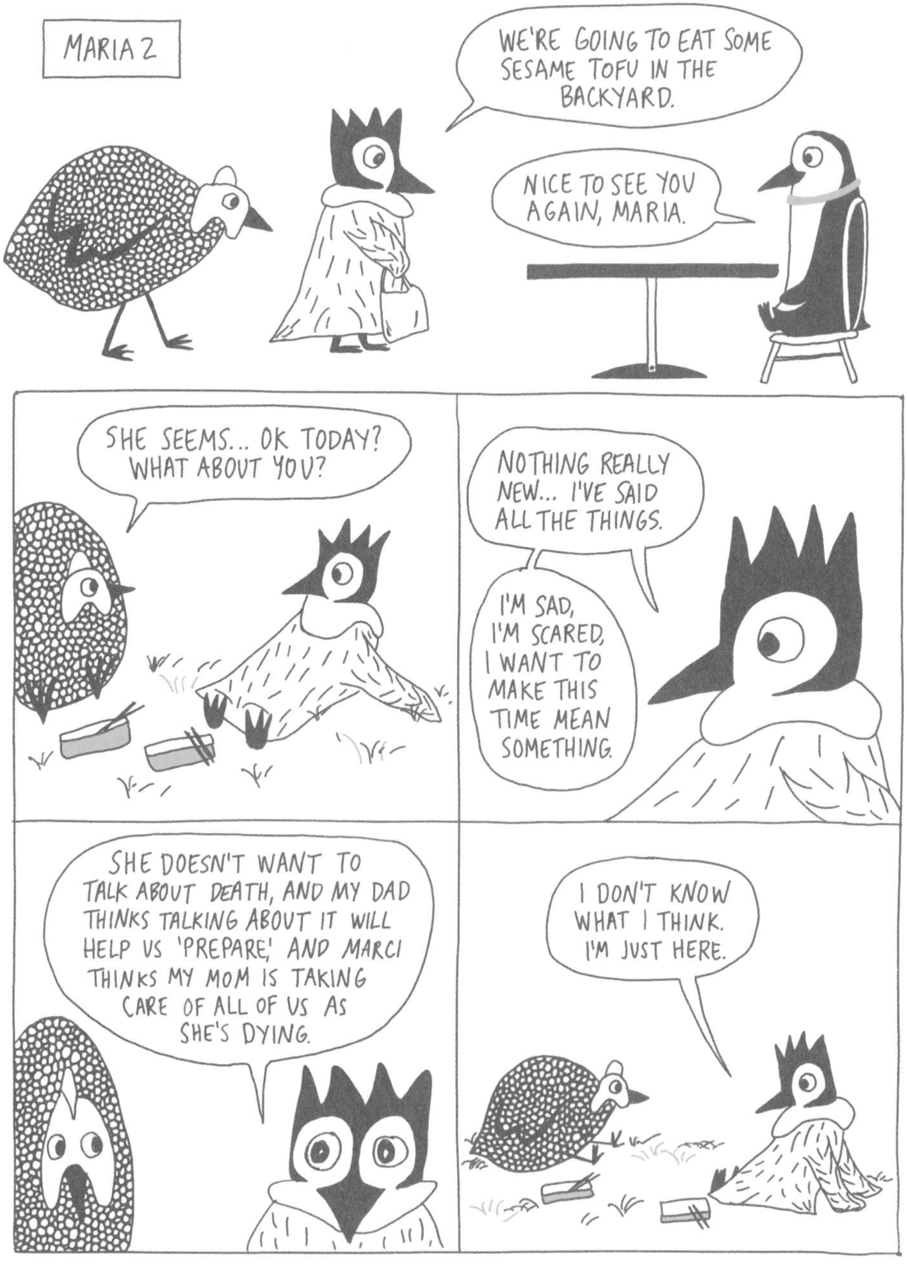
MARIA 2
WE'RE GOING TO EAT SOME SESAME TOFU IN THE BACKYARD.
NICE TO SEE YOU AGAIN, MARIA.
SHE SEEMS... OK TODAY? WHAT ABOUT YOU?
NOTHING REALLY NEW... I'VE SAID ALL THE THINGS.
I'M SAD, I'M SCARED, I WANT TO MAKE THIS TIME MEAN SOMETHING.
SHE DOESN'T WANT TO TALK ABOUT DEATH, AND MY DAD THINKS TALKING ABOUT IT WILL HELP US 'PREPARE,' AND MARCI THINKS MY MOM IS TAKING CARE OF ALL OF US AS SHE'S DYING.
I DON'T KNOW WHAT I THINK. I'M JUST HERE.

THERAPY 2

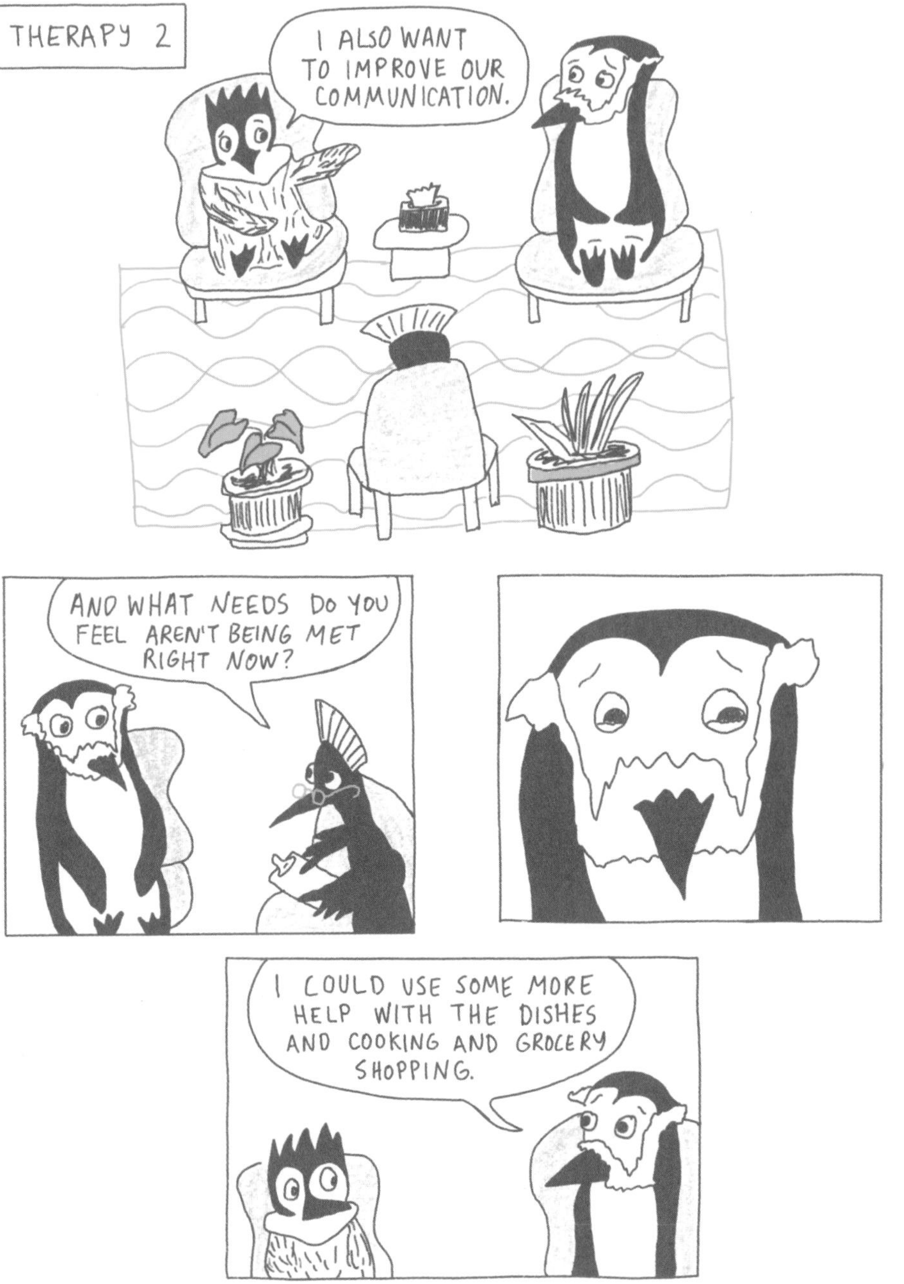
I ALSO WANT TO IMPROVE OUR COMMUNICATION.
AND WHAT NEEDS DO YOU FEEL AREN'T BEING MET RIGHT NOW?
I COULD USE SOME MORE HELP WITH THE DISHES AND COOKING AND GROCERY SHOPPING.

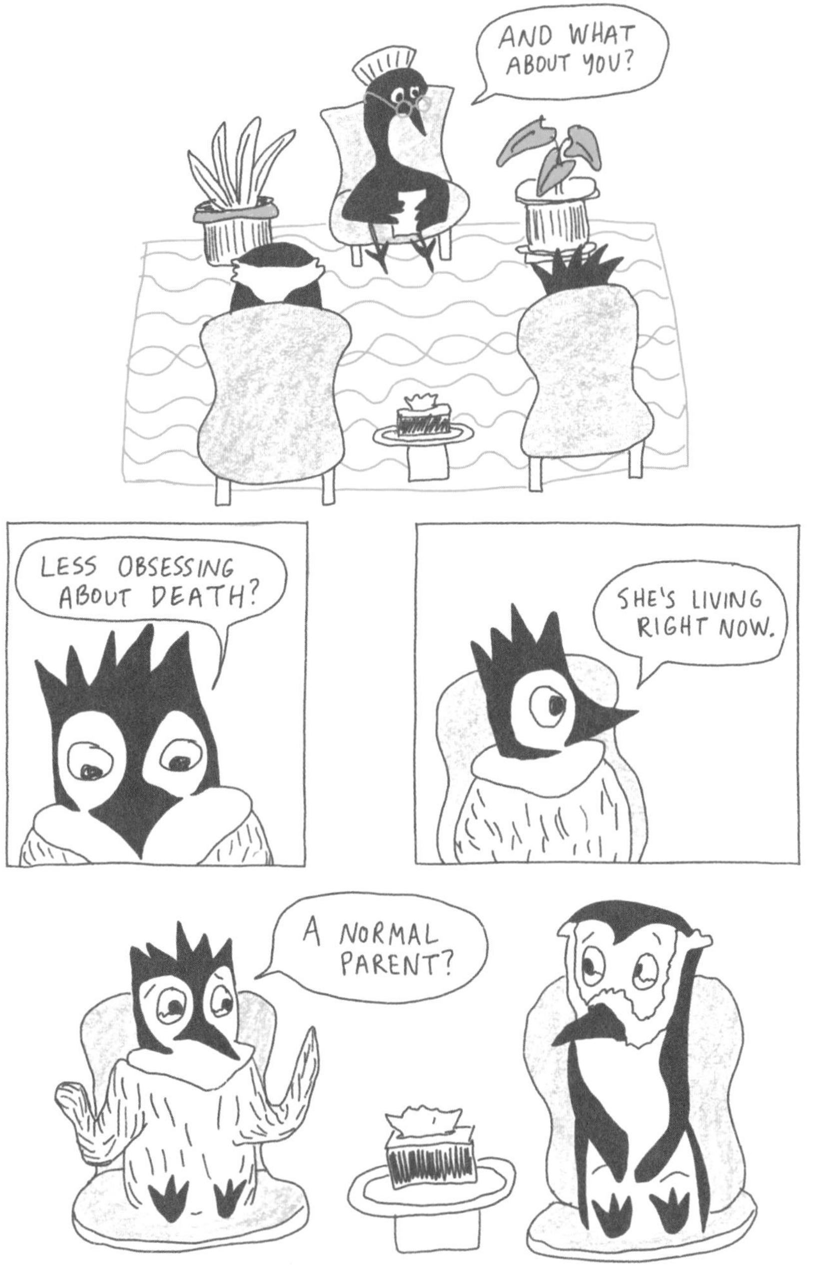
AND WHAT ABOUT YOU?
LESS OBSESSING ABOUT DEATH?
SHE'S LIVING RIGHT NOW.
A NORMAL PARENT?

GENDERQUEER 2

YOU KNOW, WE ALWAYS KNEW YOU WERE MARCHING TO YOUR OWN BEAT.
WE DIDN'T HAVE THE WORDS BACK THEN.
YOUR MOTHER AND I THOUGHT WE WERE RAISING A LESBIAN.

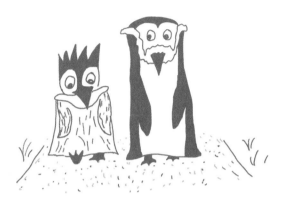

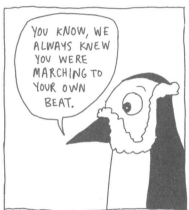

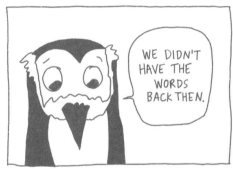

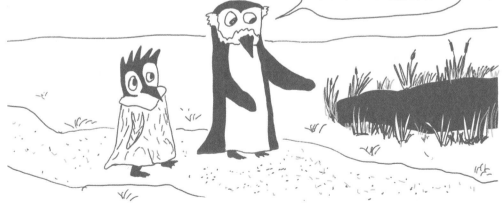

OCTOBER

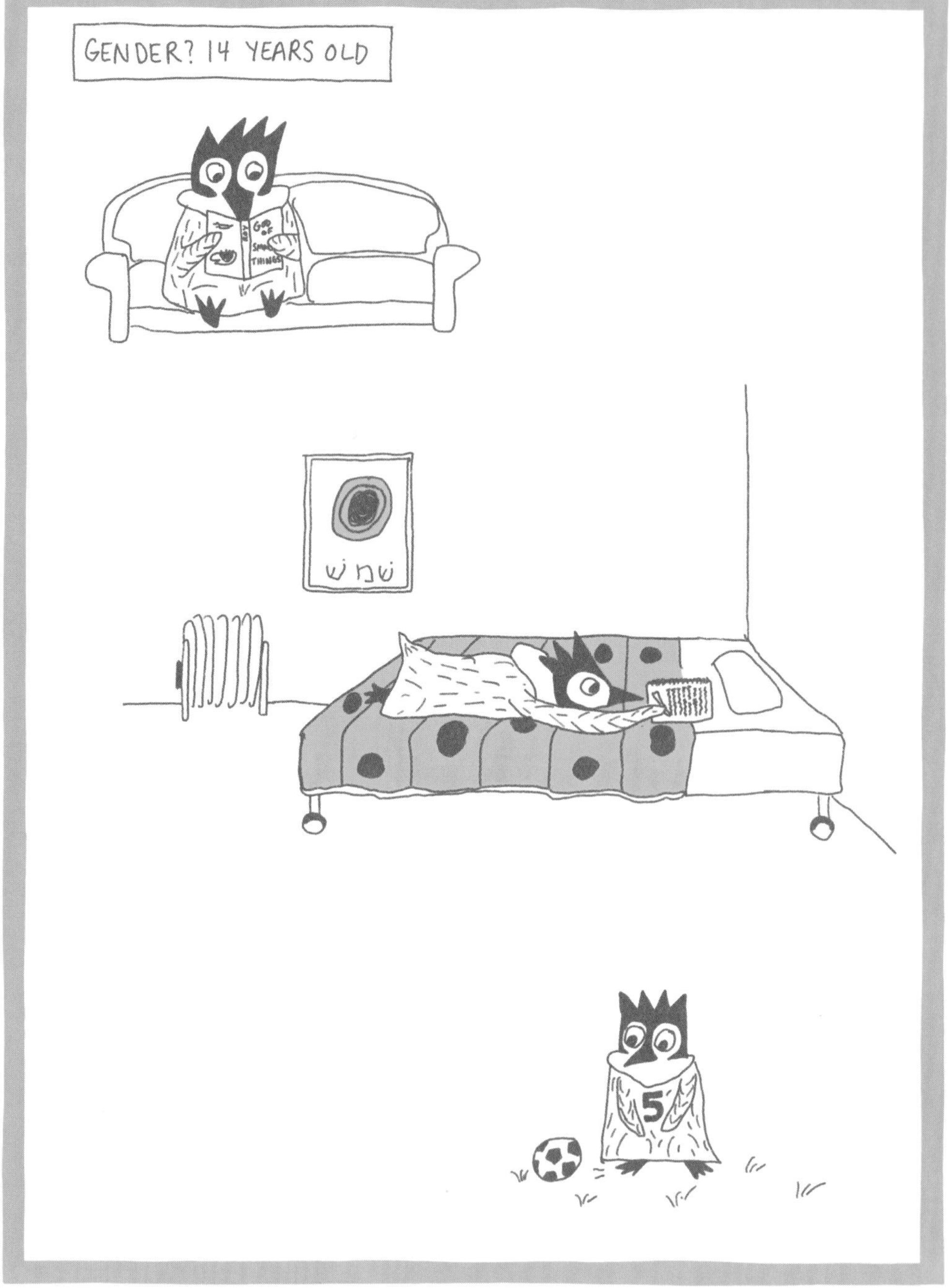
GENDER? 14 YEARS OLD
5

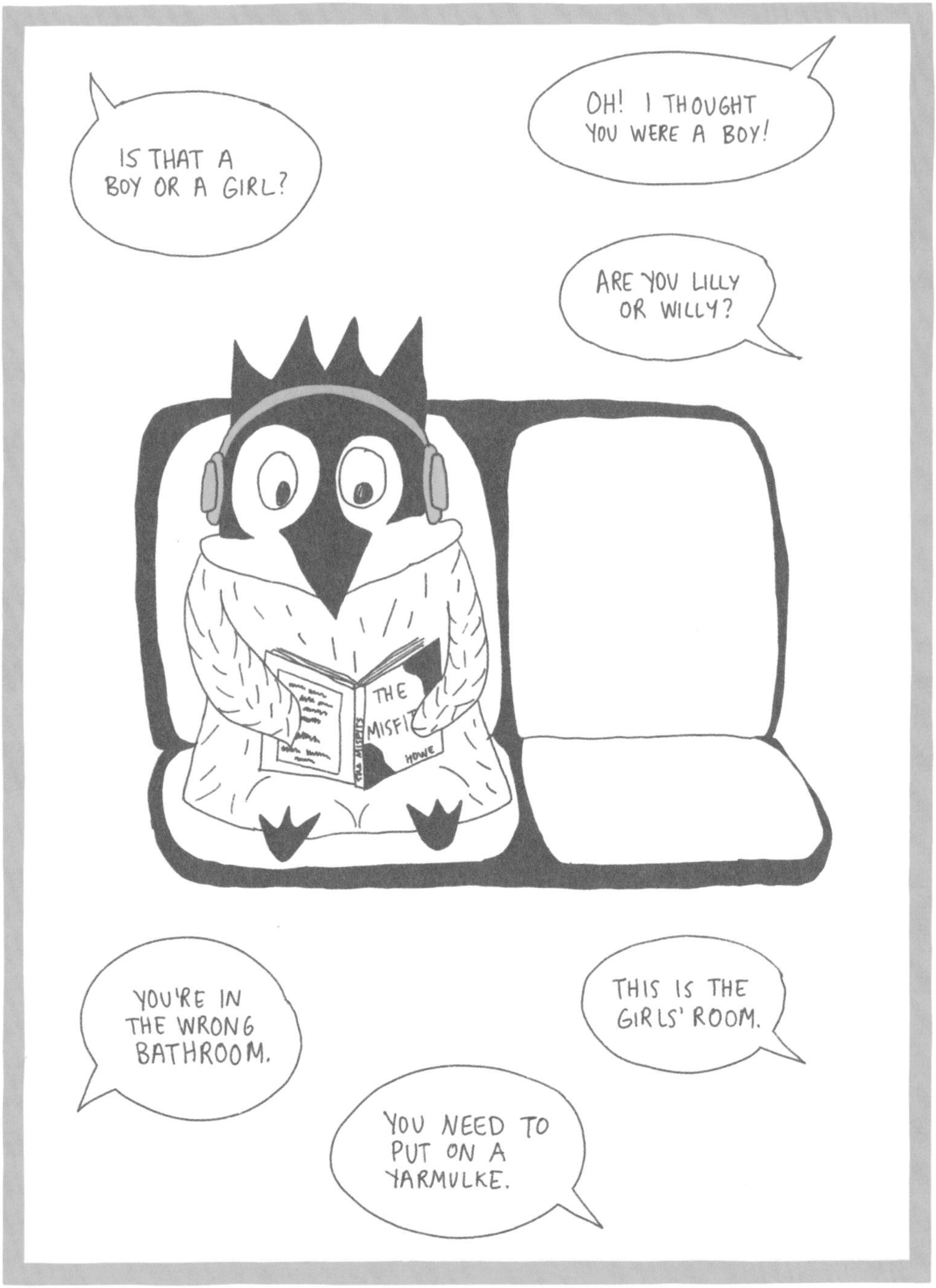
IS THAT A BOY OR A GIRL?
OH! I THOUGHT YOU WERE A BOY!
ARE YOU LILLY OR WILLY?
THE MISFITS
HOWE
YOU'RE IN THE WRONG BATHROOM.
THIS IS THE GIRLS' ROOM.
YOU NEED TO PUT ON A YARMULKE.

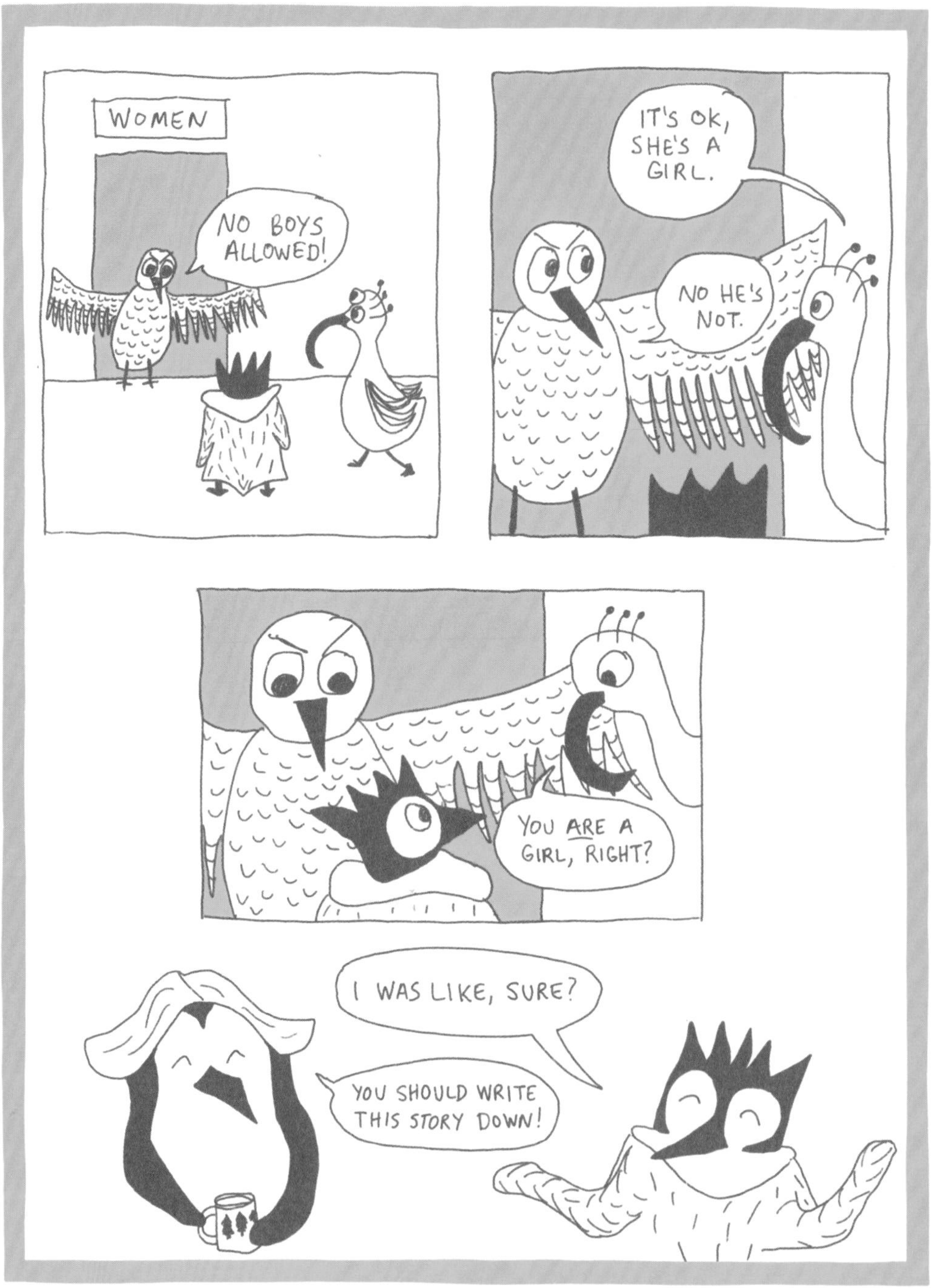
WOMEN
NO BOYS ALLOWED!
IT'S OK, SHE'S A GIRL.
NO HE'S NOT.
YOU ARE A GIRL, RIGHT?
I WAS LIKE, SURE?
YOU SHOULD WRITE THIS STORY DOWN!

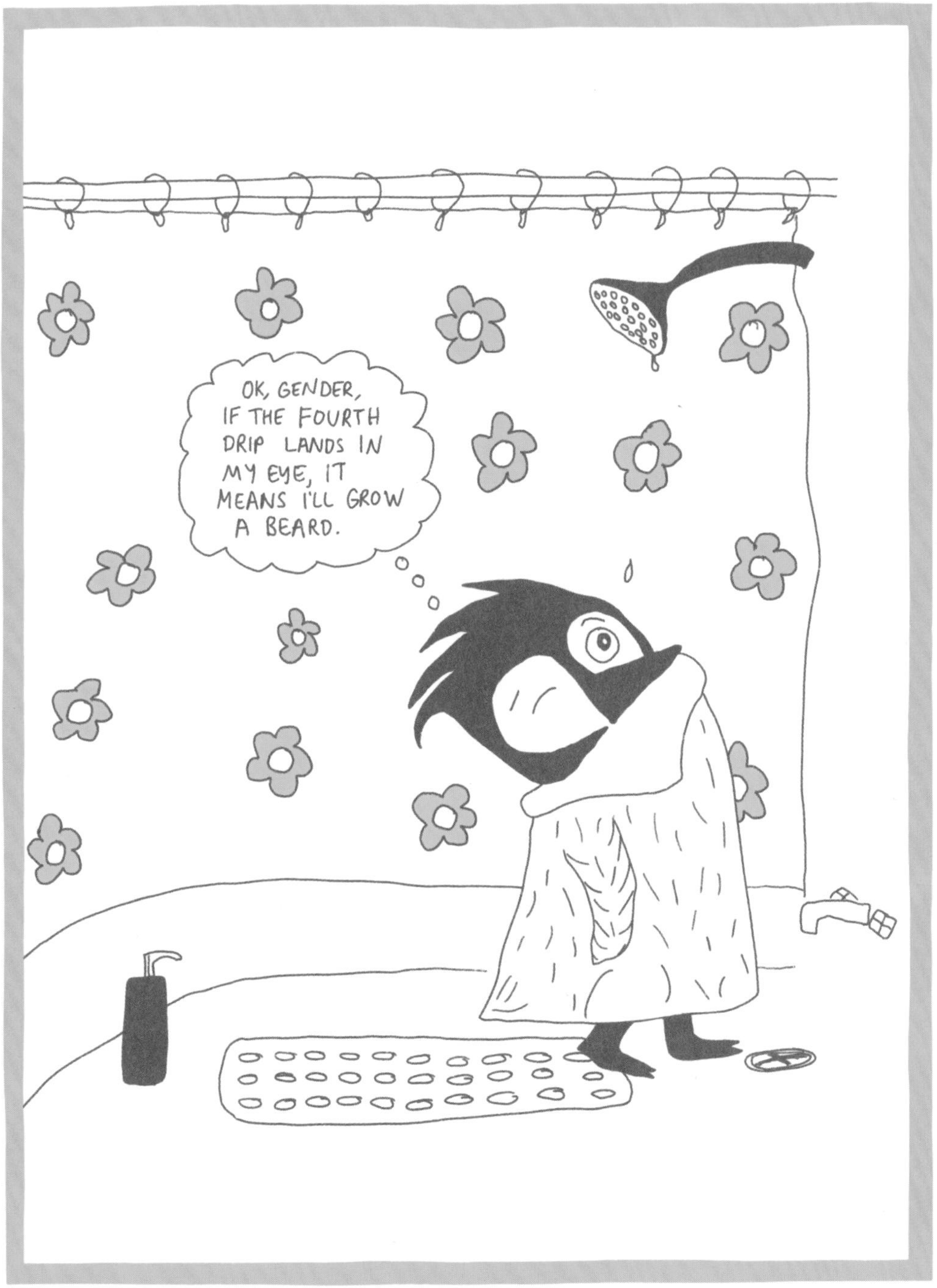
OK, GENDER, IF THE FOURTH DRIP LANDS IN MY EYE, IT MEANS I'LL GROW A BEARD.

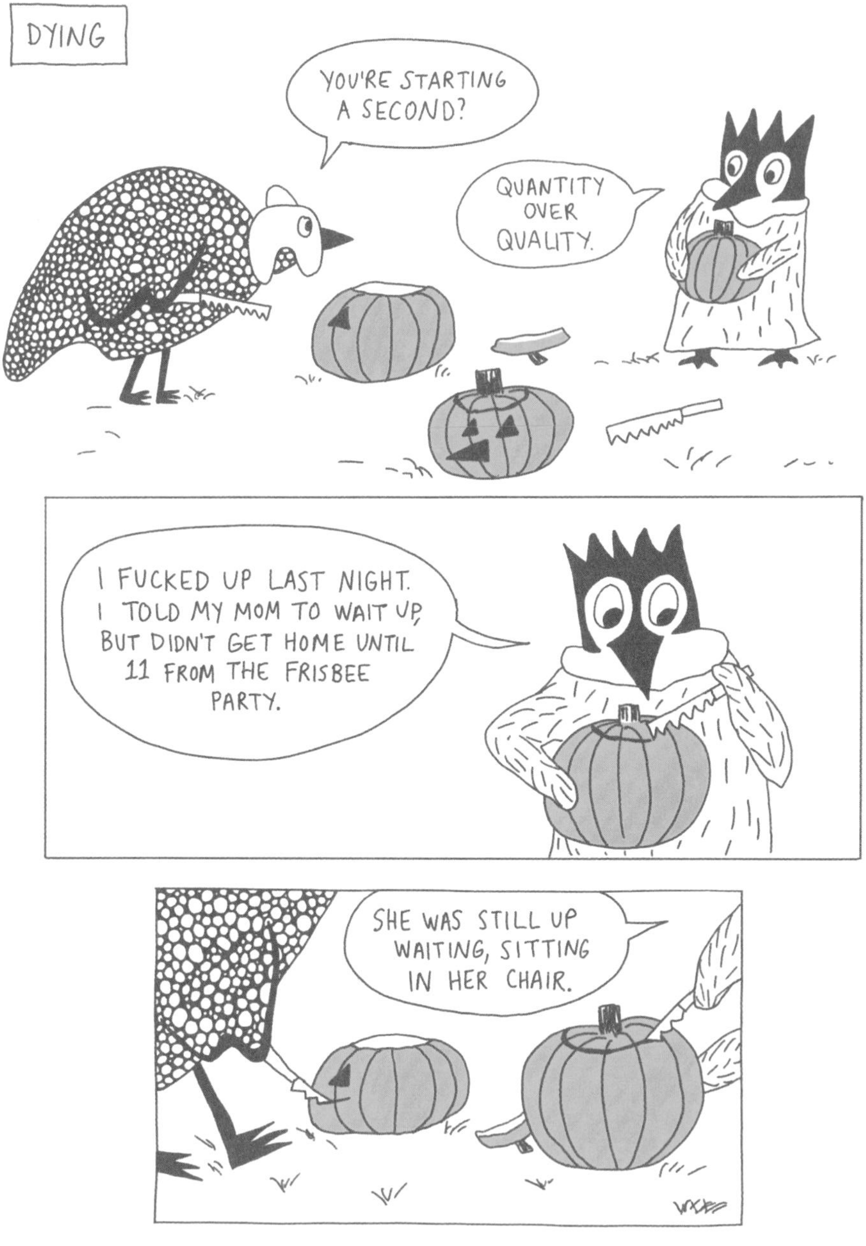
DYING
YOU'RE STARTING A SECOND?
QUANTITY OVER QUALITY.
I FUCKED UP LAST NIGHT. I TOLD MY MOM TO WAIT UP, BUT DIDN'T GET HOME UNTIL 11 FROM THE FRISBEE PARTY.
SHE WAS STILL UP WAITING, SITTING IN HER CHAIR.

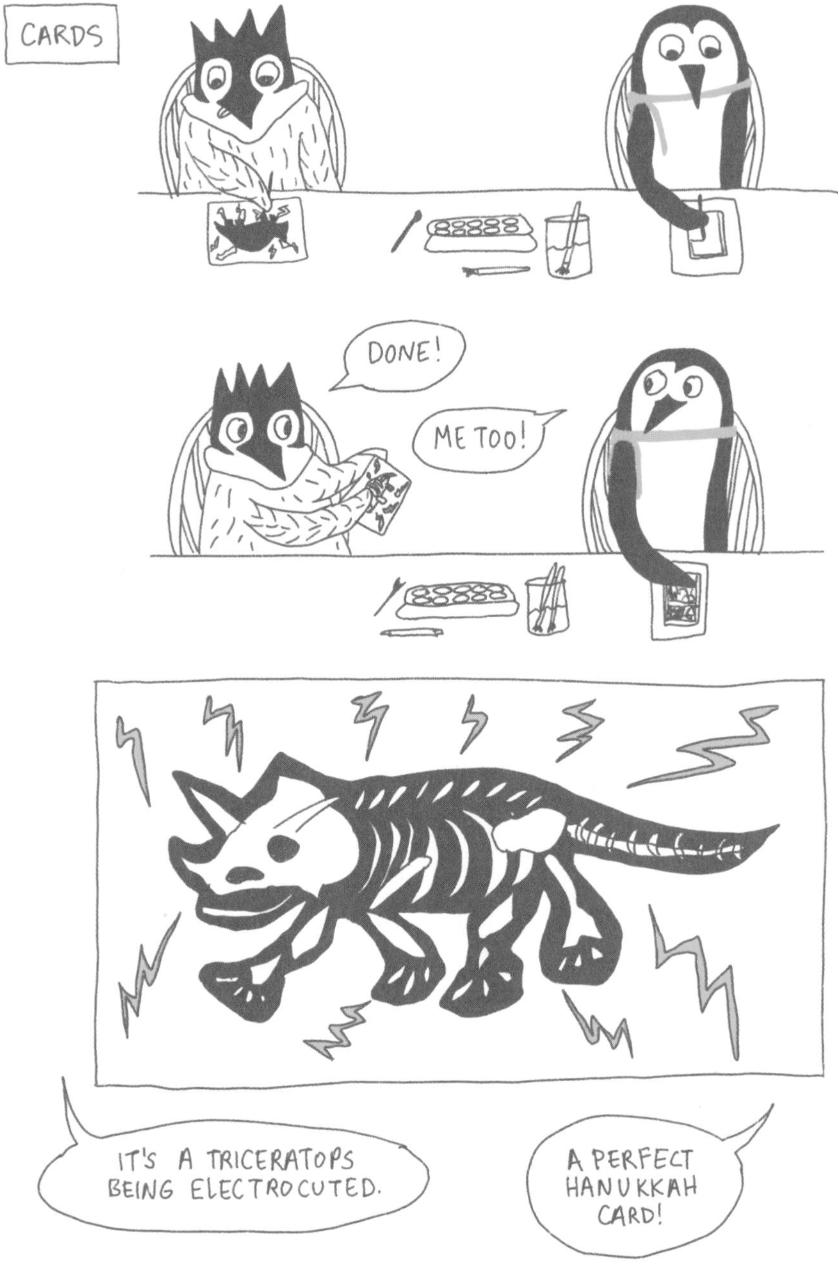
CARDS
DONE!
ME TOO!
IT'S A TRICERATOPS BEING ELECTROCUTED.
A PERFECT HANUKKAH CARD!

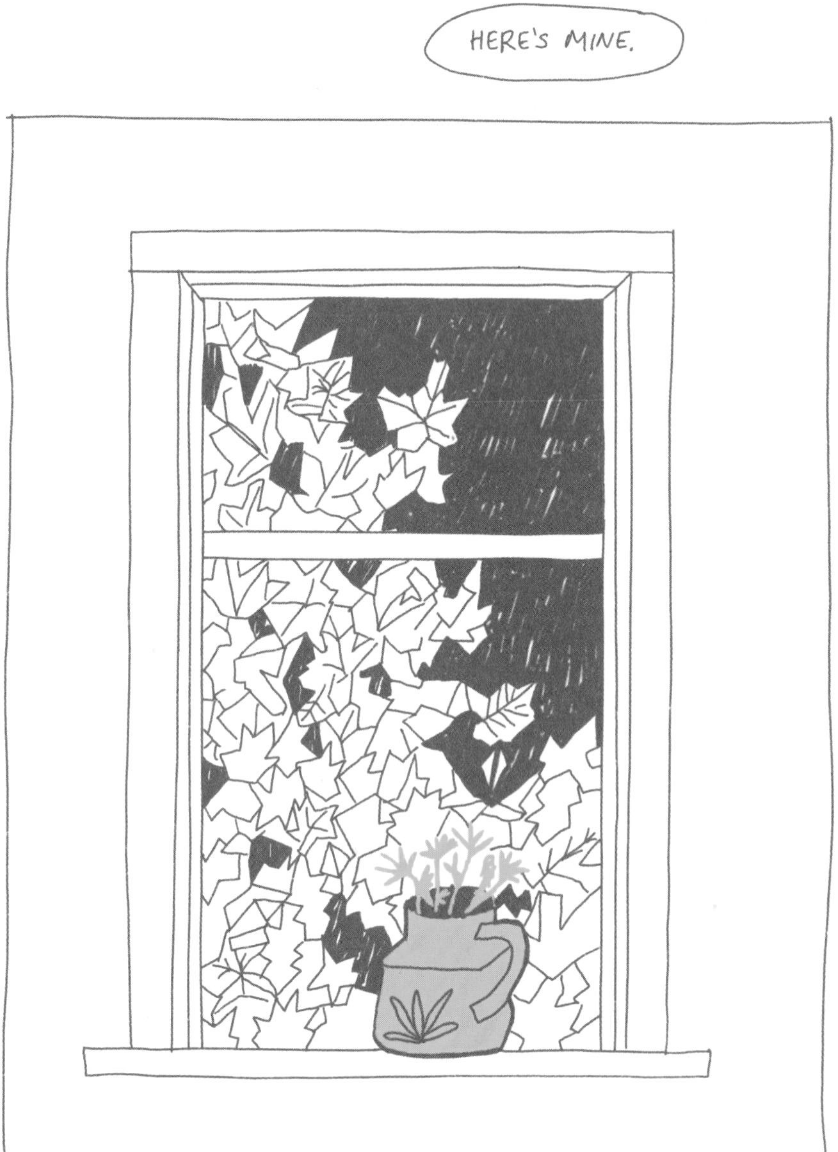
HERE'S MINE.

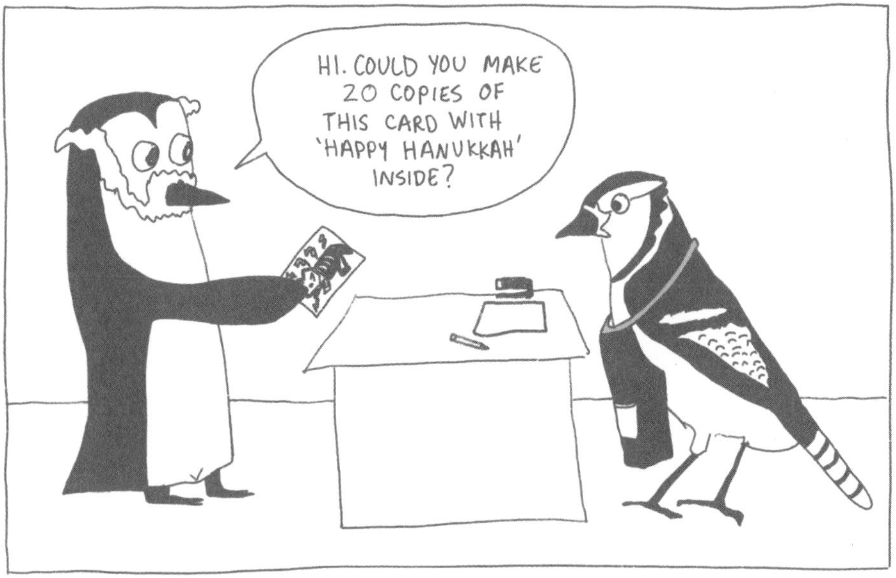
HI. COULD YOU MAKE 20 COPIES OF THIS CARD WITH 'HAPPY HANUKKAH' INSIDE?

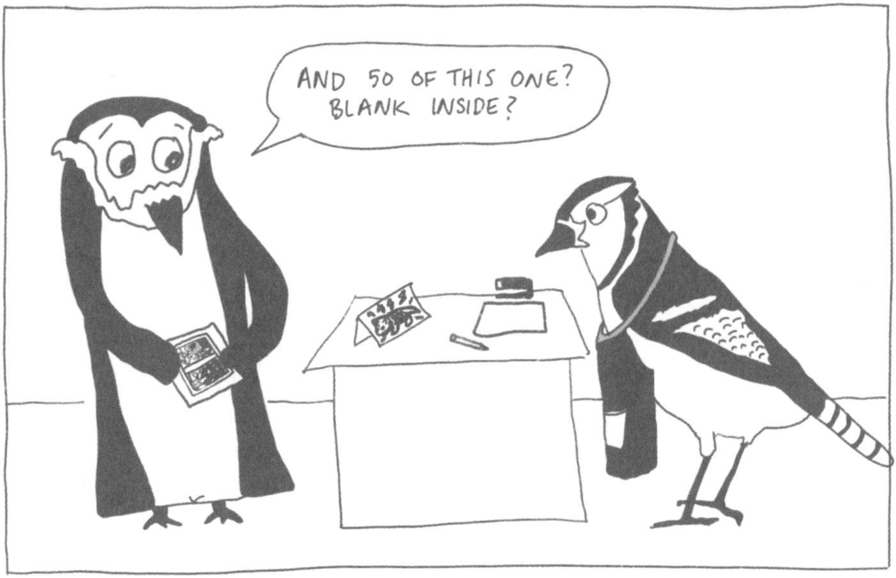
AND 50 OF THIS ONE? BLANK INSIDE?

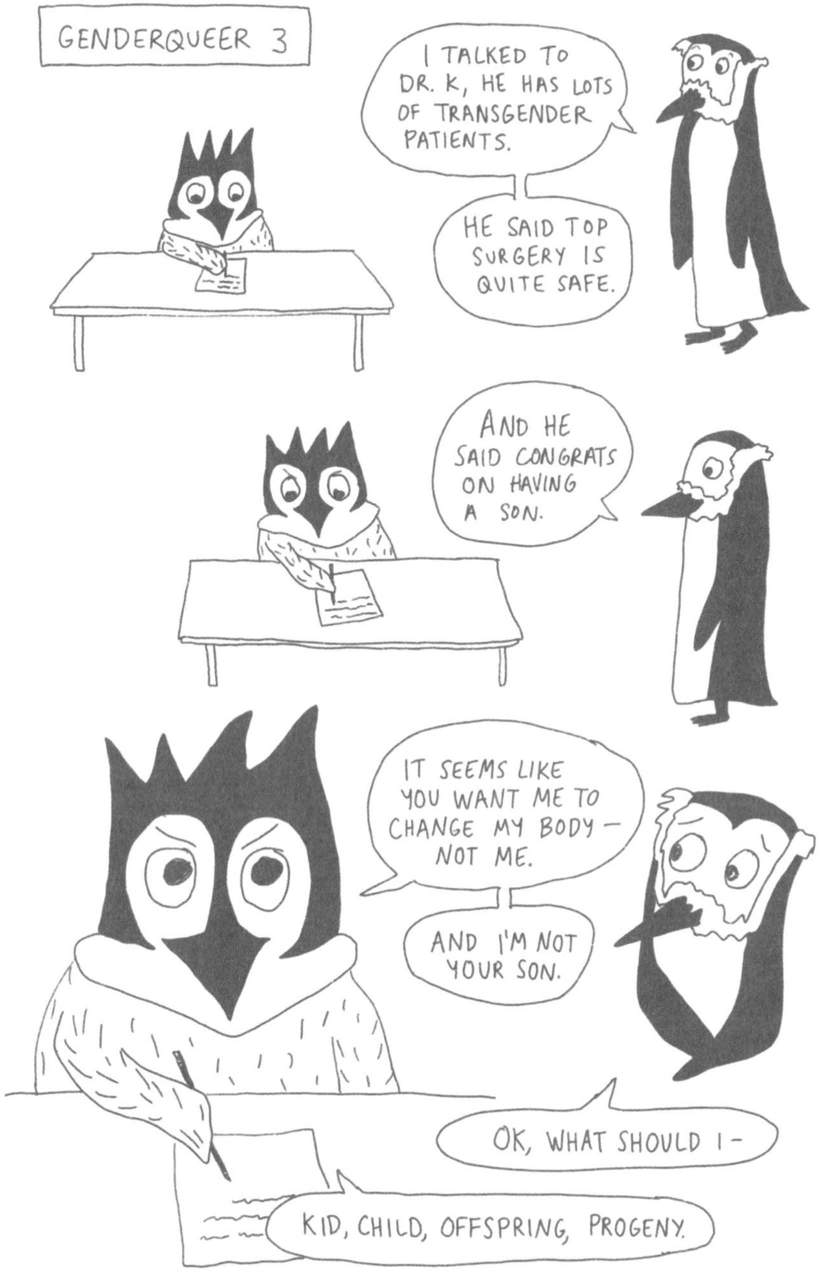
GENDERQUEER 3
I TALKED TO DR. K, HE HAS LOTS OF TRANSGENDER PATIENTS.
HE SAID TOP SURGERY IS QUITE SAFE.
AND HE SAID CONGRATS ON HAVING A SON.
IT SEEMS LIKE YOU WANT ME TO CHANGE MY BODY — NOT ME.
AND I'M NOT YOUR SON.
OK, WHAT SHOULD I-
KID, CHILD, OFFSPRING, PROGENY.

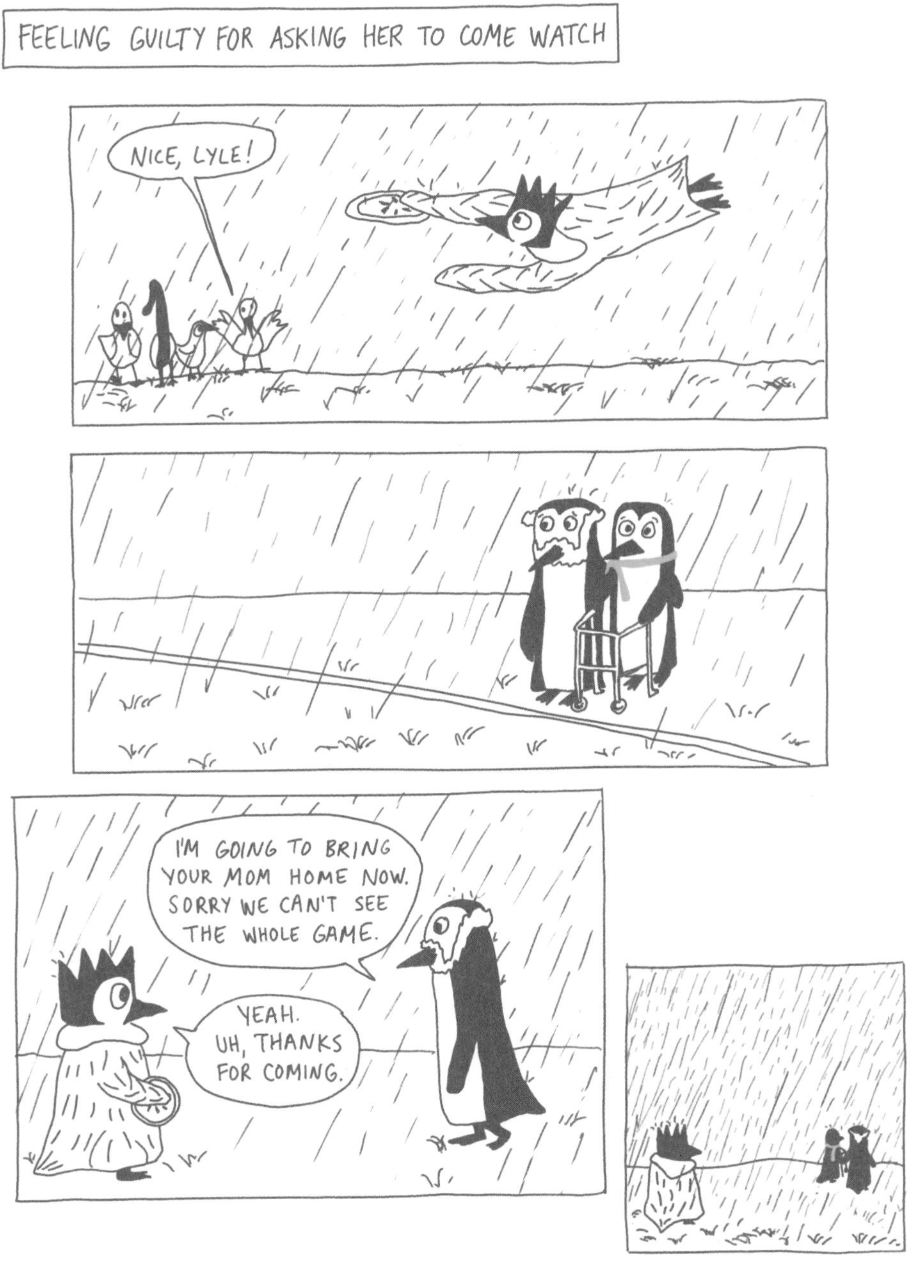
FEELING GUILTY FOR ASKING HER TO COME WATCH
NICE, LYLE!
I'M GOING TO BRING YOUR MOM HOME NOW. SORRY WE CAN'T SEE THE WHOLE GAME.
YEAH. UH, THANKS FOR COMING.

PROS AND CONS

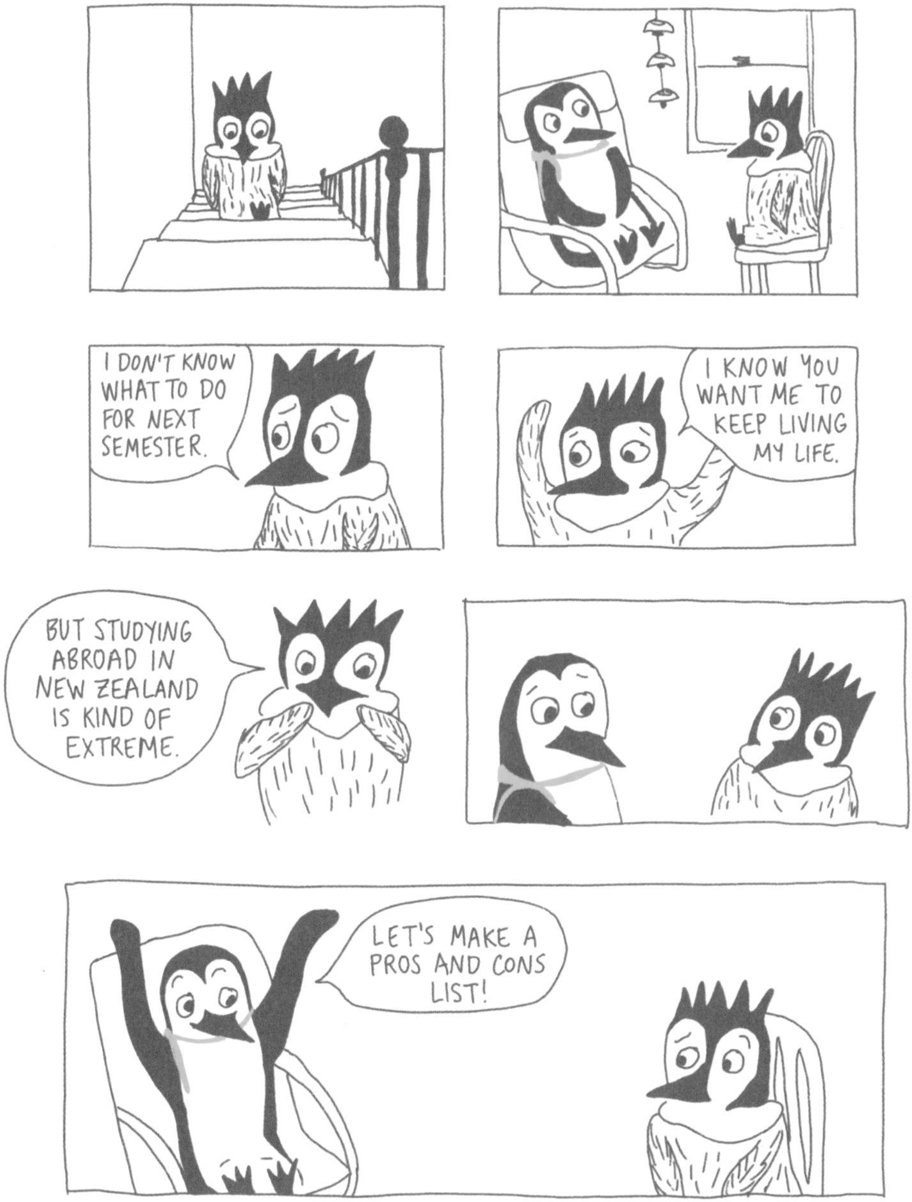
I DON'T KNOW WHAT TO DO FOR NEXT SEMESTER.
I KNOW YOU WANT ME TO KEEP LIVING MY LIFE.
BUT STUDYING ABROAD IN NEW ZEALAND IS KIND OF EXTREME.
LET'S MAKE A PROS AND CONS LIST!

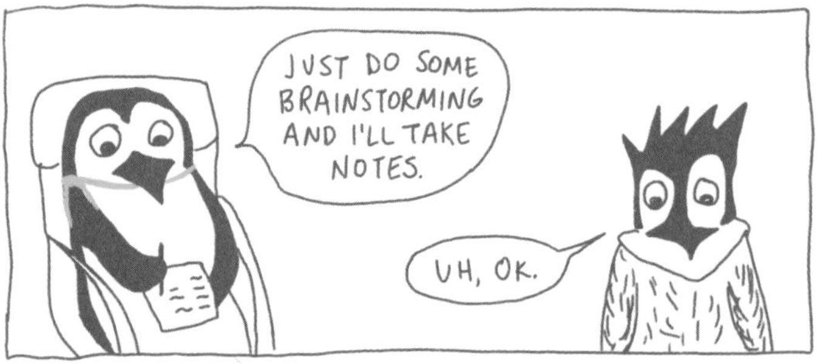
JUST DO SOME BRAINSTORMING AND I'LL TAKE NOTES.
UH, OK.

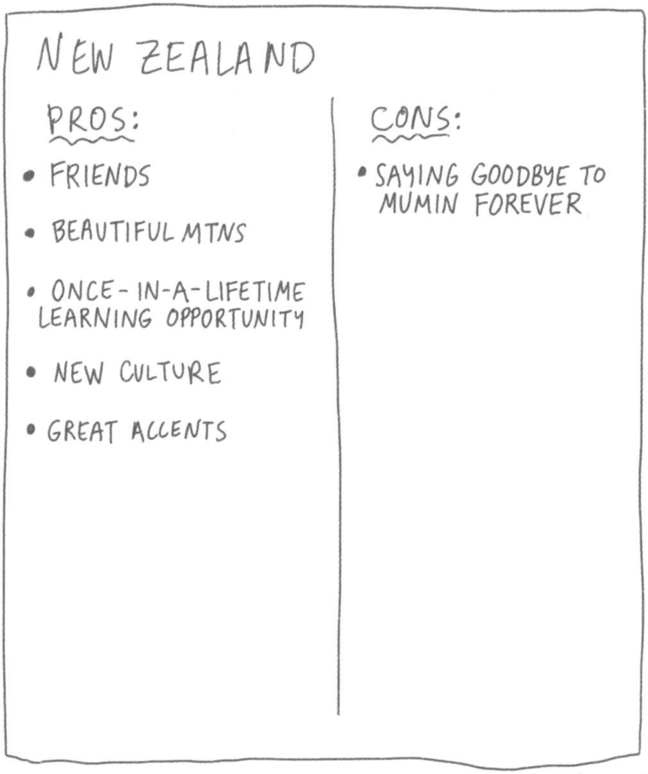
NEW ZEALAND
PROS:
• FRIENDS
• BEAUTIFUL MTNS
• ONCE-IN-A-LIFETIME LEARNING OPPORTUNITY
• NEW CULTURE
• GREAT ACCENTS
CONS:
• SAYING GOODBYE TO MUMIN FOREVER

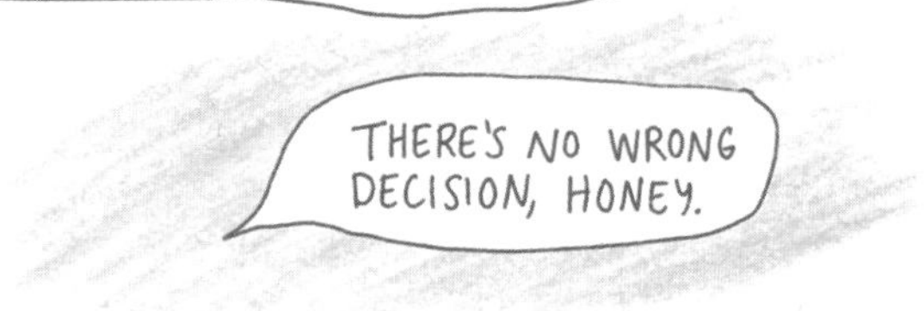
THERE'S NO WRONG DECISION, HONEY.

NOVEMBER

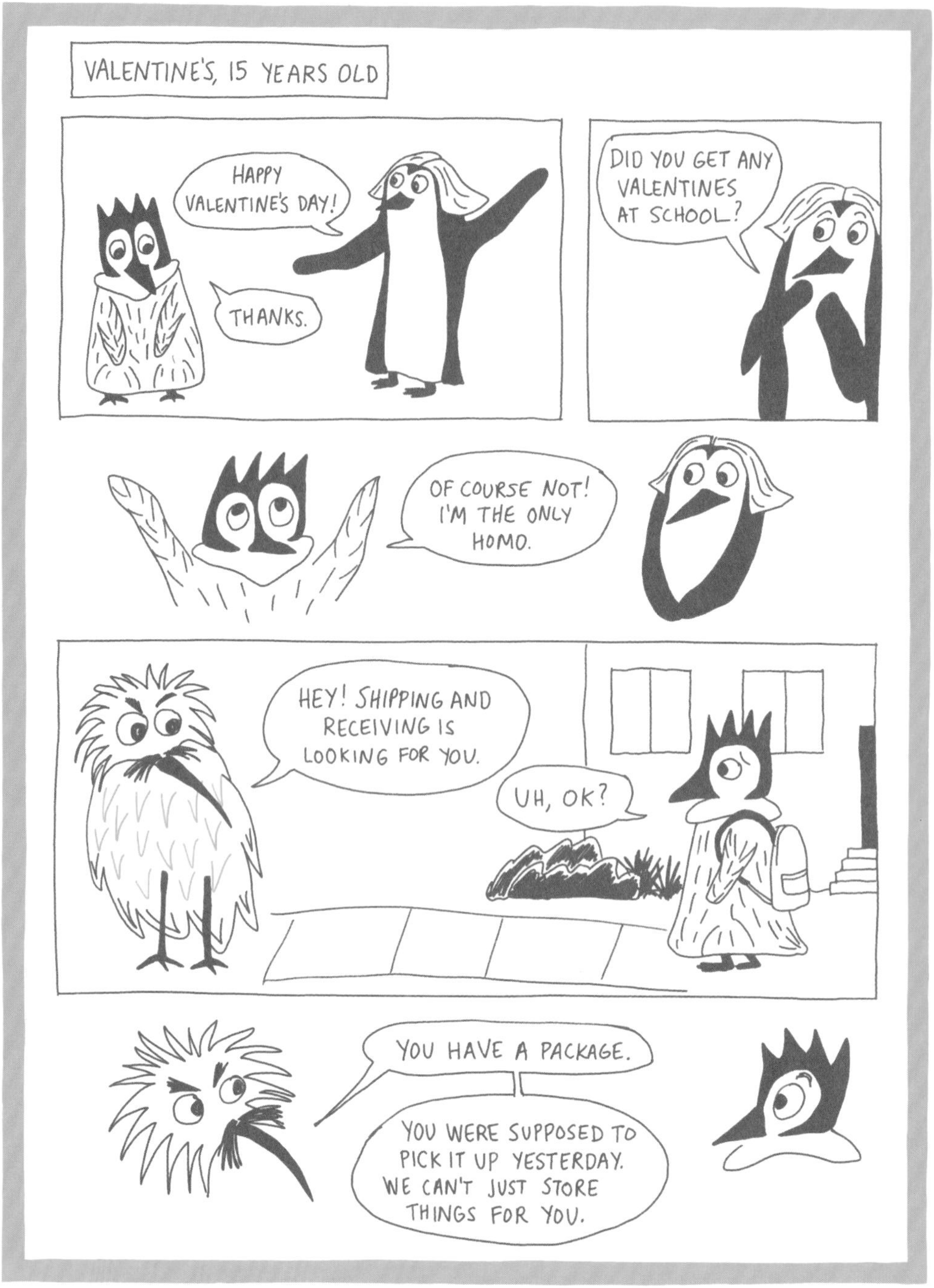
VALENTINE'S, 15 YEARS OLD
HAPPY VALENTINE'S DAY!
THANKS.
DID YOU GET ANY VALENTINES AT SCHOOL?
OF COURSE NOT! I'M THE ONLY HOMO.
HEY! SHIPPING AND RECEIVING IS LOOKING FOR YOU.
UH, OK?
YOU HAVE A PACKAGE.
YOU WERE SUPPOSED TO PICK IT UP YESTERDAY. WE CAN'T JUST STORE THINGS FOR YOU.

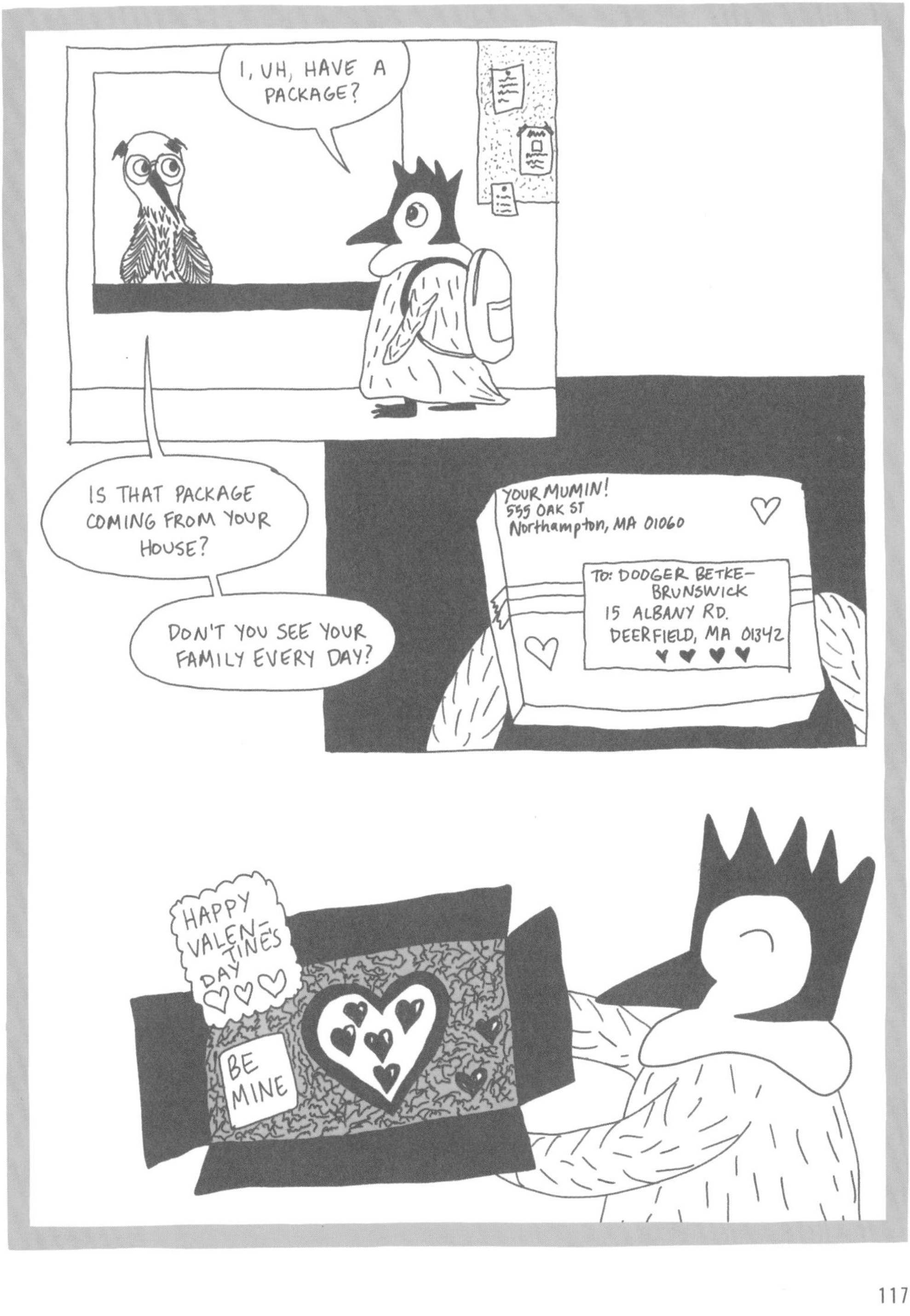
I, UH, HAVE A PACKAGE?
IS THAT PACKAGE COMING FROM YOUR HOUSE?
DON'T YOU SEE YOUR FAMILY EVERY DAY?
YOUR MUMIN!
555 OAK ST
Northampton, MA 01060
TO: DODGER BETKE-BRUNSWICK
15 ALBANY RD.
DEERFIELD, MA 01342
HAPPY VALEN-TINE'S DAY
BE MINE

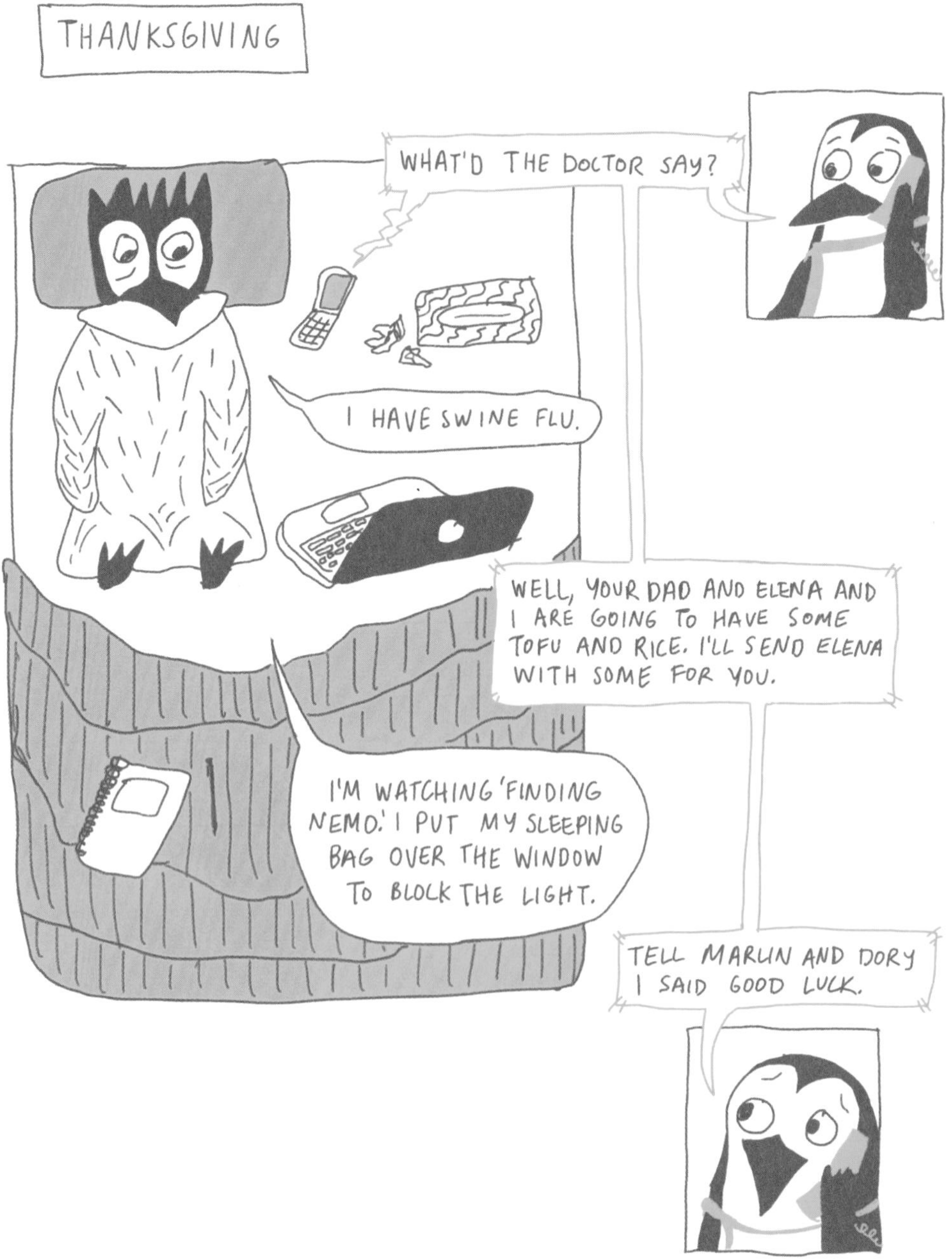
THANKSGIVING
WHAT'D THE DOCTOR SAY?
I HAVE SWINE FLU.
WELL, YOUR DAD AND ELENA AND I ARE GOING TO HAVE SOME TOFU AND RICE. I'LL SEND ELENA WITH SOME FOR YOU.
I'M WATCHING 'FINDING NEMO.' I PUT MY SLEEPING BAG OVER THE WINDOW TO BLOCK THE LIGHT.
TELL MARLIN AND DORY I SAID GOOD LUCK.

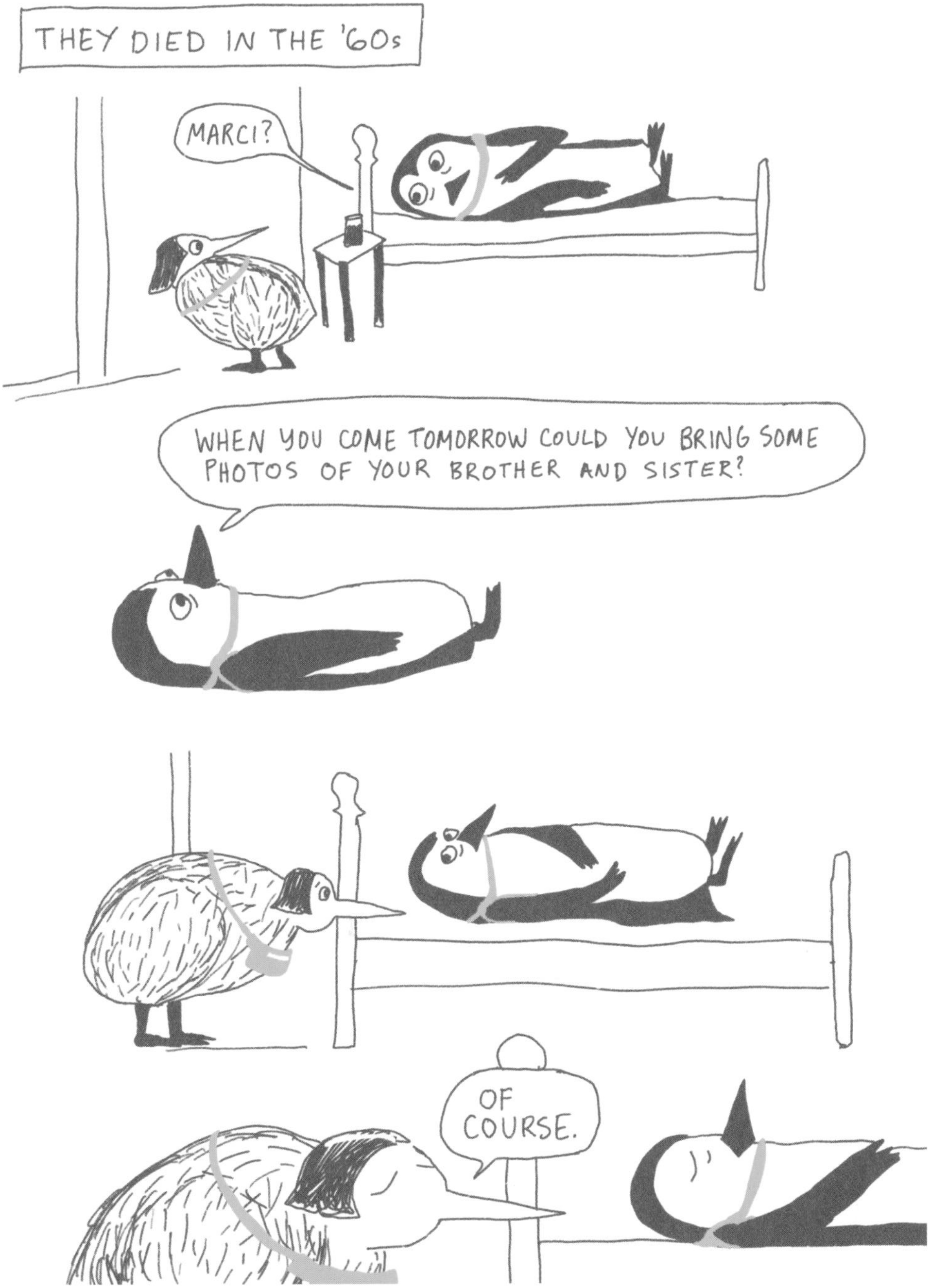
THEY DIED IN THE '60s
MARCI?
WHEN YOU COME TOMORROW COULD YOU BRING SOME PHOTOS OF YOUR BROTHER AND SISTER?
OF COURSE.

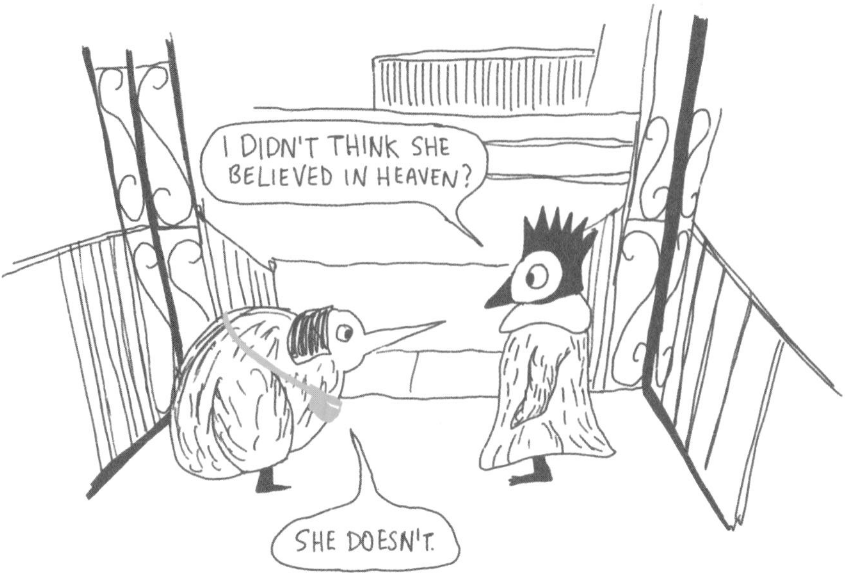
I DIDN'T THINK SHE BELIEVED IN HEAVEN?
SHE DOESN'T.

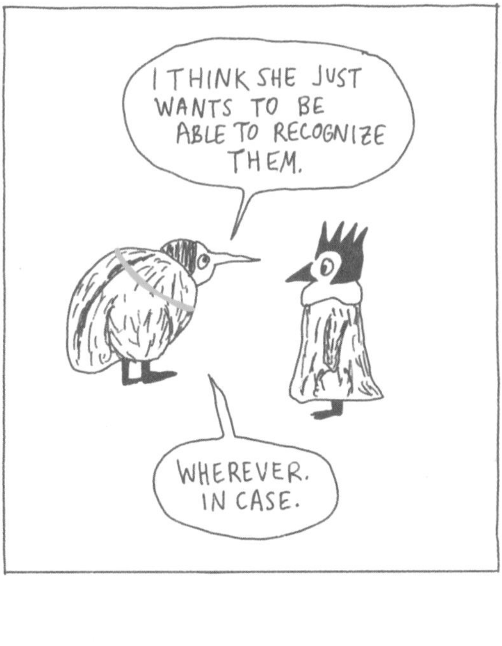
I THINK SHE JUST WANTS TO BE ABLE TO RECOGNIZE THEM.
WHEREVER. IN CASE.

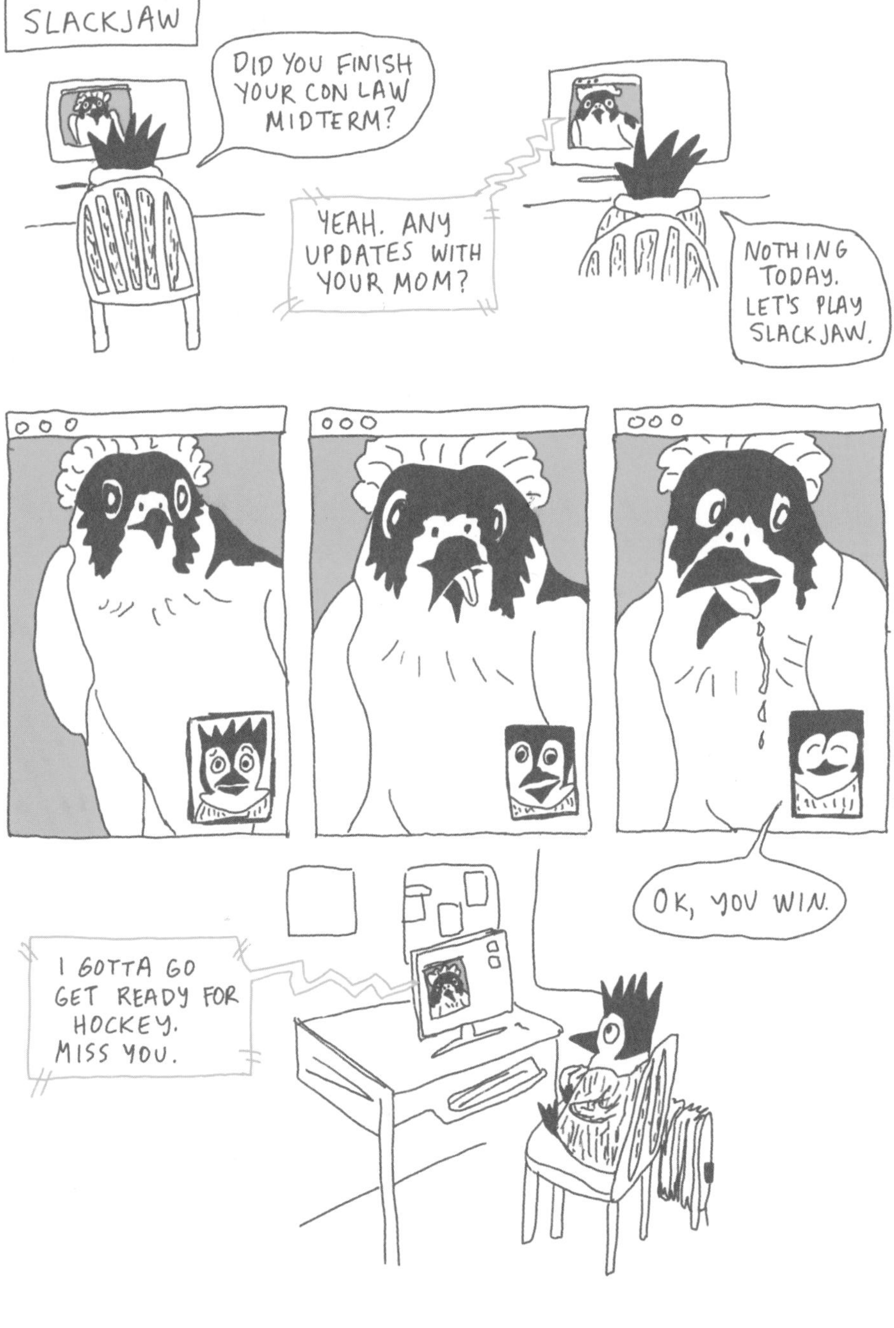
SLACKJAW
DID YOU FINISH YOUR CON LAW MIDTERM?
YEAH. ANY UPDATES WITH YOUR MOM?
NOTHING TODAY. LET'S PLAY SLACKJAW.
OK, YOU WIN.
I GOTTA GO GET READY FOR HOCKEY. MISS YOU.

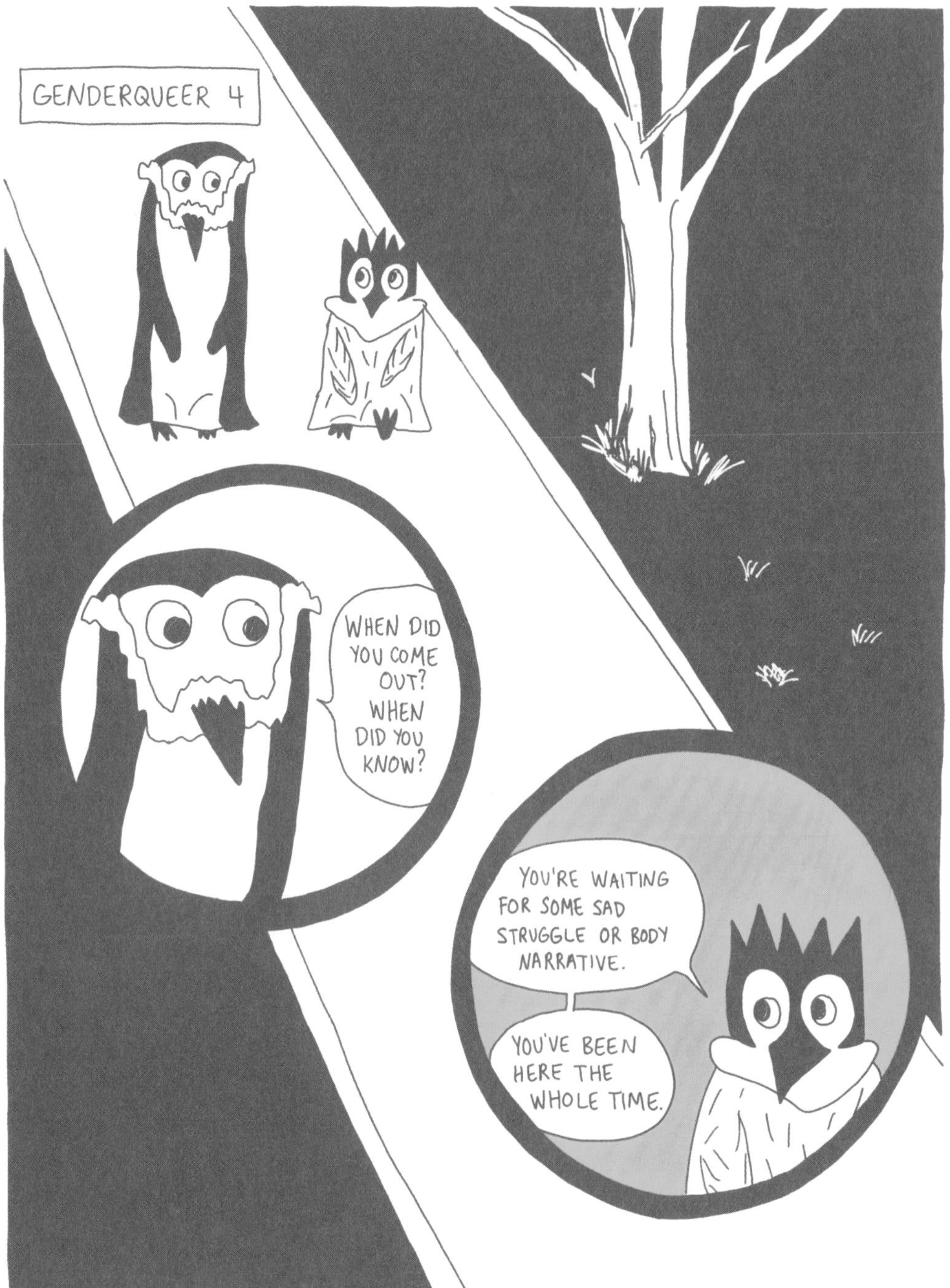
GENDERQUEER 4
WHEN DID YOU COME OUT? WHEN DID YOU KNOW?
YOU'RE WAITING FOR SOME SAD STRUGGLE OR BODY NARRATIVE.
YOU'VE BEEN HERE THE WHOLE TIME.

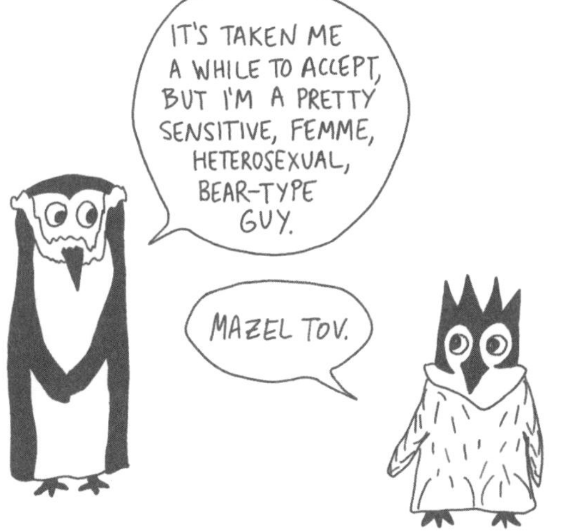
IT'S TAKEN ME A WHILE TO ACCEPT, BUT I'M A PRETTY SENSITIVE, FEMME, HETEROSEXUAL, BEAR-TYPE GUY.
MAZEL TOV.

GIFTS SHE GAVE IN THE FINAL WEEK

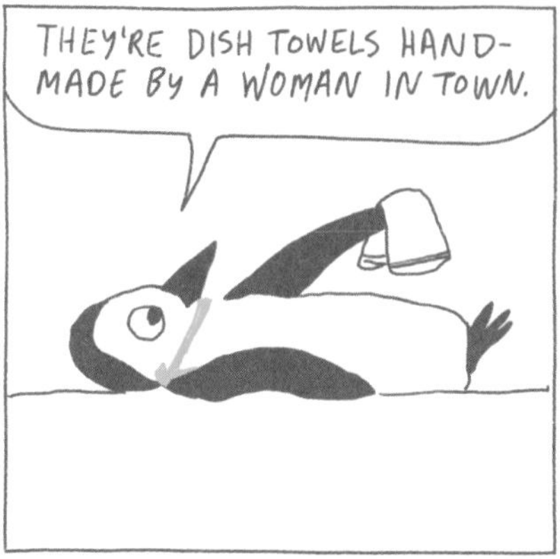
THEY'RE DISH TOWELS HAND-MADE BY A WOMAN IN TOWN.

MARCI

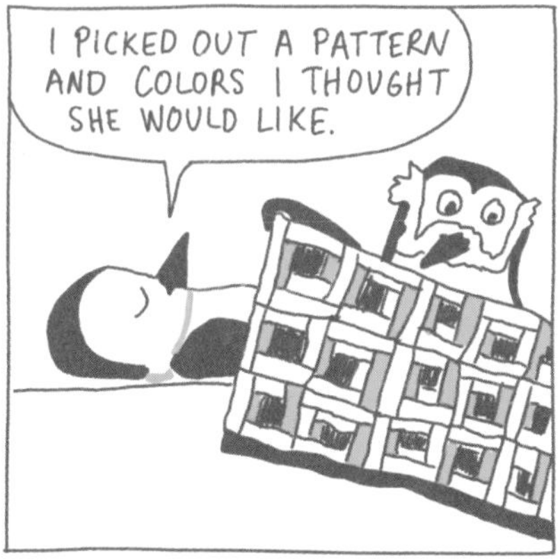
I PICKED OUT A PATTERN AND COLORS I THOUGHT SHE WOULD LIKE.

NANA (HER MOM)

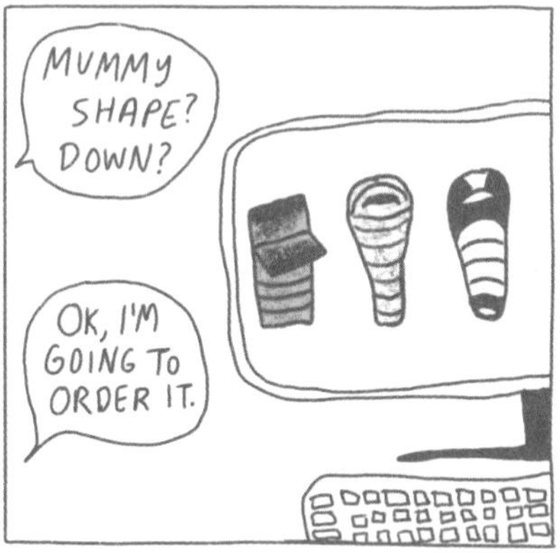
MUMMY SHAPE? DOWN?
OK, I'M GOING TO ORDER IT.

ME

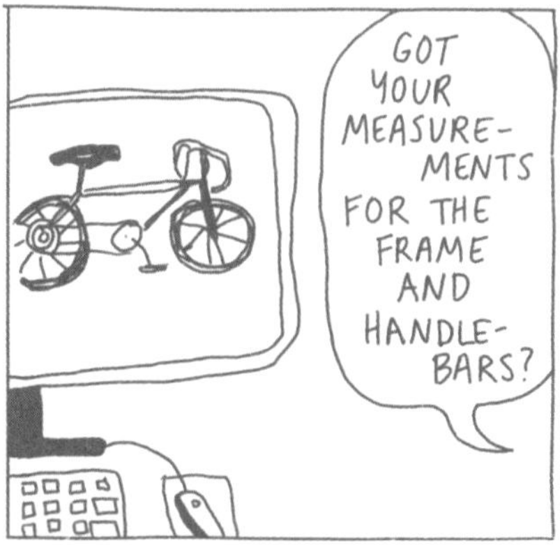
GOT YOUR MEASURE-MENTS FOR THE FRAME AND HANDLE-BARS?

MY SISTER

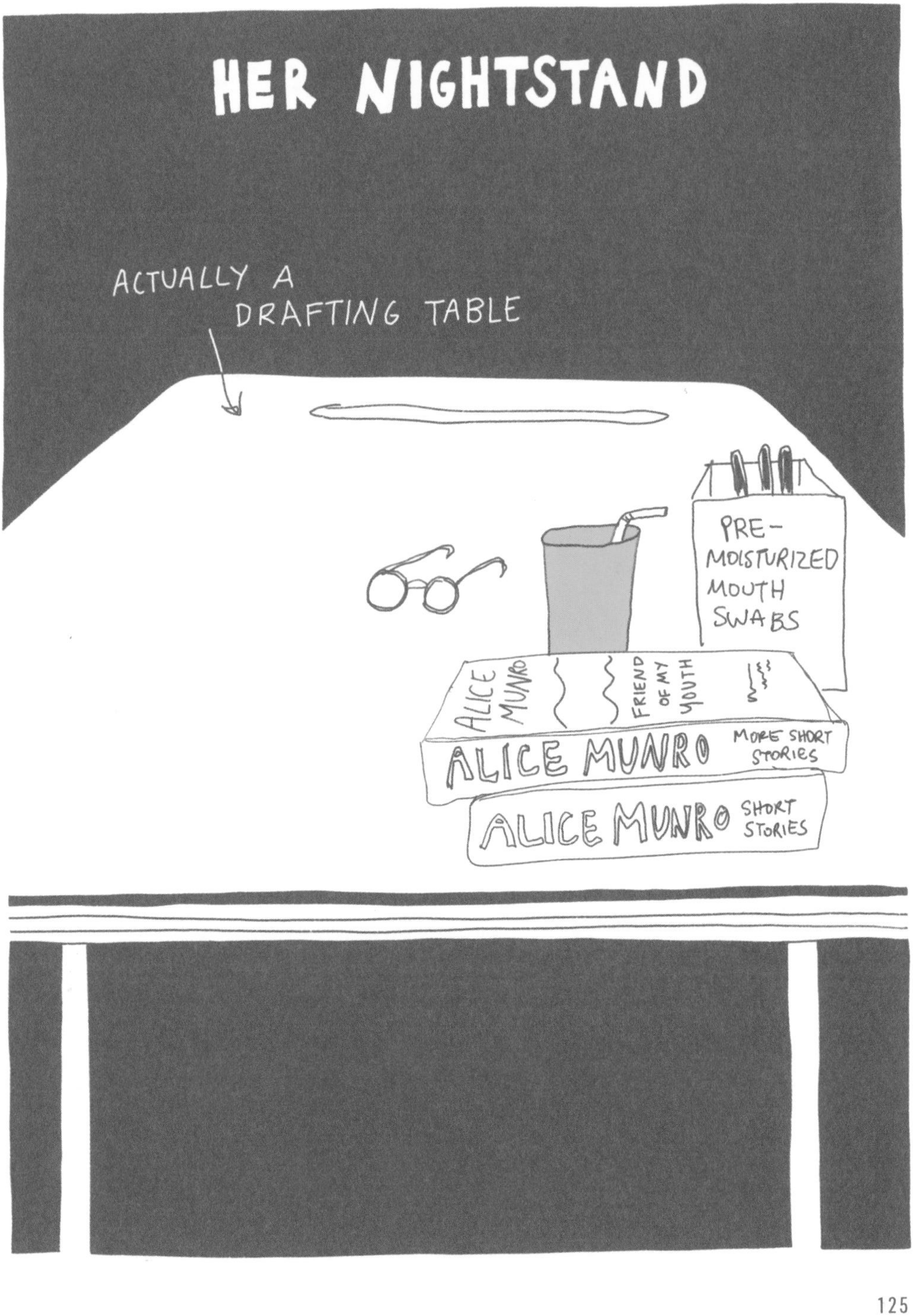
HER NIGHTSTAND
ACTUALLY A DRAFTING TABLE
PRE-MOISTURIZED MOUTH SWABS
ALICE MUNRO
FRIEND OF MY YOUTH
ALICE MUNRO
MORE SHORT STORIES
ALICE MUNRO
SHORT STORIES

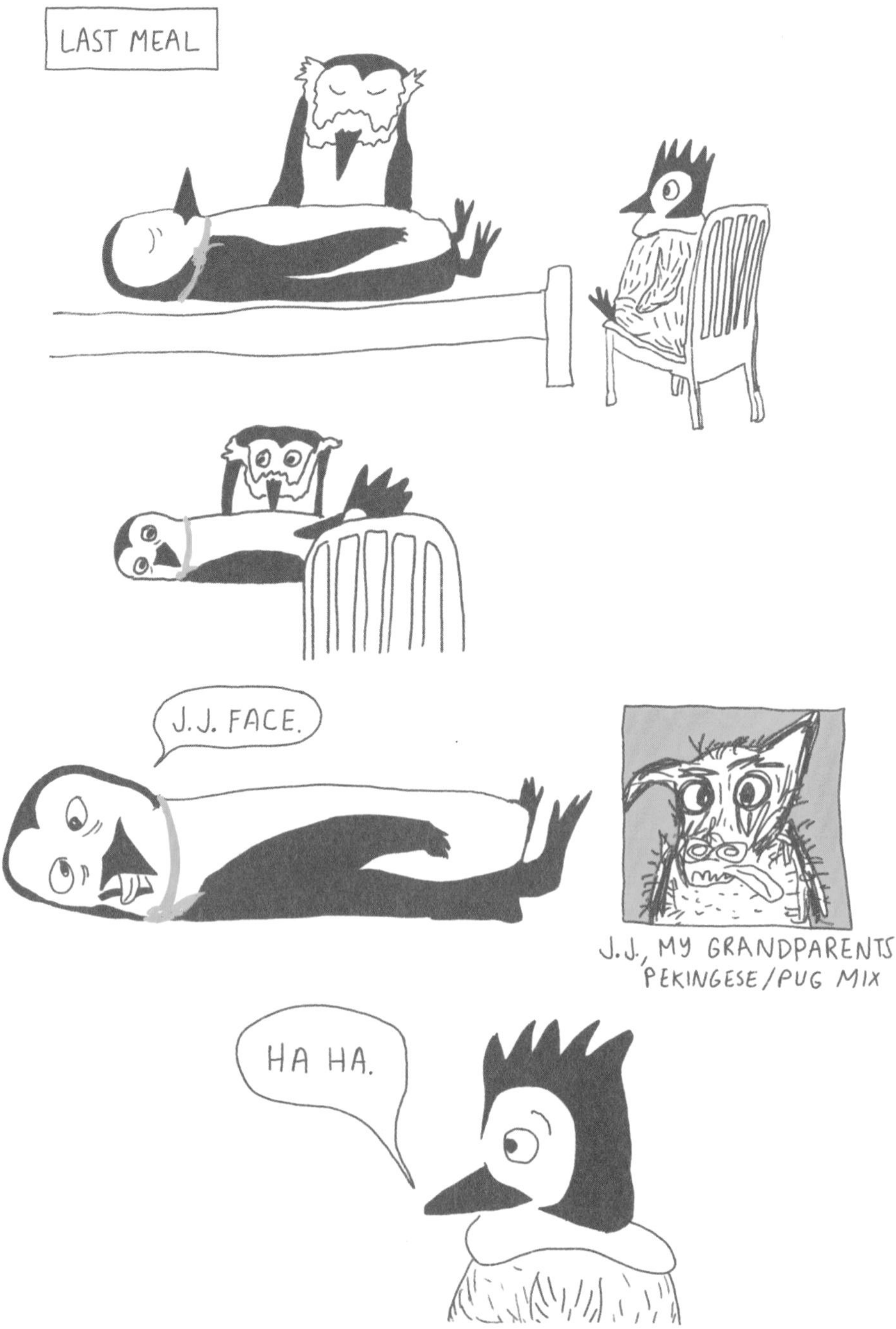
LAST MEAL
J.J. FACE.
J.J., MY GRANDPARENTS' PEKINGESE/PUG MIX
HA HA.

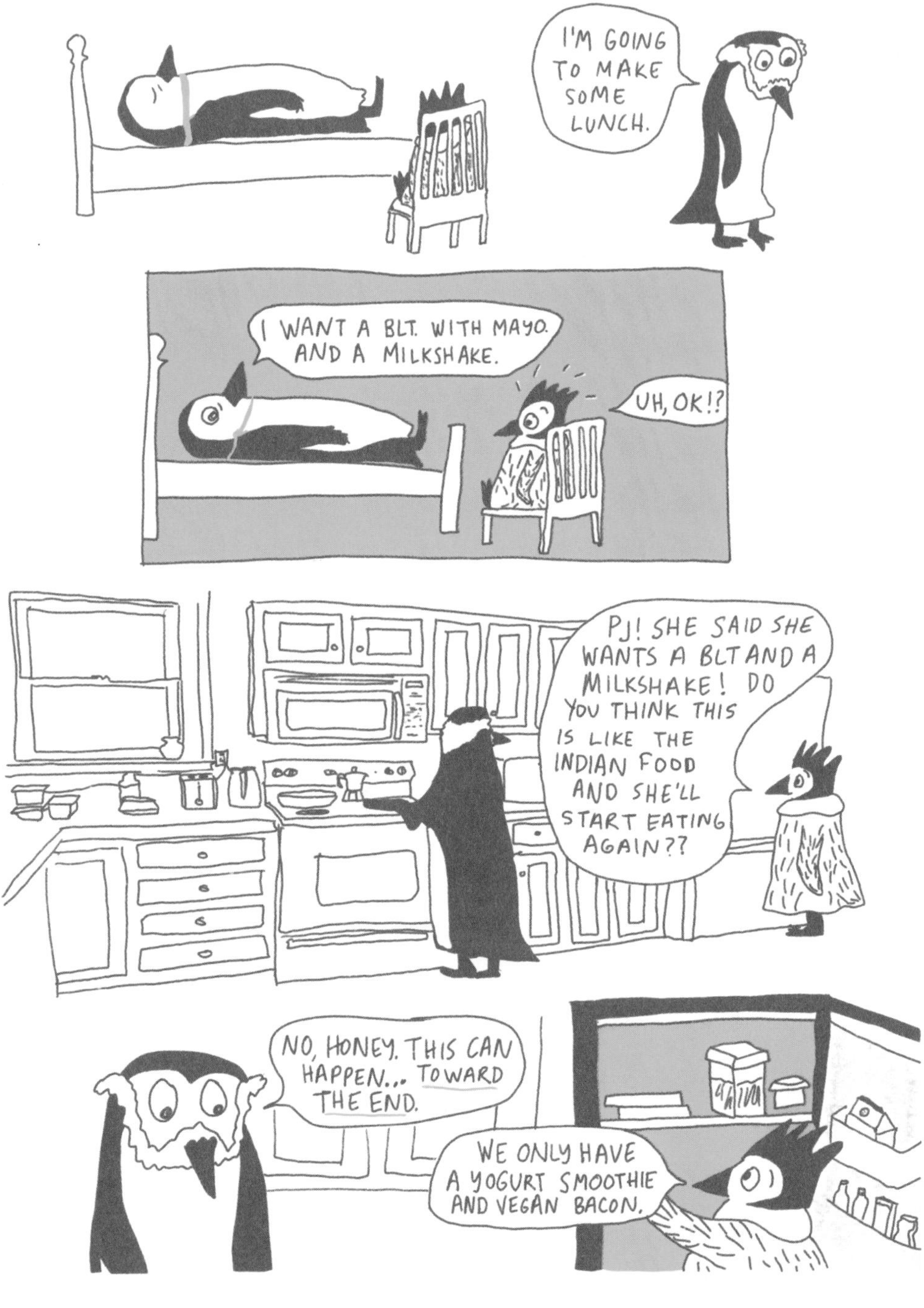
I'M GOING TO MAKE SOME LUNCH.
I WANT A BLT. WITH MAYO. AND A MILKSHAKE.
UH, OK!?
PJ! SHE SAID SHE WANTS A BLT AND A MILKSHAKE! DO YOU THINK THIS IS LIKE THE INDIAN FOOD AND SHE'LL START EATING AGAIN??
NO, HONEY. THIS CAN HAPPEN... TOWARD THE END.
WE ONLY HAVE A YOGURT SMOOTHIE AND VEGAN BACON.

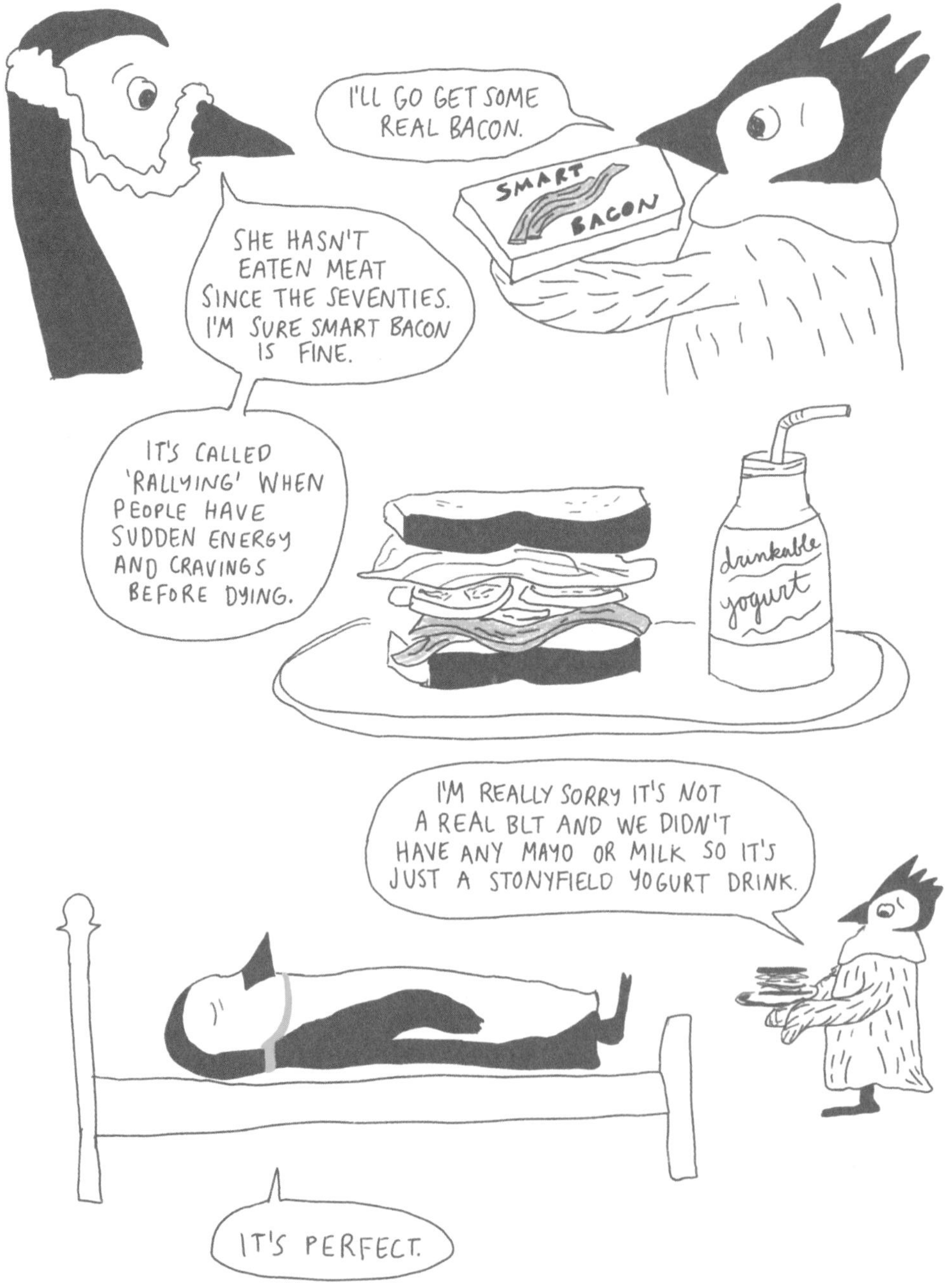
I'LL GO GET SOME REAL BACON.
SMART BACON
SHE HASN'T EATEN MEAT SINCE THE SEVENTIES. I'M SURE SMART BACON IS FINE.
IT'S CALLED 'RALLYING' WHEN PEOPLE HAVE SUDDEN ENERGY AND CRAVINGS BEFORE DYING.
drinkable yogurt
I'M REALLY SORRY IT'S NOT A REAL BLT AND WE DIDN'T HAVE ANY MAYO OR MILK SO IT'S JUST A STONYFIELD YOGURT DRINK.
IT'S PERFECT.

DECEMBER

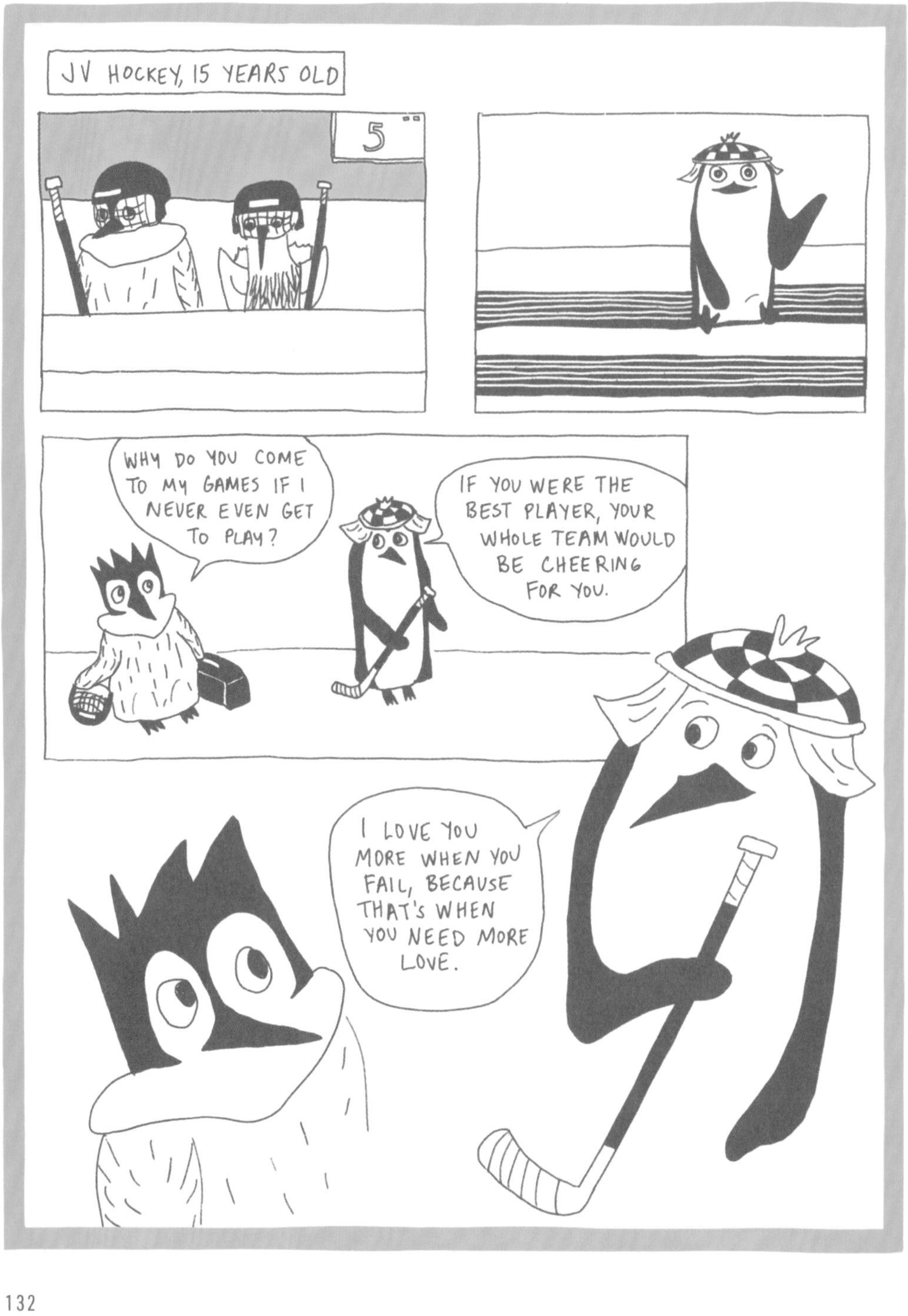
JV HOCKEY, 15 YEARS OLD
5
WHY DO YOU COME TO MY GAMES IF I NEVER EVEN GET TO PLAY?
IF YOU WERE THE BEST PLAYER, YOUR WHOLE TEAM WOULD BE CHEERING FOR YOU.
I LOVE YOU MORE WHEN YOU FAIL, BECAUSE THAT'S WHEN YOU NEED MORE LOVE.

DEATHDAY

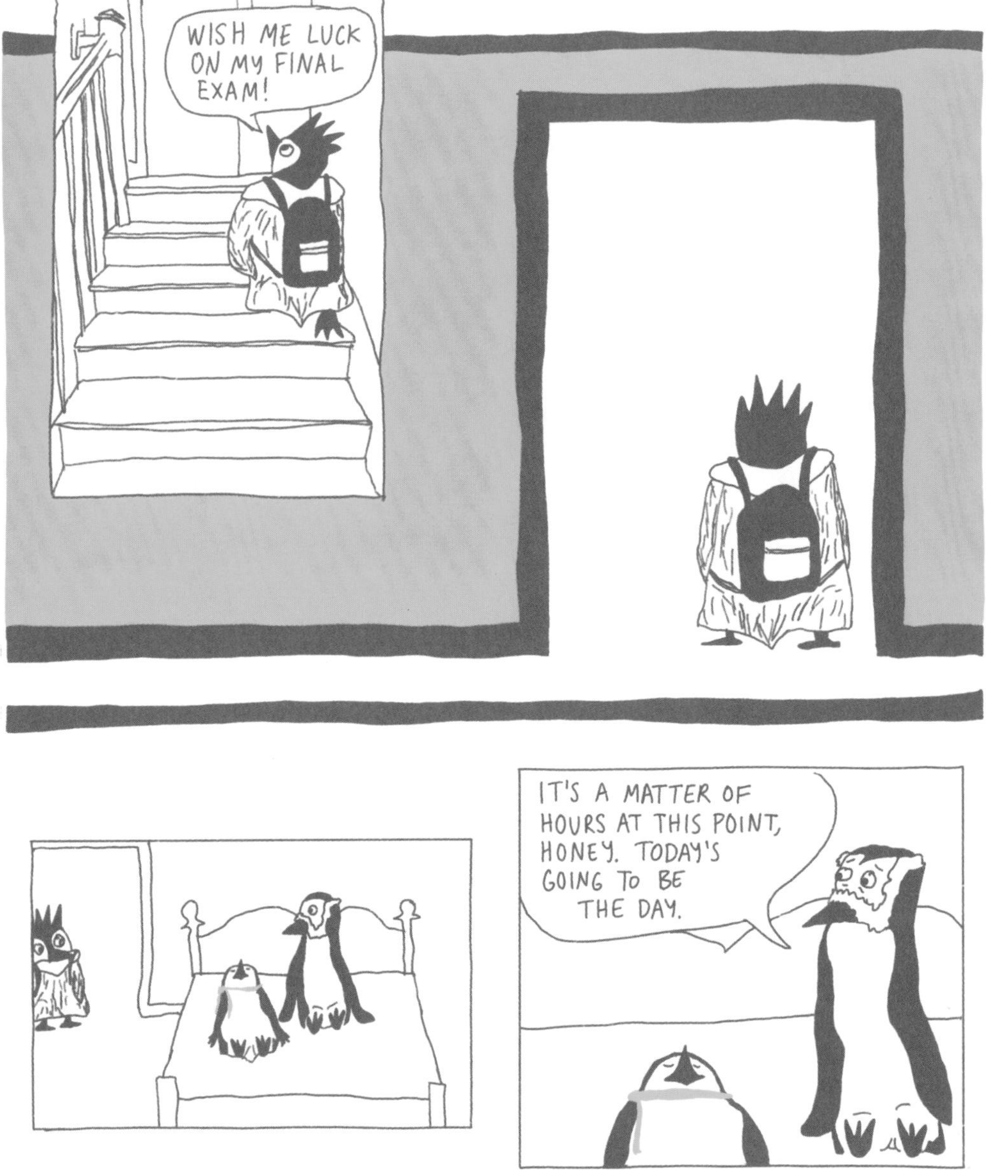

WISH ME LUCK ON MY FINAL EXAM!
IT'S A MATTER OF HOURS AT THIS POINT, HONEY. TODAY'S GOING TO BE THE DAY.

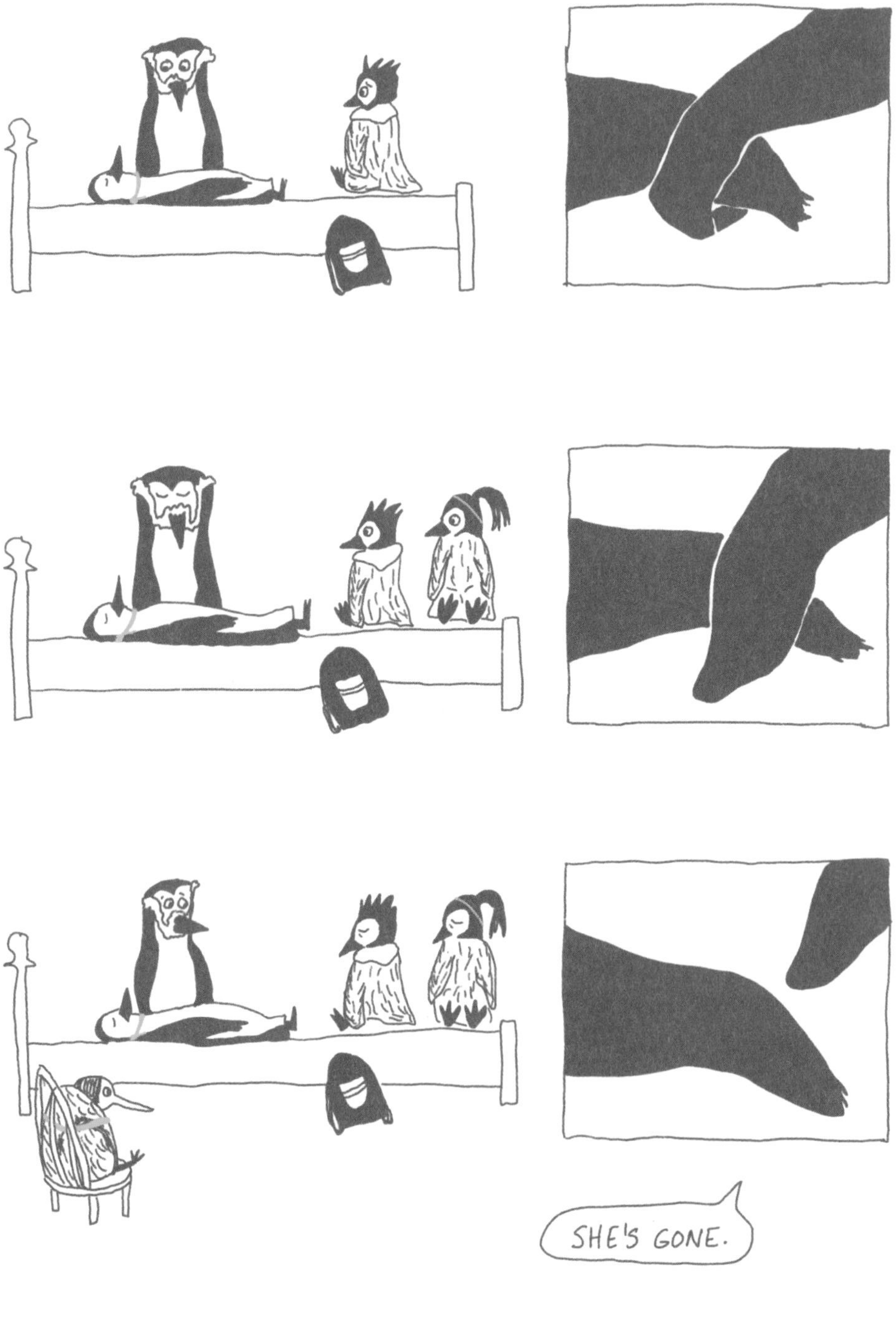
SHE'S GONE.

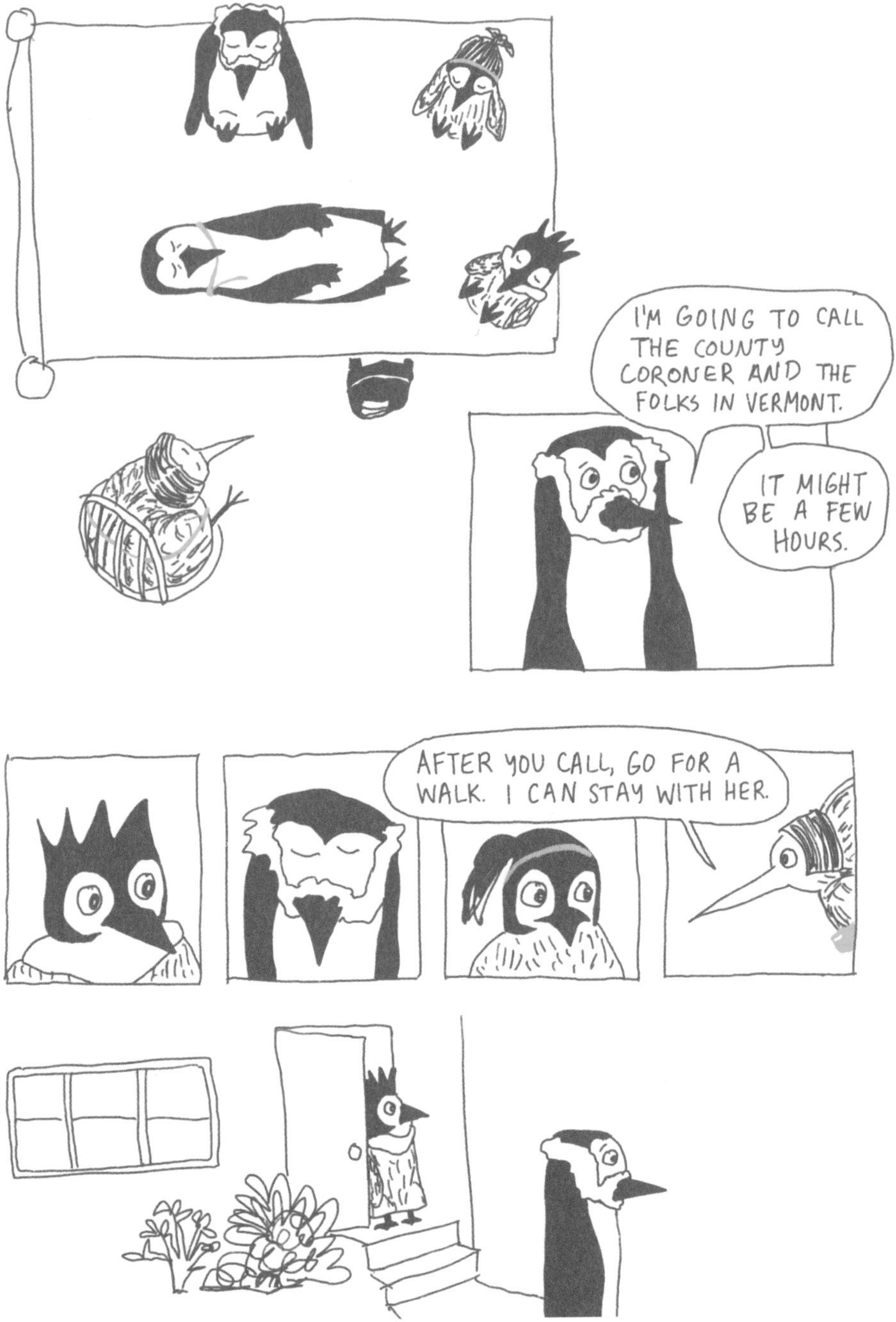

I'M GOING TO CALL THE COUNTY CORONER AND THE FOLKS IN VERMONT.
IT MIGHT BE A FEW HOURS.
AFTER YOU CALL, GO FOR A WALK. I CAN STAY WITH HER.

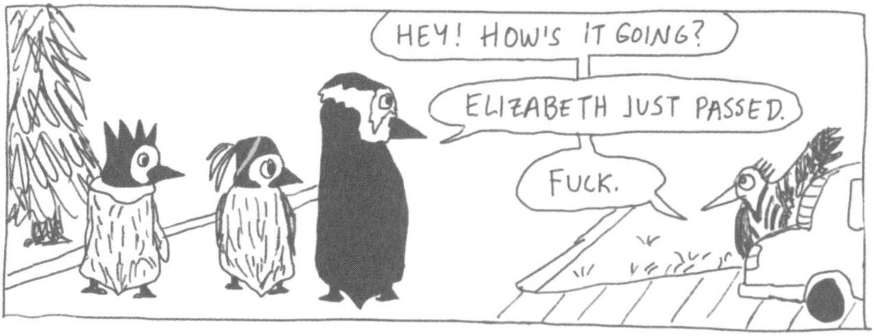
HEY! HOW'S IT GOING?
ELIZABETH JUST PASSED.
FUCK.

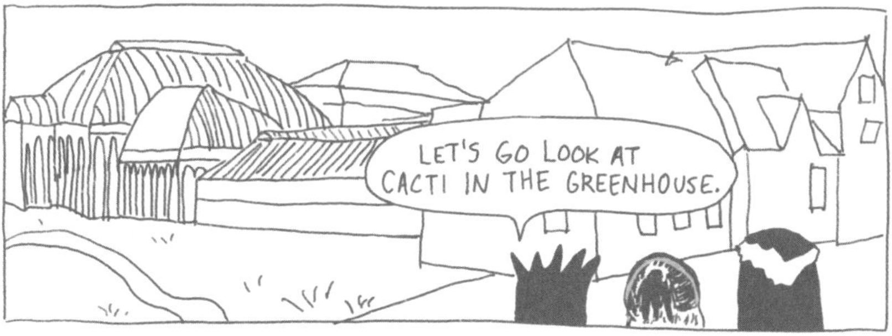
LET'S GO LOOK AT CACTI IN THE GREENHOUSE.

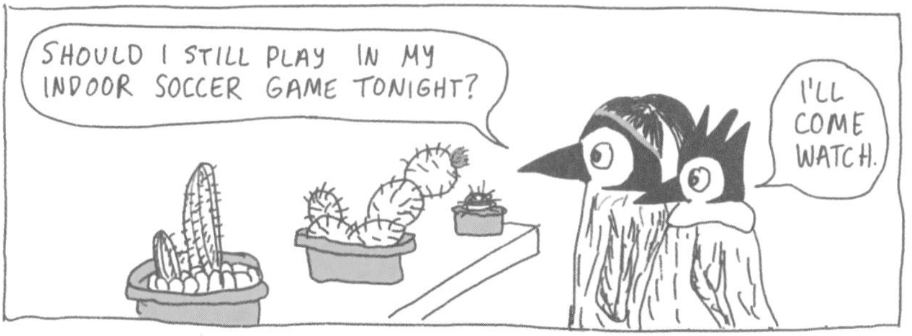
SHOULD I STILL PLAY IN MY INDOOR SOCCER GAME TONIGHT?
I'LL COME WATCH.

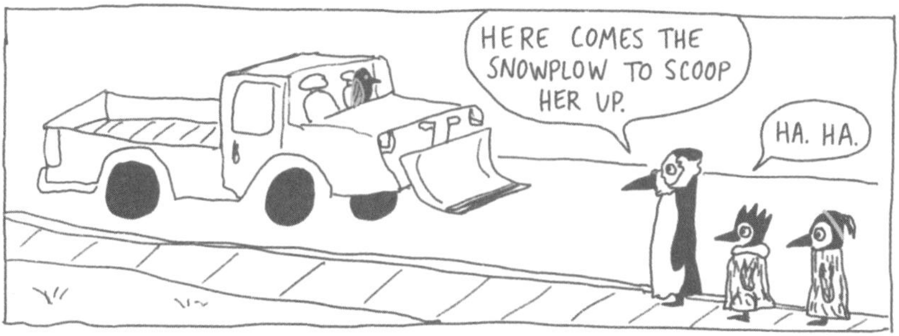
HERE COMES THE SNOWPLOW TO SCOOP HER UP.
HA. HA.

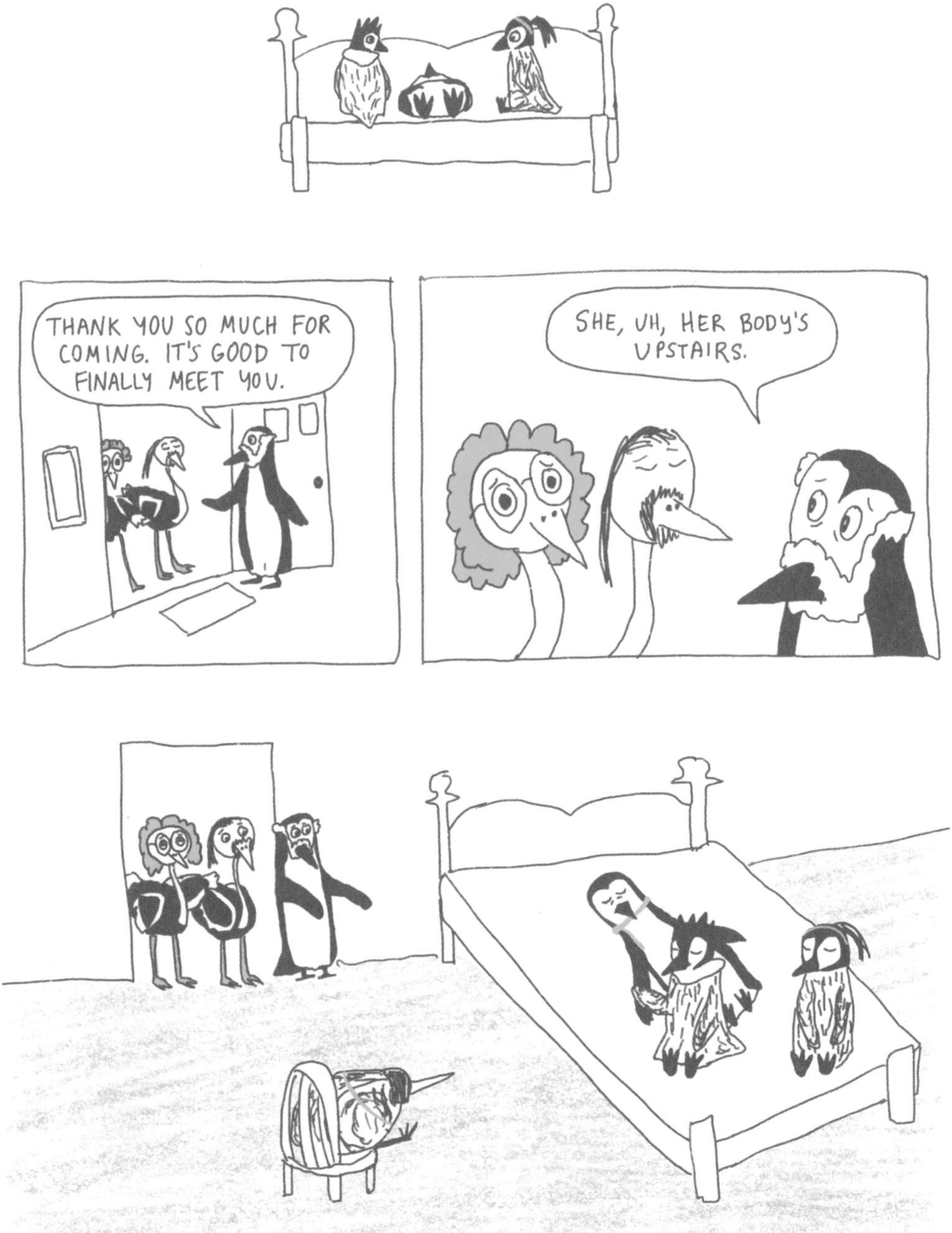
THANK YOU SO MUCH FOR COMING. IT'S GOOD TO FINALLY MEET YOU.
SHE, UH, HER BODY'S UPSTAIRS.

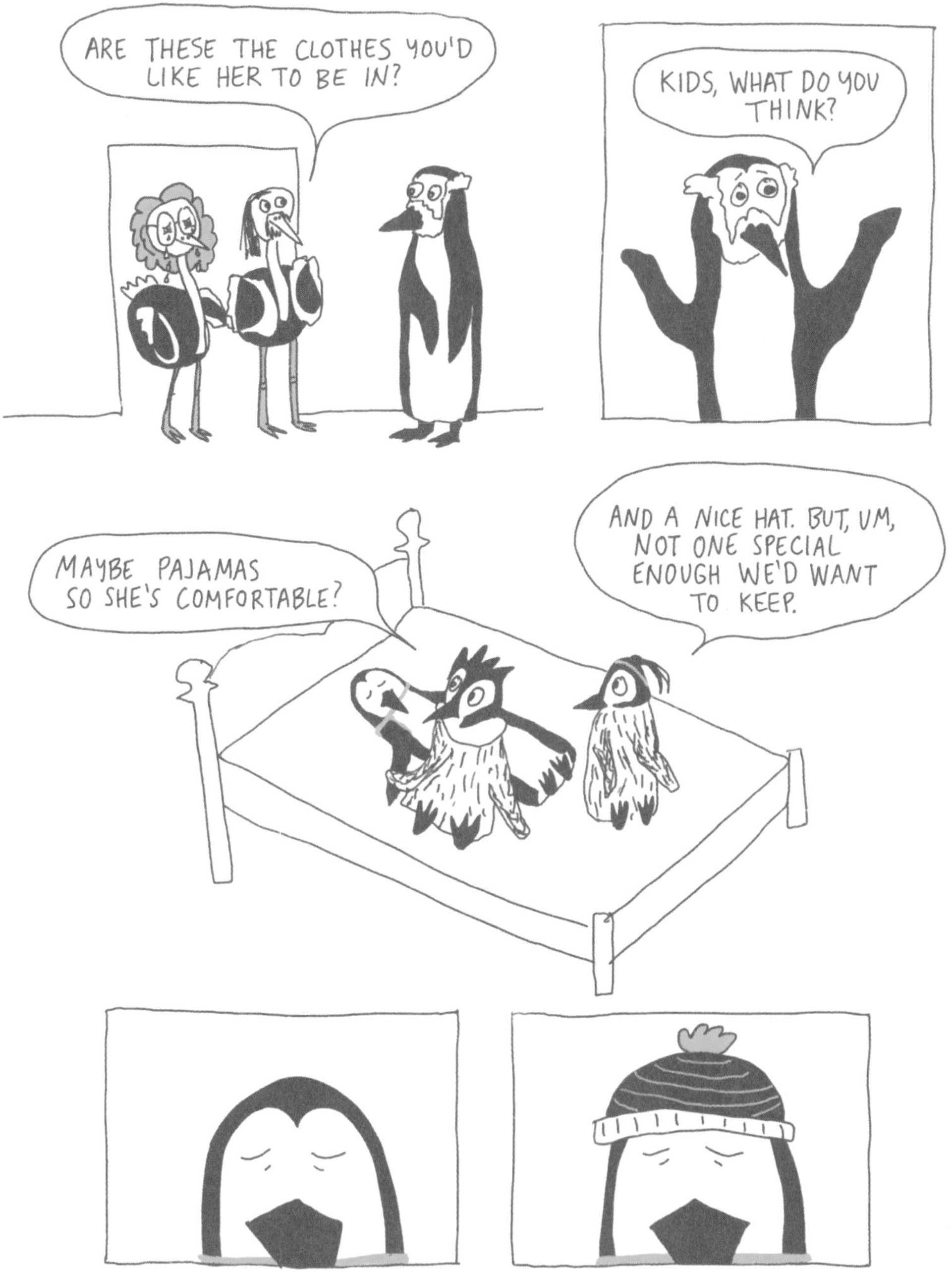
ARE THESE THE CLOTHES YOU'D LIKE HER TO BE IN?
KIDS, WHAT DO YOU THINK?
MAYBE PAJAMAS SO SHE'S COMFORTABLE?
AND A NICE HAT. BUT, UM, NOT ONE SPECIAL ENOUGH WE'D WANT TO KEEP.

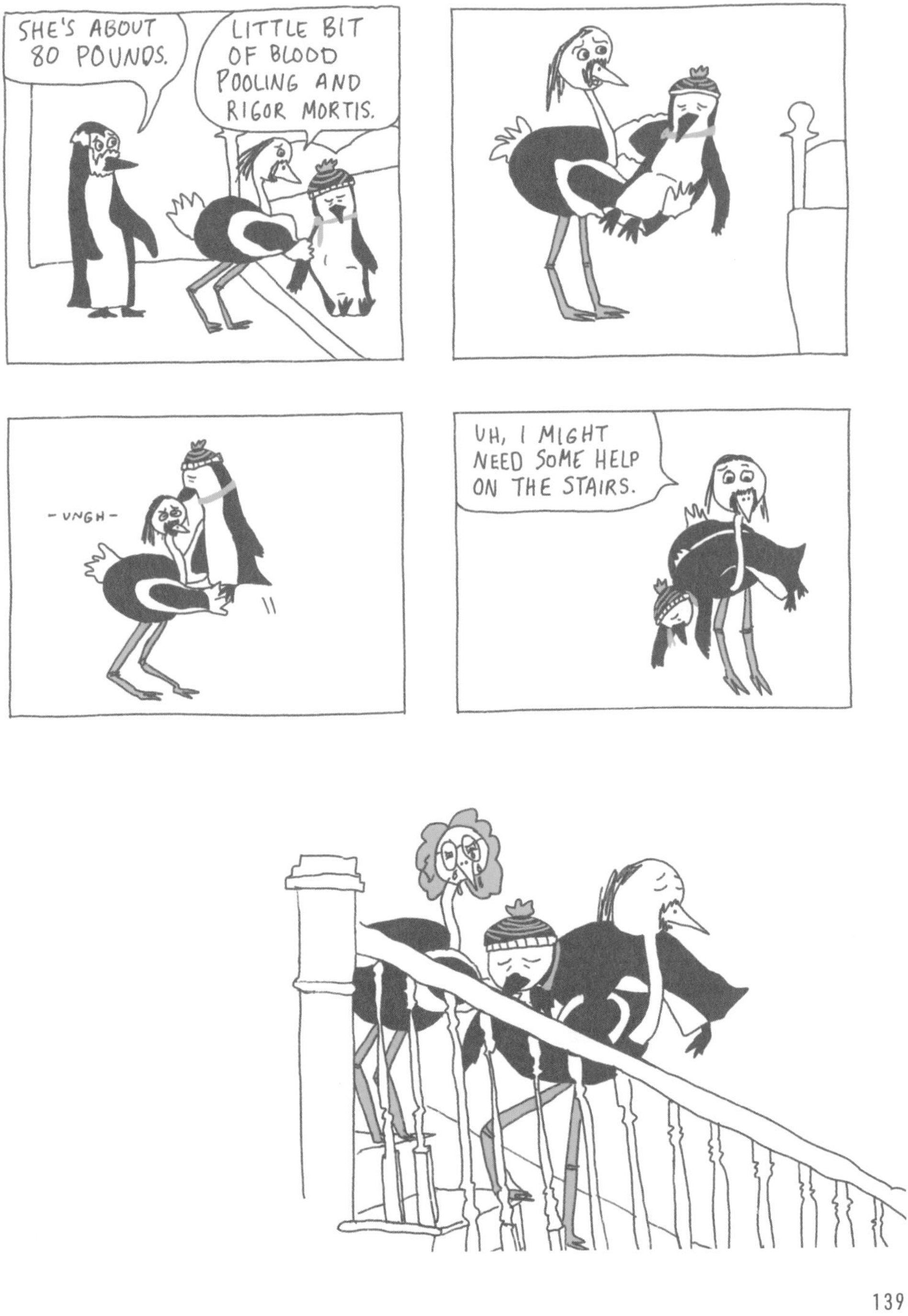
SHE'S ABOUT 80 POUNDS.
LITTLE BIT OF BLOOD POOLING AND RIGOR MORTIS.
-UNGH-
UH, I MIGHT NEED SOME HELP ON THE STAIRS.

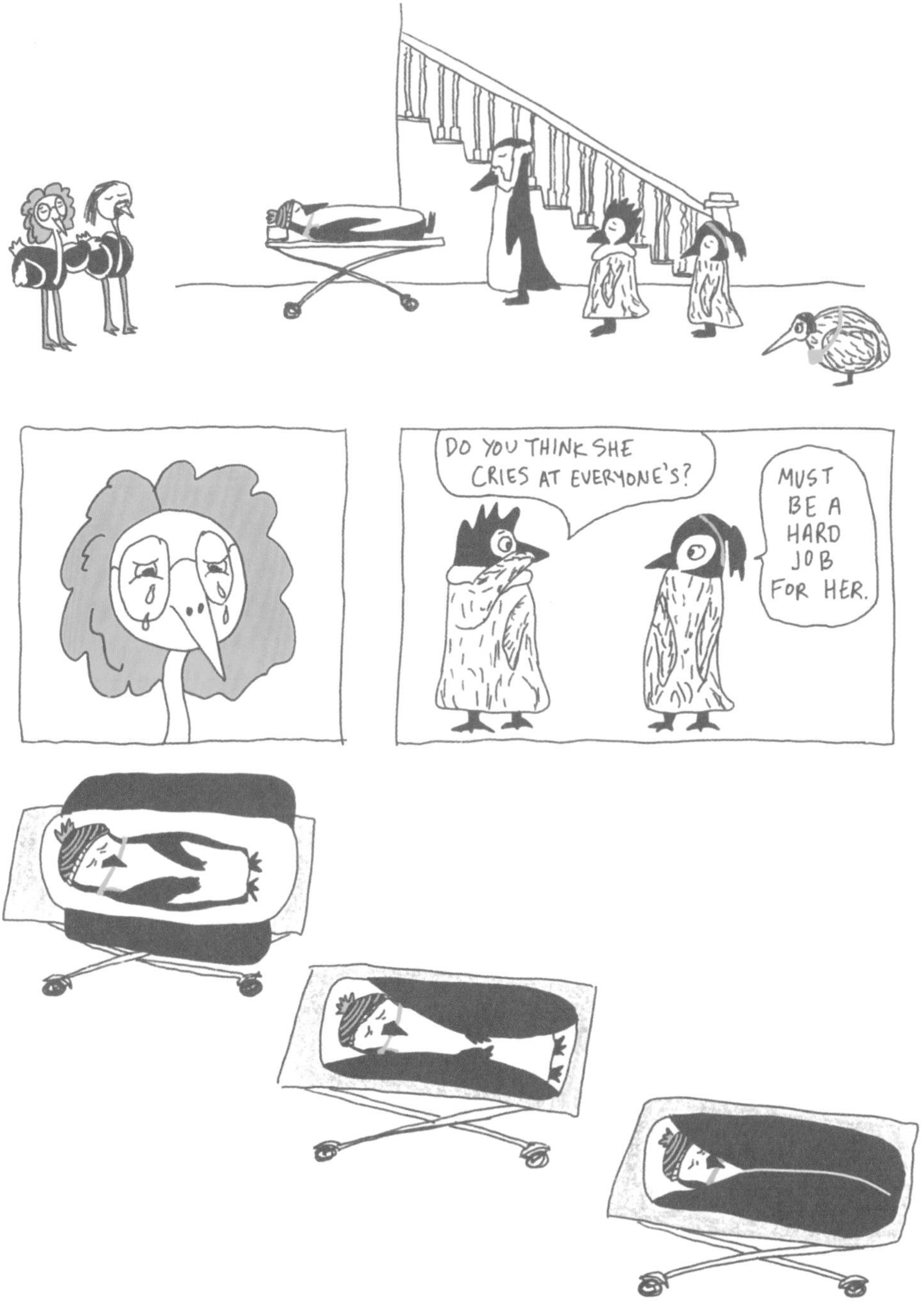
DO YOU THINK SHE CRIES AT EVERYONE'S?
MUST BE A HARD JOB FOR HER.

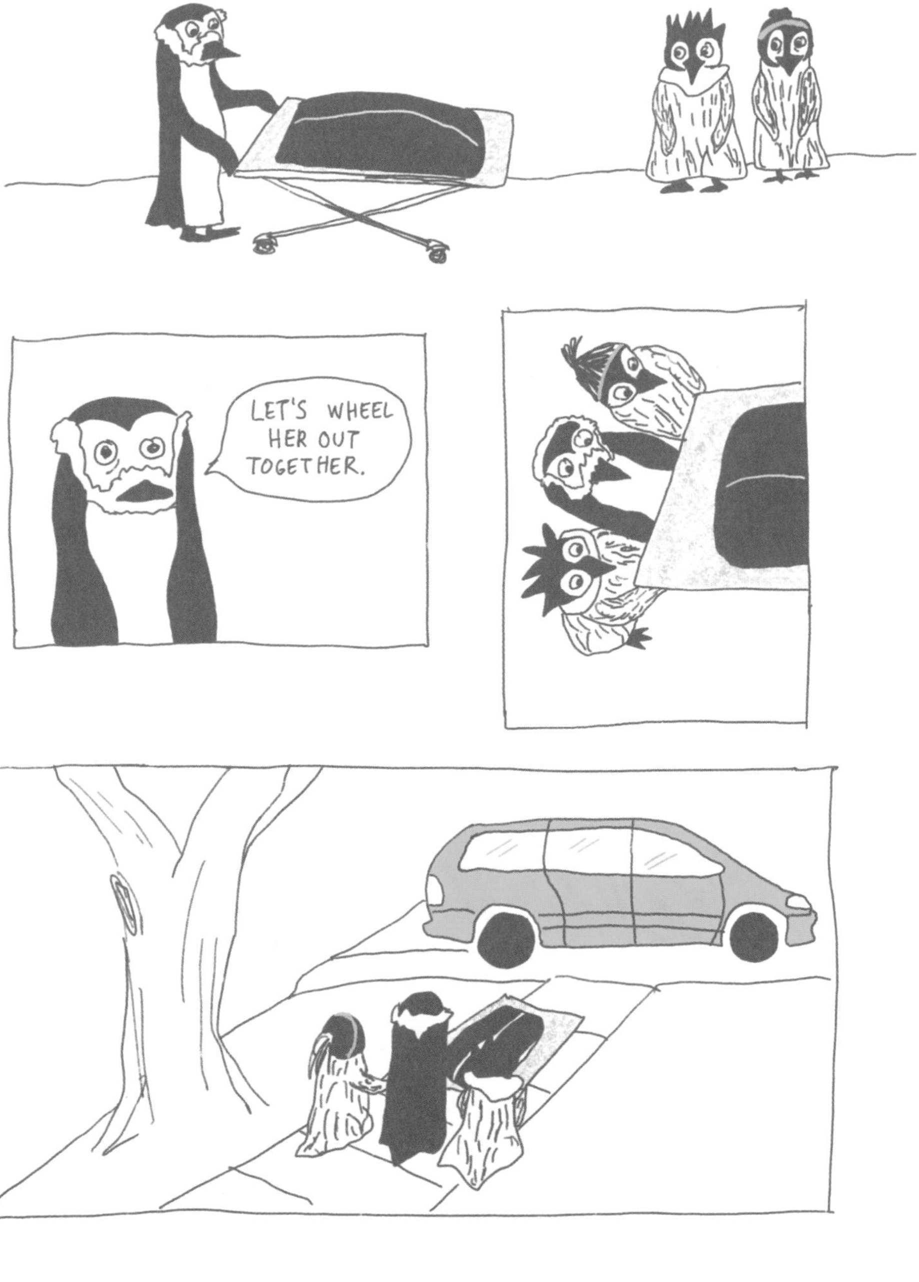
LET'S WHEEL HER OUT TOGETHER.

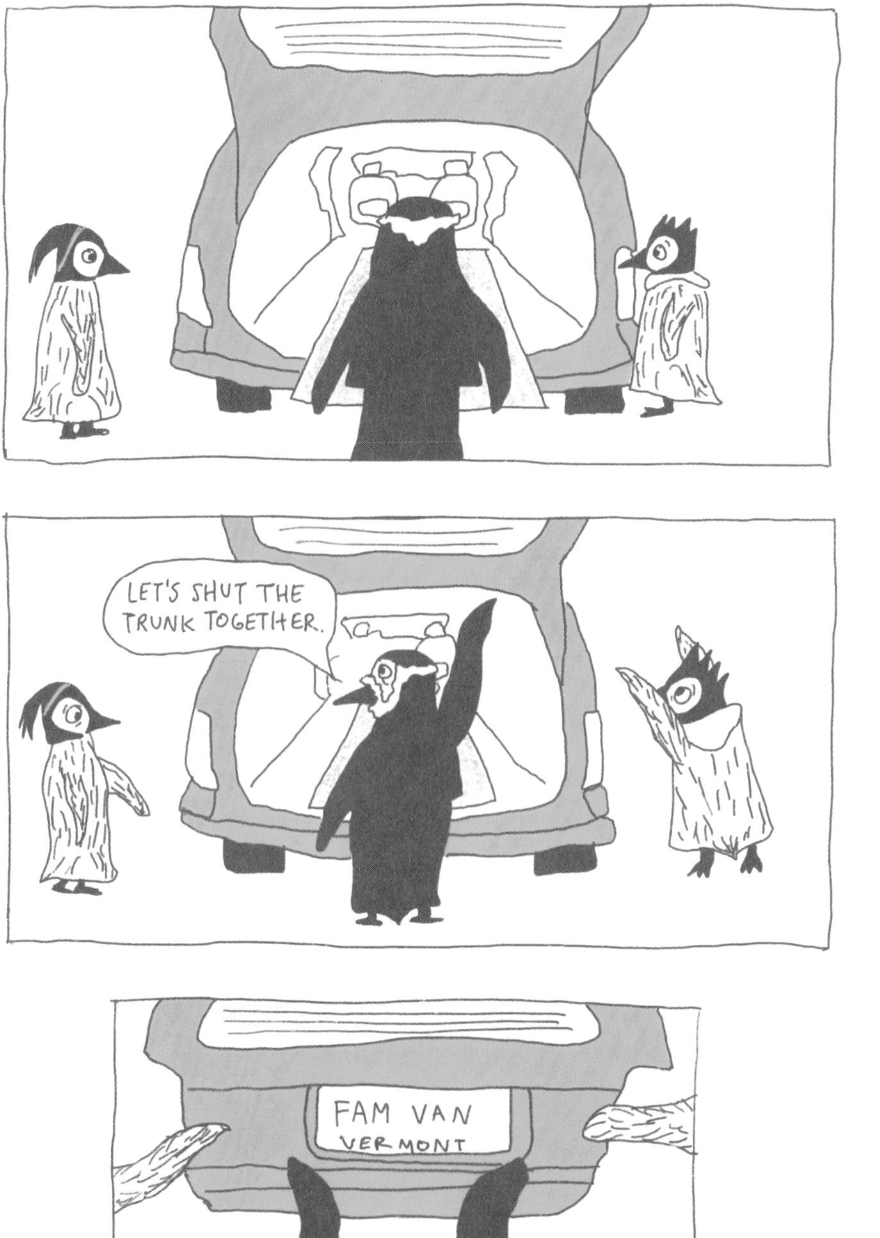
LET'S SHUT THE TRUNK TOGETHER.
FAM VAN
VERMONT
-THUCK-

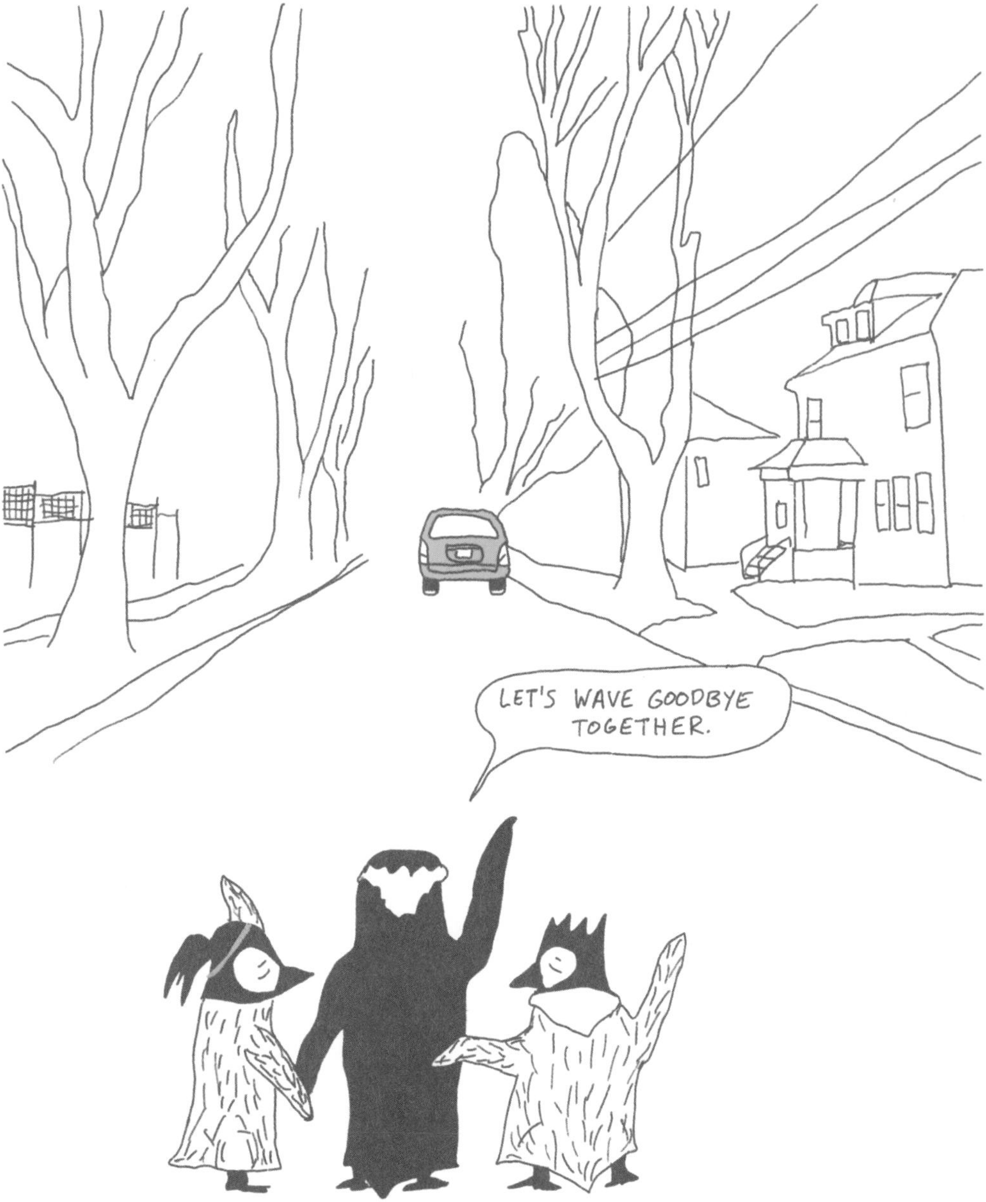
LET'S WAVE GOODBYE TOGETHER.

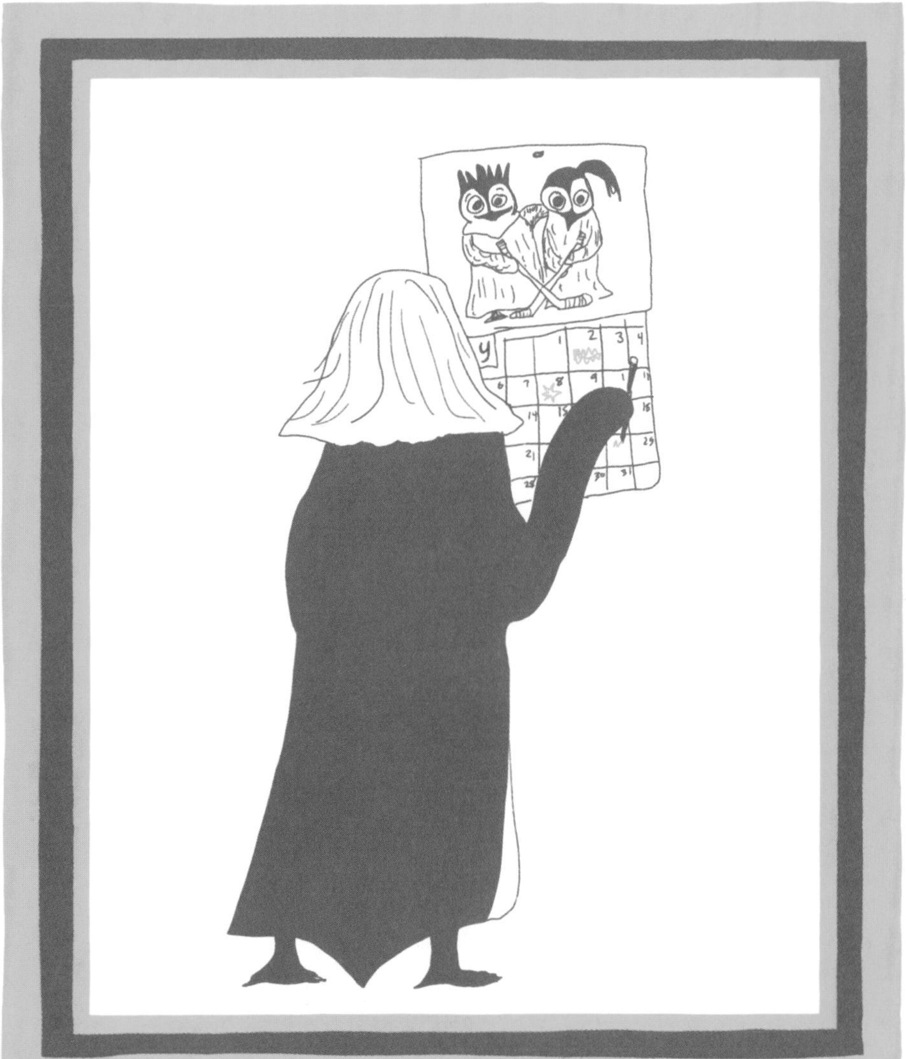

AFTER

FOOD PEOPLE DROPPED OFF

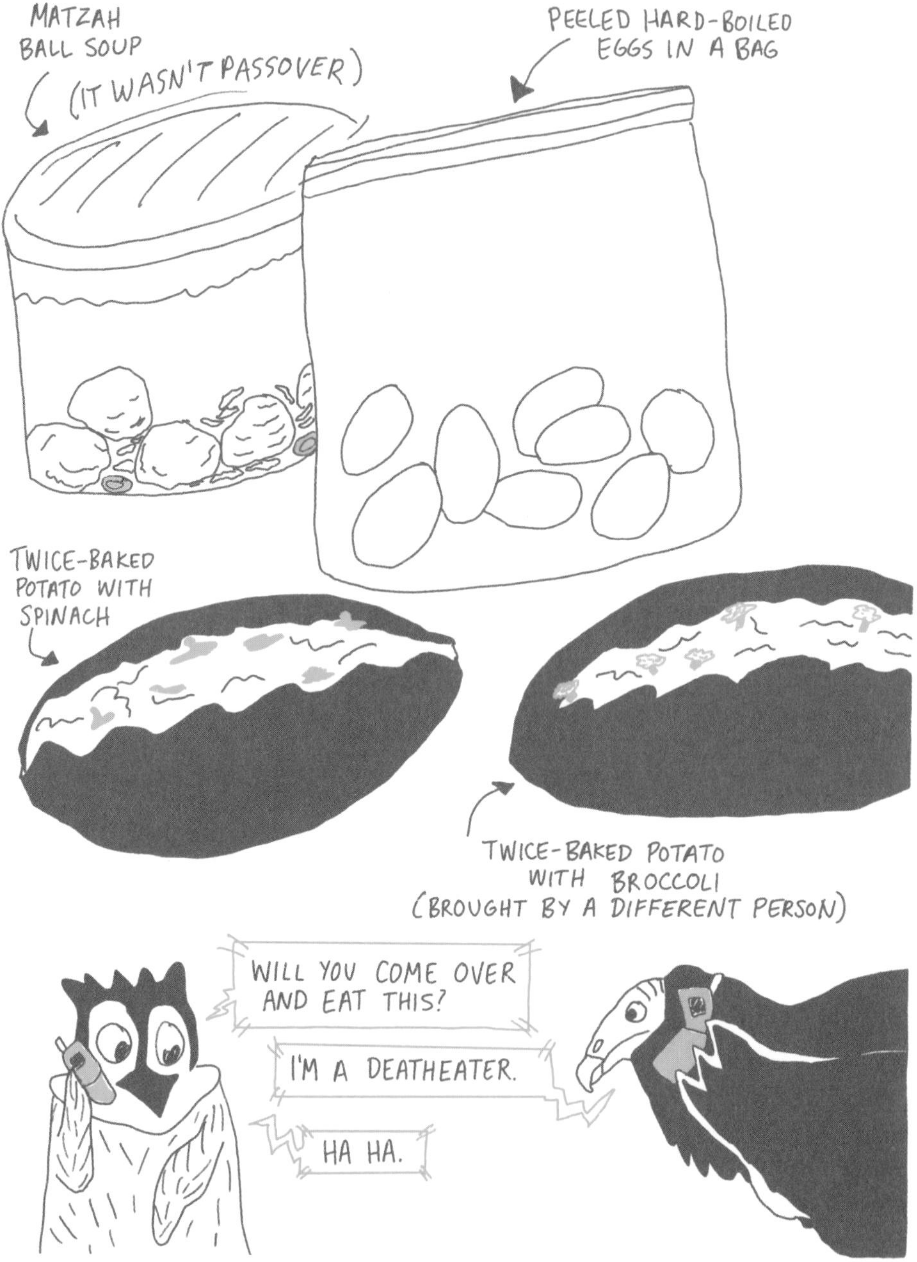
MATZAH BALL SOUP
(IT WASN'T PASSOVER)
PEELED HARD-BOILED EGGS IN A BAG
TWICE-BAKED POTATO WITH SPINACH
TWICE-BAKED POTATO WITH BROCCOLI (BROUGHT BY A DIFFERENT PERSON)
WILL YOU COME OVER AND EAT THIS?
I'M A DEATHEATER.
HA HA.

ASHES

DOES ANYONE WANT TO DO ANY READINGS OR ANYTHING?

UH, I'M GOING TO READ A LETTER FROM BEFORE SHE GOT SICK.

147

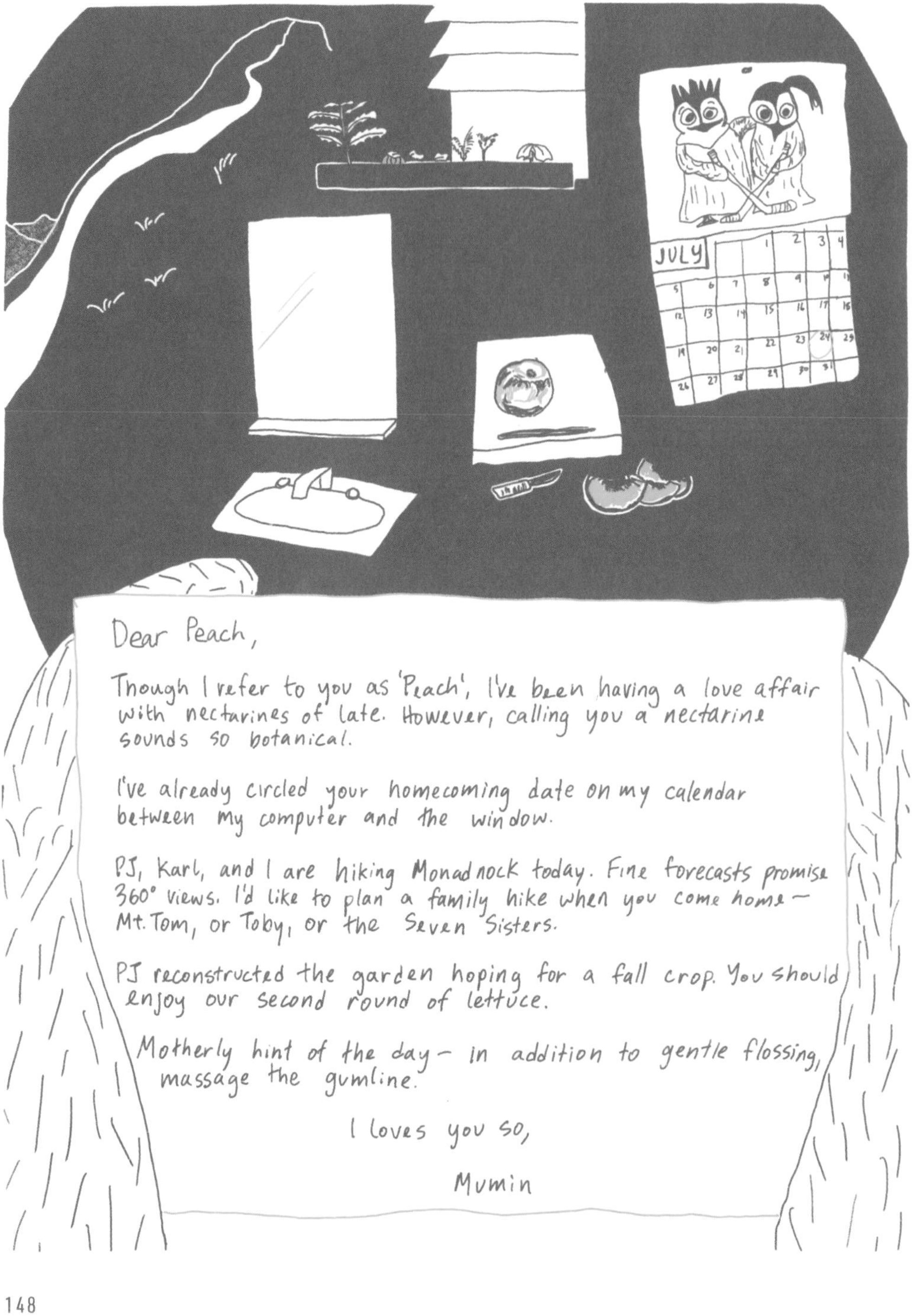
JULY
Dear Peach,
Though I refer to you as 'Peach', I've been having a love affair with nectarines of late. However, calling you a nectarine sounds so botanical.
I've already circled your homecoming date on my calendar between my computer and the window.
PJ, Karl, and I are hiking Monadnock today. Fine forecasts promise 360° views. I'd like to plan a family hike when you come home – Mt. Tom, or Toby, or the Seven Sisters.
PJ reconstructed the garden hoping for a fall crop. You should enjoy our second round of lettuce.
Motherly hint of the day – in addition to gentle flossing, massage the gumline.
I loves you so,
Mumin

OK, LET'S TAKE TURNS.

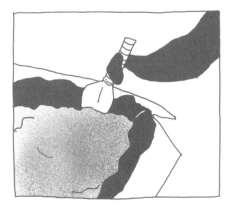

THIS IS GOING TO TAKE FOREVER WITH A TROWEL.

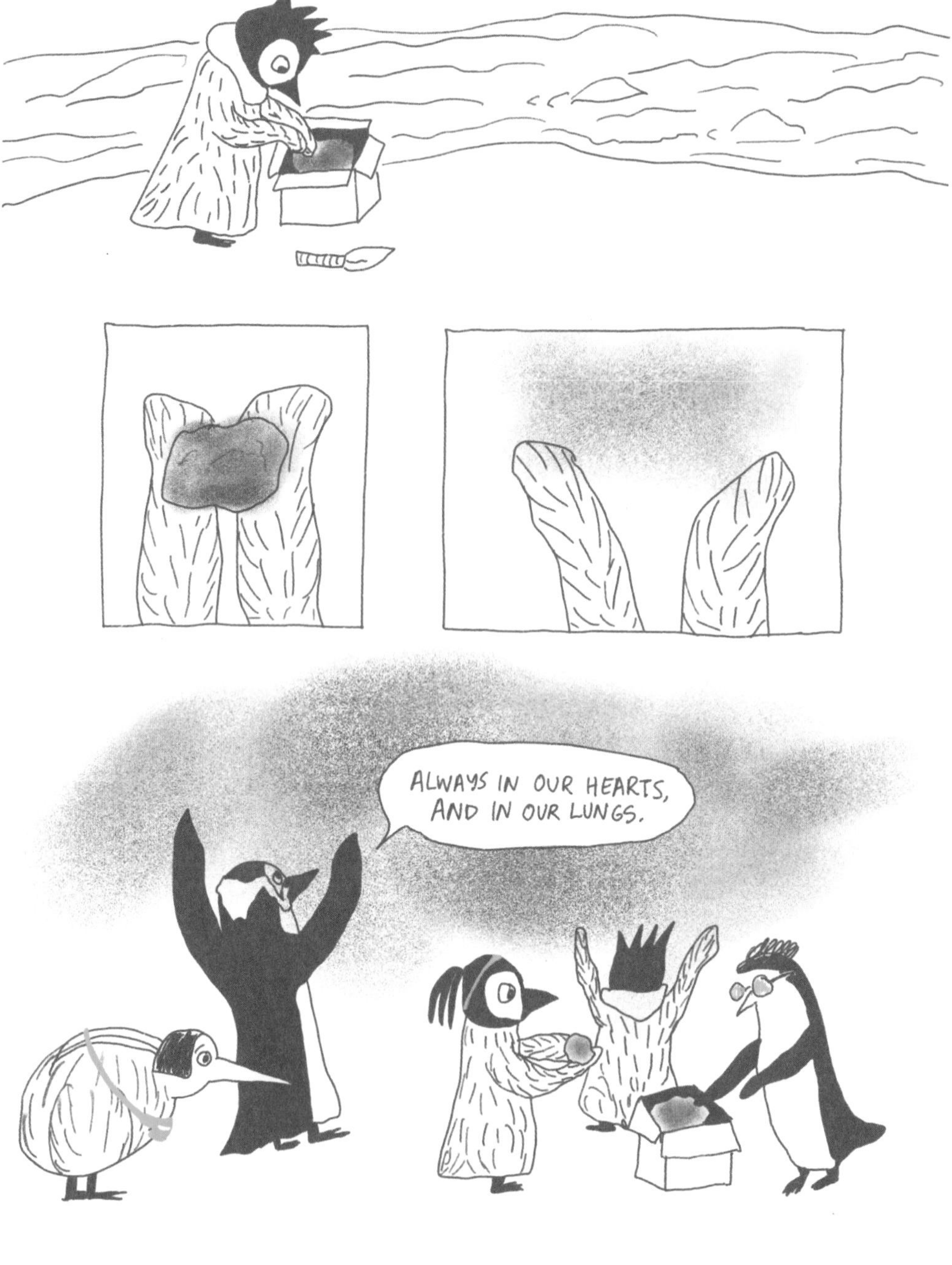
ALWAYS IN OUR HEARTS,
AND IN OUR LUNGS.

GONE

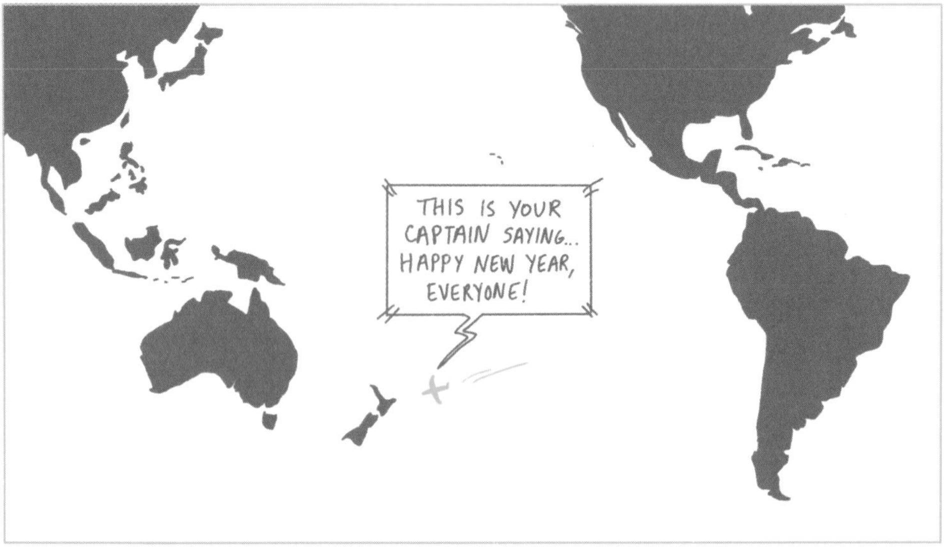
THIS IS YOUR CAPTAIN SAYING... HAPPY NEW YEAR, EVERYONE!

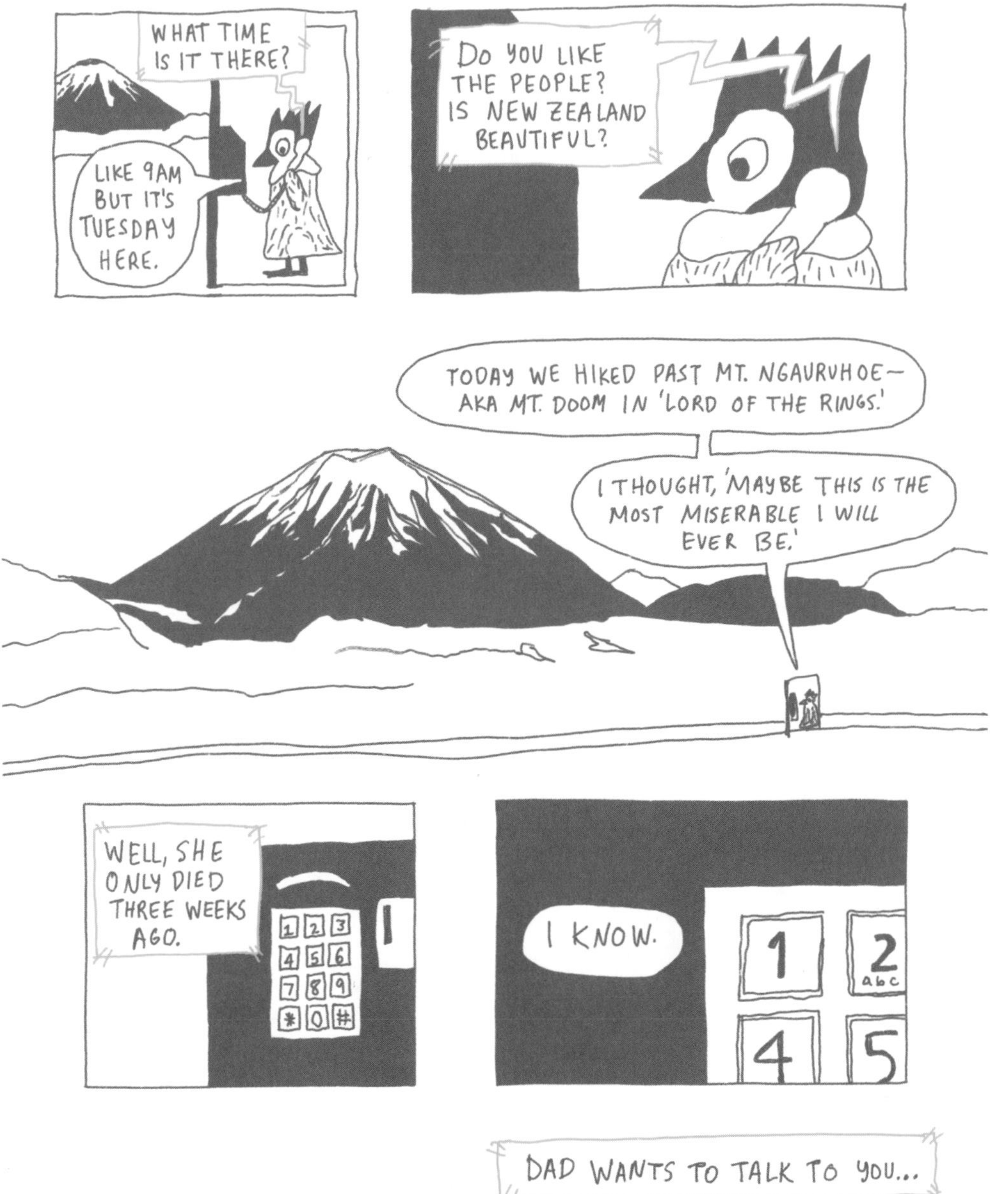
WHAT TIME IS IT THERE?
LIKE 9AM BUT IT'S TUESDAY HERE.
DO YOU LIKE THE PEOPLE? IS NEW ZEALAND BEAUTIFUL?
TODAY WE HIKED PAST MT. NGAURUHOE— AKA MT. DOOM IN 'LORD OF THE RINGS.'
I THOUGHT, 'MAYBE THIS IS THE MOST MISERABLE I WILL EVER BE.'
WELL, SHE ONLY DIED THREE WEEKS AGO.
I KNOW.
DAD WANTS TO TALK TO YOU...

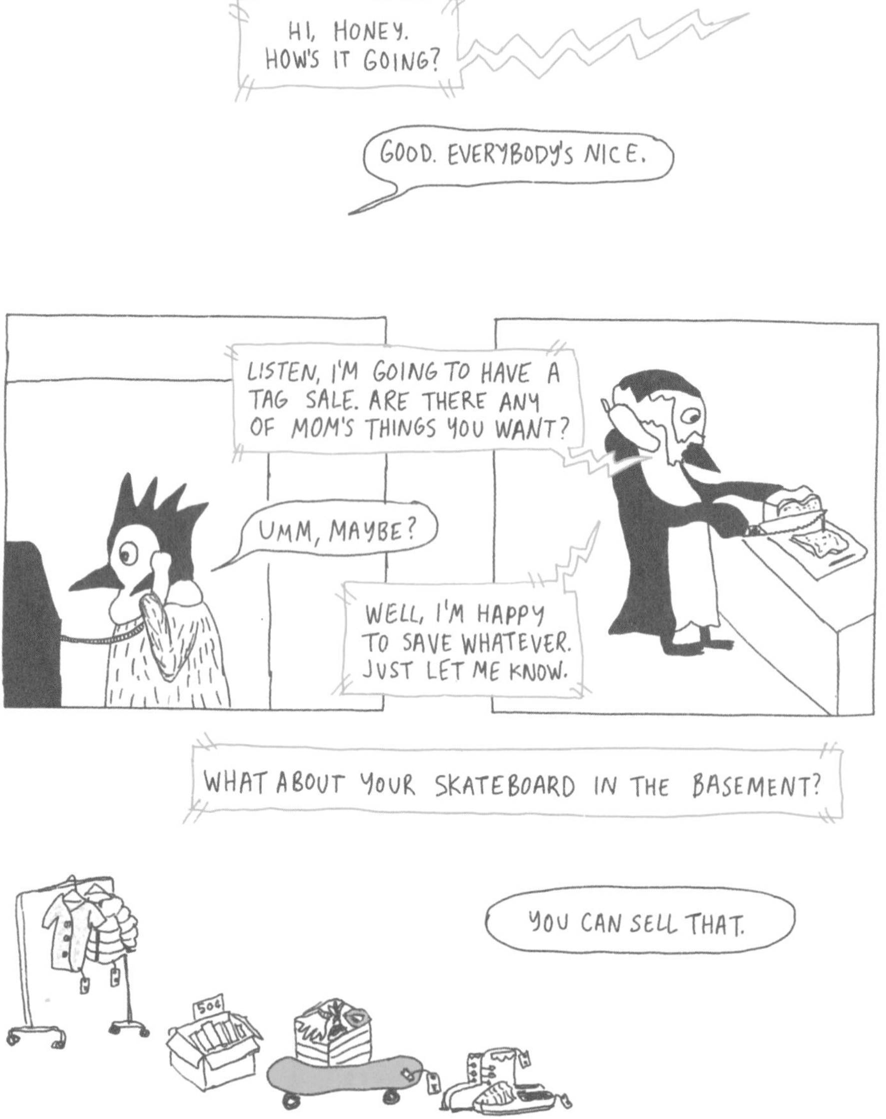
HI, HONEY. HOW'S IT GOING?
GOOD. EVERYBODY'S NICE.
LISTEN, I'M GOING TO HAVE A TAG SALE. ARE THERE ANY OF MOM'S THINGS YOU WANT?
UMM, MAYBE?
WELL, I'M HAPPY TO SAVE WHATEVER. JUST LET ME KNOW.
WHAT ABOUT YOUR SKATEBOARD IN THE BASEMENT?
YOU CAN SELL THAT.
50¢

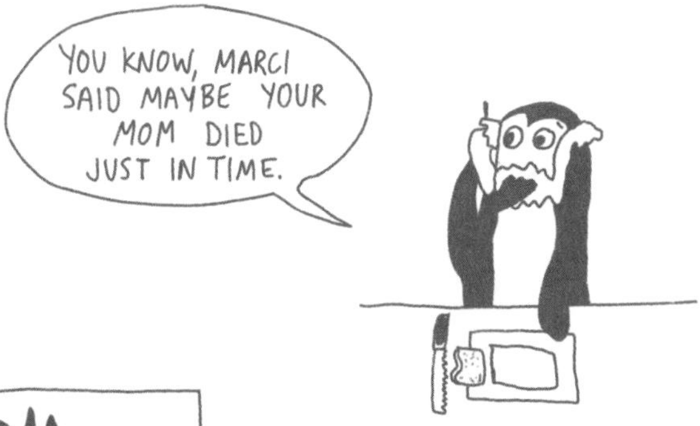
YOU KNOW, MARCI SAID MAYBE YOUR MOM DIED JUST IN TIME.

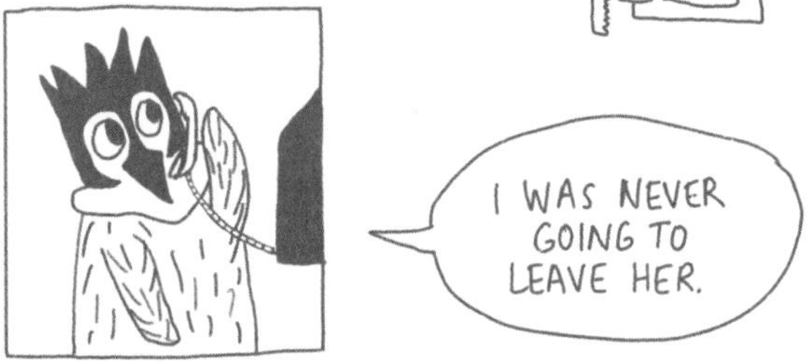
I WAS NEVER GOING TO LEAVE HER.

ACKNOWLEDGEMENTS

THANK YOU, TIN HOUSE
ALYSSA OGI, MASIE COCHRAN, DIANE CHONETTE, BECKY KRAEMER, NANCI MCCLOSKEY, CRAIG POPELARS, ALEX GONZALES, SANGI LAMA, JAKOB VALA, DAVID CALIGIURI, ELIZABETH DEMEO.

THANK YOU, MAGGIE COOPER.

THANK YOU, CALIFORNIA COLLEGE OF ARTS MFA IN COMICS FACULTY
MATT SILADY, JUSTIN HALL, NICOLE J GEORGES, JOHN JENNINGS, THI BUI, MELANIE GILLMAN, ED LUCE, JOYCE RICE, ELIZABETH BEIER.

THANK YOU, CCA MFA COHORT.

THANK YOU, SHING YIN KHOR, MAIA KOBABE, KIT FRASER, OLIVER NORTHWOOD, MIKE ROSSI, KRIS THURRELL, RANDY CLANCY, MARGOT ROBINSON, AMY HINKLEY, ADRIANNA BEAUDETTE, SCOTTIE BURON, KELSEY DUTTON, EVI VAN ITALLIE, REBA RICHARDSON, NICOLE ARULANANTHAM, BECCA ABUZA.

THANK YOU, MARCI YOSS, BARRY FEINGOLD, PATTY DANA, MARY GUSTAFIK.

THANK YOU, RICHARD BRUNSWICK + ELENA BETKE-BRUNSWICK.

THANK YOU, EDUARDO PARRA.

THANK YOU, MOM.